AF841647

A SIXTH-CENTURY TAX REGISTER
FROM THE HERMOPOLITE NOME

American Studies in Papyrology

Series Editors
James G. Keenan, Kathleen McNamee, and Arthur Verhoogt

Volume 51
A Sixth-century Tax Register
from the Hermopolite Nome
by
Roger S. Bagnall, James G. Keenan, and Leslie S. B. MacCoull

A Sixth-century Tax Register from the Hermopolite Nome

by

Roger S. Bagnall
James G. Keenan
Leslie S. B. MacCoull

AMERICAN SOCIETY OF PAPYROLOGISTS
DURHAM, NORTH CAROLINA

A Sixth-century Tax Register
from the Hermopolite Nome
by
Roger S. Bagnall, James G. Keenan, and Leslie S. B. MacCoull

© 2011
The American Society of Papyrologists

ISBN 13-978-0-9799758-4-4

ISBN 10-978-0-9799758-4-0

Library of Congress Cataloging-in-Publication Data

Bagnall, Roger S.
A sixth-century tax register from the Hermopolite Nome / by Roger S. Bagnall, James G. Keenan, and Leslie S.B. MacCoull.
p. cm. -- (American studies in papyrology ; v. 51)
Includes bibliographical references and indexes.
Text in Greek with introduction and commentary in English.
ISBN 978-0-9799758-4-4 (hardcover : alk. paper)
1. Manuscripts, Greek (Papyri)--Egypt--Hermopolite Nome. 2. Taxation--Egypt--History. 3. Hermopolite Nome (Egypt)--Antiquities. I. Keenan, James G. II. MacCoull, Leslie S. B. III. British Library. IV. Title.
PA3304.B34 2011
487'.3--dc23

2011023961

Preface

This edition has been in preparation longer than any of the editors would have wished. It began with a version prepared by Leslie MacCoull from autopsy in the British Library in 1984–1986 as well as from microfilm and photographs. She wishes to thank the successive directors of the then Department of Oriental Manuscripts, Dr. Emanuel Silver and Dr. Vrej Nersessian, and their staff for their assistance, as well as the Interlibrary Loan Service of Hayden Library, Arizona State University. She also wishes to commemorate Mirrit Boutros Ghali (1908–1992). The other two editors took over the revision of the text and preparation of the introduction and commentary, both from autopsy (Roger Bagnall has read through the original once, James Keenan twice) and with the assistance of digital images made by the British Library. Our work in London and the making of the images were supported by research funding from Columbia University and from a grant to Bagnall by the Andrew W. Mellon Foundation, which also made possible a semester's leave for Keenan to devote to the project. We would like to thank Jean Gascou, Todd Hickey, Bernhard Palme, and Kathleen McNamee for reading the manuscript. They offered many useful observations, discussed problems with us, and saved us from numerous errors. Alain Delattre kindly helped us with some questions about the section on names.

As an abbreviation for this volume we suggest *P.Lond.Herm.*

June 2011

Contents

Illustrations

Introduction

1. Acquisition, Provenance, Codicology

In the British Library's handwritten *List of Oriental MSS. acquired from 1890–1908. Or. 4047–6947* (ORC / GEN / MSS / 6), an entry on p. 226 for 1901 refers to "Or. 5987–6146" as consisting of "Miscellaneous fragments, Coptic and Arabic." These include the codex presented here, presumably catalogued as "Oriental" upon quick impression because of Coptic letters present in the text and perhaps because of the other manuscripts accompanying it. A few years later, however, in the first published description of the codex, Crum would write: "The text is Greek, except for a number of curious Egyptian names and words in which Coptic letters are employed" (Crum 1905: 445). Since the first physical description of the codex is by the Rev. C. Murch (*apud* Crum 1905: 445), one may guess that Murch himself had on behalf of the British Museum negotiated the purchase in Egypt of the codex and, probably also, the entire lot here recorded (*Who Was Who in Egyptology*[3] 302).

The codex, with its 27 folios and one unplaced fragment, is shelved in the Asia, Pacific and Africa Collections (formerly the Department of Oriental Manuscripts) of the British Library as Or. 6046. It is mounted in 14 different glass sandwiches, two folios per sandwich until the last, which houses Folio 27 and the unplaced fragment. The sheets of glass measure exactly one foot square. They are bound by leather frames that reduce the effective visual space by 3/8″ on all four sides. This circumstance poses no problem for visual access to the full range of writing side to side, but reduces the effective range of folio heights to 28.7 cm. Since the folio heights are usually slightly more than this, it is impossible to measure them exactly; the best that can be said is that all folio heights (except for Fol. 21 and the fragment) are slightly more than 28.7 cm. An unfortunate consequence of this mounting is that the tops of first lines are frequently compromised; less often, so are the bottoms of last lines. Folio widths tend to run about 13 cm. (More on this and related matters below.) Individual folio widths accompany the introductions to each. In mounting, blobs of glue appear to have been used at the corners to hold the leaves in place.

The codex derives from the Hermopolite nome, along with Aphrodito the most prolific source of documentary codices. It is probably from Hermopolis itself, but its concern is with tax payments recorded for the village Temseu Skordon (21r.1, 24r.1; Drew-Bear 1979: 278–279 and J. Sheridan, *P.Col.* IX, p. 157) and for a hamlet, ἐποίκιον (*SPP* X 25 B.10), Topos Demeou (22v.1, 23r.44, 25v.1, 27r.1, 27v.1; Drew-Bear 1979: 90). The text was not dated by Crum, but was subsequently assigned without discussion (Drew-Bear 1979: 278, 398) to the seventh/eighth century. It was Jean Gascou who first saw that the codex was a record of payments in money and not in kind. And it was such monetary concerns, especially the codex's use of the 18-carat solidus, that led him to date the codex to the first half of the sixth century (Gascou 1989: 84/2008: 364; his reference to 19 carats is a slip). The codex itself refers half a dozen times to a tenth indiction, and no other (20v.1, 21r.2, etc.). A likely tenth indiction is that of A.D. 546/7, to which palaeographical considerations well conform. See further below Sections 2 (Palaeography), 5 (Money), and 6 (Chronology).

Murch described the codex as consisting of 27 consecutive folios plus the fragment. He described the folios as mostly "double"; "several," however, were "single." These were supplied with extensions to their inner edges "to allow of a fold and so of their being pierced by the two small leathern thongs, which, penetrating the whole mass at top and bottom, held it together" (Murch *apud* Crum loc.cit.). Murch must have seen the codex before its mounting, while it was still in Egypt. The "leathern thongs" are now gone, the holes impossible to locate, except perhaps in the aforementioned extensions. But if Murch was correct about the double character of most of the folios, he was referring to a situation before the cutting of the original sheets into the present single folios. Without dismounting the glass sandwiches, we cannot come further in reconstructing the original state. In the mounting of its sister text, *P.Lond.Copt.* I 1076 = Or. 6047, each bifolio is uncut and mounted in its own glass sandwich; and these bifolios are significantly wider (13 inches to 10 by Murch's measurements) than any reconstructed hypothetical bifolio of the present codex.

The "several" sheets with extensions, or stubs, turn out in fact to be three: Folios 8 (only upper half of stub preserved), 12 (Plate 2), and 13. The short and narrow Folio 21 is a later insert (Plate 3). The ordering of pages for the first twenty folios, from 1r to 20r, is assured by their numbering from 2 to 40, although this could postdate their original writing. The original first folio of the codex, with a presumed cover page (recto) and page 1 (verso), is accordingly lost. Problems arise at the end of the codex, where the numbering, from 1 to 6, as far as it is preserved or capable of restoration (based on a matching of page totals with the relevant "page-by-page" summary, *kataselis*, 22v.2–7), goes in reverse order (more on this below). This is presumably what inclined Gascou to refer to the codex's pagination as "incohérente" (1989: 75 n. 19 and 84 = 2008: 355 n. 19 and 364).

A table of folios with their fiber directions was worked out by MacCoull. We give that table here, including the original pagination, and indicate those folios where *kolleseis* seem to be present with a K. These joins seem to be random and are therefore unhelpful in determining the character of the roll or rolls from which were cut the folios for our codex. We have added entries for the missing first folio, numbered here zero. For Folio 26, we have for purposes of this table kept the current numbering in the mounting; see below on its correct orientation.

[Fol. 0r (↓)	Cover]	
[Fol. 0v (→)	1]	
Fol. 1r (↓)	2	
Fol. 1v (→)	3	
Fol. 2r (↓)	4	
Fol. 2v (→)	5	
Fol. 3r (↓)	6	
Fol. 3v (→)	7	
Fol. 4r (↓)	8	K
Fol. 4v (→)	9	
Fol. 5r (↓)	10	
Fol. 5v (→)	11	
Fol. 6r (↓)	12	K
Fol. 6v (→)	13	K
Fol. 7r (↓)	14	K
Fol. 7v (→)	15	
Fol. 8r (↓)	16	
Fol. 8v (→)	17	
Fol. 9r (↓)	18	K
Fol. 9v (→)	19	
Fol. 10r (→)	**20**	K
Fol. 10v (↓)	**21**	
Fol. 11r (↓)	22	K
Fol. 11v (→)	23	
Fol. 12r (↓)	24	
Fol. 12v (→)	25	
Fol. 13r (↓)	26	K?
Fol. 13v (→)	27	
Fol. 14r (↓)	28	K
Fol. 14v (→)	29	
Fol. 15r (↓)	30	
Fol. 15v (→)	31	
Fol. 16r (↓)	32	K
Fol. 16v (→)	33	
Fol. 17r (↓)	34	
Fol. 17v (→)	35	
Fol. 18r (→)	36	
Fol. 18v (↓)	37	
Fol. 19r (→)	38	
Fol. 19v (↓)	39	
Fol. 20r (→)	40	K?
Fol. 20v (↓)		
Fol. 21r (→)		
Fol. 21v (↓)		
Fol. 22r (→)		
Fol. 22v (↓)		
Fol. 23r (→)		
Fol. 23v (↓)		
Fol. 24r (→)		K
Fol. 24v (↓)		
Fol. 25r (→)	6	
Fol. 25v (↓)	[5]	
Fol. 26r (↓)	[3]	K
Fol. 26v (→)	4	
Fol. 27r (→)	[2]	
Fol. 27v (↓)	[1]	

Murch's description of a codex of mainly double leaves and several independent leaves has led later scholars (first Gascou 1989 = 2008) to consider the codex to have been constructed mainly as a "cahier" or notebook, with papyrus leaves stacked and then vertically folded in half and stitched at the spine, top and bottom. Neither Murch nor Gascou asks how the extensions of single Folios 8, 12 and 13 could have avoided obscuring some of the writing on neighboring folios, over which they would have lain. This problem would have existed whether the codex was created after the inscription of its folios or the extensions were part of a blank manufactured codex then used for writing the tax account, or even if the extra folios were inserted after both they and the codex had been written on.

The codex displays a pattern of pages with alternating fiber directions. The first part of the codex, from Folio 0 through Folio 17, with the exception of Folio 10, follows the ↓→ pattern. From Folio 18 onward this is reversed to →↓ (emboldened in the table), except for Folio 26, with its reversal of page numbers as compared with its neighboring Folios 25 and

27 (cf. below). The logical conclusion would be that the codex began with a stack of sheets with fibers horizontal on the top; this was then folded so that it formed a single quire with the fibers vertical on the first half of the rectos, then horizontal on the remainder. Apparently Folio 10 was put in with vertical fibers up.

If all of this is correct, we should be able to match the verso sides of folios in the first part of the codex with the rectos starting with Folio 18, omitting inserts (Folios 8, 12, 13, and 21). Morover, the right edges of those versos and left edges of those rectos should be cleanly cut, and added together they should be roughly consistent in width. We can in fact do this for 17v+18r, 16v+19r, and 15v+20r. It is conceivable that 14v+22r (despite the ragged edges; we have no photograph of 22r and cannot judge fibers) could belong together, and 5v+27r show reasonable fiber match. But 9v+24r, 7v+25r, and 6v+26r do not look as favorable, either for matching fibers or for seeing the clean cutting that should be visible throughout if in fact the entire codex in Murch's time had been in bifolia. Given the difficulty of working with a few glassed frames at a time, we do not think we can go further in reconstructing the situation of the codex at the time of acquisition. It is conceivable that Murch was ignoring the existence of some folia that had already been damaged at the fold and come apart from their original mates, or that some damage occurred between when he saw the codex and it reached the Museum.

A final anomaly: in their present glass housings Folios 24–27 are inexplicably mounted upside down. Something happened in the course of conservation; we do not know what. It should be clear from the table that a simple fix on the codex is to flip Folio 26 over so its current recto becomes verso and current verso becomes recto. This restores Folio 26 to the fiber pattern of Folios 18–25 and 27, making this section now entirely uniform in that regard. More importantly, it removes the incoherence of the 1–6 pagination of Folios 25–27. The pagination still goes in reverse from the back of the codex inward, but now the numerical sequence is straight: Folio 26r, now become Folio 26v, is Topos Demeou, page [3]. Folio 26v, become Folio 26r, is now, as it always was, and was clearly so marked, page 4. And of course the proper dating sequence of the respective pages is restored: Page 3 preserves a Tybi 5 date (line 10), page 4 continues Tybi 5 entries (see line 1) but shifts to Mecheir 4 entries at line 9. In our text, we present the text with our correction of the sequence incorporated. We have rejected a broader reordering of Folios 25–27 and their respective sides, because the exceptional damage to Folio 27 seems to suggest it always stood closer to the vulnerable end of the codex than Folios 25 and 26. The unplaced fragment must belong either to a folio later than 27, or to another insert (after 20v, most likely), but we cannot tell which. The original codex should have had (on the assumption that our enumeration of inserted leaves is correct) additional leaves, attached at the time to Folios [0], 1, 2, 3, and 4; the fragment could come from one of those. Whether the others were written on, or (for example) were torn out in antiquity for other use, we have no way of knowing. Murch's description does not acknowledge the problem that they pose for reconstruction of the codex.

2. Palaeography

Murch (*apud* Crum 1905: 445) identified the codex as having been written "by two scribes" (cf. Gascou 1989: 84 = 2008: 364: "émanant de deux scribes distincts"). It is easiest to say that, according to Murch, the principal scribe was responsible for everything except for what the second scribe wrote. He credited the latter with "foll. 10*b* (mid.)—12*a* (mid.), 22*b*, 23 (part), 26*a* (part)."

We think that overall the scribal exchanges may have been more complicated than Murch allowed—that is, there were more than two scribes, with scribes beyond the first and second pitching in from time to time, but in very limited ways. In any case, one hand dominates the text, being responsible for the page-by-page entries both for Temseu Skordon (1r–20v) and for Topos Demeou (24r–27r and the central portion of 27v). We do not see any switch to a second scribe from Folios 10v through 12r, but do believe, in apparent accord with Murch, that the two page-by-page summaries (*kataselides*) at 22v.1–8 (for Topos Demeou) and on 23r (Plate 4; for Temseu Skordon) were written by a second, less skilled, hand. It is more upright and certainly more regular, albeit within a restricted repertoire and space, than the principal hand. Possibly he was also responsible for the oblique strokes placed in the left margins against individual entries as well as the other, more occasional checking marks (small X's in the left margin above the oblique strokes, doubled strokes, dots in the right-hand margin) that suggest a second party totting up and checking the work of a first.

Pages and page sections other than those just mentioned, that is, the *kataselides*, are surely not the work of the codex's second, or tally, hand, but may (again) be the work of the principal scribe (21rv, 22v.9–23). The central (crossed out) portion of 27v also seems to be the work of the main scribe, but the sections written both above and below are surely by a different hand—and not the second hand. The unplaced fragment, positioned at the end of our edition, looks (once again) like the work of our first hand, but there are several other, more problematic cases, as follows:

(1) At 5v MacCoull identified a second hand at work, lines 26–27, where two payments for Choiak 10 are entered. This looks possible, but the specimen is too brief for absolute certitude.

(2) On 9v (Plate 1) there seem to be numerous changes of hand, or handwriting styles, including and in addition to the principal scribe's, especially but not exclusively between lines 5 and 11. The eye is quickly drawn to the uncial style of the name CENIKION in line 6—but comparisons with other writings of this name (2v.25 CINIKION, cf. 12r.6, 16r.18, 20v.25) shows that the main scribe writes the name in like fashion elsewhere, though perhaps not so majestically. Among other considerations, the handwriting of the symbols and ciphers in Cols. 2 and 3, including his neglect specially to mark numbers in

the thousands, remains consistent in appearance with the hand of our principal scribe. Also noteworthy is the typical leftward drift of Cols. 2 and 3, while Col. 1 shows the usual fondness for tremas. The ink does show variations in thickness: thick at lines 1–8, thin at 9–27, very thick at 28–36. This lends an impression of a different hand, but the sudden shift in the thickness of the writing is probably to be attributed to use of a different pen, or to a pen newly pared (lines 9–27), or newly and more frequently dipped in ink (1–8, 28–36). Since our main hand is legible, but often internally irregular (see below), it seems best to accept 9v as being predominantly if not exclusively his work. That others contributed lines or parts of lines remains possible.

(3) MacCoull (perhaps partly following Murch) identified a different hand at work from 10v.16–17 until 12v.1–2, but this is a difficult call. It is true the writing beginning at 10v.16–17 looks different, but all that follows is visually consistent with expectations by now long familiar from the first hand, including matters of alignment and fondness for tremas. It is true nonetheless that this section identified by MacCoull exhibits some unique spellings, e.g., Στεκς (11r.3) for the usual Στεξ, ϫιϭ (11r.4) for ϫιϫ, ϩελήνα (11r.9) for ϩελένα.

(4) 21r is written large and thick, but the text is short with plenty of room to spare; probably by a third hand not elsewhere represented.

(5) MacCoull perceived a second hand to be picking up the text at 24r.12 (or 13?)—"Here the second scribe reappears"—but did not specify how far it ran. It is true that for several lines (the canceled line 11; lines 12–14) the names are written small. But the rest of the page seems consonant with the hand of the main scribe.

(6) The tiny hand at the top of 27v (lines 1–2) is surely not the main scribe's.

Thus in the codex the presence of hands other than the main hand is exceptional or short-term. The main hand is one whose normally medium size tends to be influenced by availability of space. It can be larger when there was ample papyrus (21r if by the main hand; the unplaced fragment). But it is normally (there are exceptions) driven to fit as much as possible (vertically) on a single page, with more compression toward the bottom than at top. It is also driven, insofar as possible, to limit entries to single lines even if that requires extraordinary horizontal compression and abbreviation (12v.25–26 is an exemplary exception). This especially happens when payments in one party's name have been made "through" (διά) another party. Such entries, even so, will tend to drive the scribe's second and third columns into a realignment rightward, momentarily offsetting a characteristic tendency of his second and third columns to drift progressively to the left as his writing moves down the page.

The hand was seemingly first identified as Coptic because of its occasional use of Coptic letters in some of the distinctively Egyptian personal names. Most common are hori and djandja. Much less frequent are schima (especially in the word or name ϭεc) and shai (most examples of this letter thanks to names in the Topos Demeou pages of the codex). Fai is found only once (6v.13), chai and ti not at all.[1] The hand is also distinguished by its frequent use of tremas, especially over initial iotas in commonly found names like Ioannes, Iosephis, and Ieremias; also over iotas in numbers in the ten-to-nineteen range. Tremas over medial iotas (Ἡσαΐας, Σοΐου) and final iotas (Κουϊ, ϩαμποϊ) also occur. Tremas over upsilon can be found, though opportunities for their use are limited: over the upsilon for 400, for example. It is also found frequently over the iota of υἱός. As earlier mentioned, the scribe does not specially mark numerals in the thousands.

The hand, generally upright and legible, is variable in its degree of cursiveness and in its tendency toward ligatures. For some reason the name CENIKION, as mentioned, is regularly and strikingly written as if in majuscules. The hand also varies its letter forms. Beta, for example, appears both as B and with an open top. It is regularly B in Βίκτωρ, but see 13r.13–14 (B in 13, open in 14). It is regularly open-topped in its medial position in the common name Φῖβις, e.g., 1r.9, 10, 13, but see 11. Nu varies between N and a form that looks like eta. This variation can occur within a single name, notably in the patronymic ΠανηΧνου—first nu as N, second nu as n. Eta-like nus are especially deceptive in the name Πινουτίων and in the Coptic word φομντ. Tau is written in standard form (T), but in ligature is written as v. The latter is most easily observed in the letter string epsilon-tau-rho found in the name Πέτρ(ος) and the word σιτομέτρ(ης). The symbol for ½ is written in a form somewhere between L and S; that is, the shape is that of a splayed L. The scribe's standard practice was to follow that sign with a mid-height dot. This is not always observable, but that is probably the result of fading and abrasion for the most part.[2]

The main hand employs a variety of modes to indicate abbreviation depending on the letter at point of abbreviation, Perhaps most distinctive are abbreviations at rho and phi and even iota (in Φοι(βάμμων)) where the letters' descenders are (sometimes sharply) fish-hooked to the right and crossed by an oblique stroke: the effect is "chrismatic." Abbreviations at kappa and lambda are by oblique strokes through the letters' extended right legs. After mu, the indication of abbreviations is usually roughly "sinusoidal" (S). Abbreviations at tau and gamma begin at the right tip of the crossbar with strokes dropping down with moderate curving. In genitive endings in omicron-upsilon, upsilon is sometimes written over omicron as a short horizontal stroke, sometimes as an umbrella, or occasionally as even more elaborately curving horizontal strokes.

---

[1] On the absence of ti in documentary texts from this region, see *P.Bal.* I, pp. 148-49.

[2] We have noted dots clearly at 1r.2-3, 6; 1v.7-8, 24, 26; 2r.9; 2v.7; 3r.3; 3v.5, 14, 18; 4r.2; 4v.4; 5r.7; 5v.8, 12, 15; 6v.2, 9, 12-13, 20, 28; 7r.8, 13, 18; 7v.4, 6, 14, 17, 19, 24, 25; 8r.6, 25; 9r.5, 9; 9v.19, 22; 10r.19; 10v.7-8; 11r.18; 12r.3; 12v.8; 13r.8, 24; 13v.14, 32; 14r.13?; 14v.19; 15r.2, 7, 12, 23; 15v.30; 16r.4; 16v.22; 17v.24; 18r.10, 24, 26, 30?; 18v.5, 10, 13, 14, 21, 31; 19r.8, 14, 27, 31, 33; 19v.3, 14; 20r.3, 8, 13, 15; 20v.4, 10-11; 22v.11, 12; 23r.51-52; 24r.15, 27, 32; 25r.2, 5; 25v.25; 26v.18-20; 27r.8, 15, 18, 31; 27v.21. The absence on 26r is noteworthy.

3. Language

The codex is a syntactically impoverished document owing to a virtually complete absence of verbs and cases other than nominative and genitive. It is nevertheless of interest especially because the main scribe and the supposed secondary scribes in effect slide between two linguistic worlds, the Greek and the Coptic, perhaps not even thinking of them as distinct codes. Discussion of the codex's language cannot of course be entirely separated from the preceding discussion of palaeography. If there are indeed two or more distinguishable scribes, their linguistic usages should be discussed separately; conversely, linguistic idiosyncrasies should be helpful in distinguishing between writers. Investigations along these lines, however, have not proved successful. As discussed above, it has been difficult to identify the different hands at work in different segments of the codex; moreover, as pertinent here, linguistic usage between the supposedly different hands is remarkably consistent and of little use in distinguishing between writers. Thus it is possible to discuss the language of the codex as a whole under the assumption, and with the caution, that *almost* everything said here of the codex as a whole can be held true of the main scribe.

Obviously, those who first examined the codex, that is, Murch and Crum, were struck by its frequent use of Coptic letters. MacCoull's editorial practice in her preliminary edition was to print all names with Coptic letters in them fully in Coptic type. We have chosen, following Maspero (in *P.Cair.Masp.*) and Gascou (in *P.Sorb.* II 69), to print only the individual letters as Coptic within otherwise typographically Greek names. But there may be wisdom in MacCoull's practice, since it gives a better, or at least different, visual impression of scribes sliding back and forth between linguistic codes.

If the use of the Coptic letters is the first sign that the scribes were Egyptians writing Greek, a second cue is the codex's vagaries in case uses. On most pages the majority (though not always a decisive one) of taxpayers will be identified by names and patronymics. The frequent entries for the Holy Church and the less common entries for the Holy Martyrion are, perhaps tellingly, cast in the genitive case (Index IV for references); but declinable personal names in first position (let us call this the "first" or "name position") are usually in the nominative case, while names in second position (let us call this the "second" or "patronymic position") are usually in the genitive. But there are numerous exceptions, where the first position is occupied by names morphologically genitive (e.g., Ἀπολλῶτος, Ἁτρῆτος, Ἰακυβίου, Μονίου, Ὥρου); when the name of an occupation or trade follows in second position a name in the genitive in first position, this too is regularly cast in the genitive case (1v.9, 6v.24, etc.). Then, too, there is the case of the stonecutter Kyros, whose name is always cast in the nominative (Κῦρος), but whose trade, with one exception (11v.19), is always (in the seven remaining examples: 1r.20, 3r.13, etc.) produced as a genitive (λαξόου; see LSJ s.v. λαξόος for the form). Less often but frequently enough, the second position is taken by a name in the nominative case. The best example is Ἠλίας, which is never abbreviated and retains its nominative form in second position, and in other places where the genitive is called for (e.g., 9v.27, 13r.15, with κλ(ηρονόμοι), 10r.11, with τοῦ οἴκ(ου)). This phenomenon occurs so often and with such consistency that, were it not for rare exceptions (alpha genitive at 18v.32, omicron-upsilon at 20v.21 and 23), it might seem to have been treated as fully indeclinable. A special problem is created by the word or name Κόμες, always in second position, never first: is it then an undeclined patronymic or does it mean *comes*, i.e., "count"? If the latter is the case, we find the title would have been applied to two names, Monis and Psas (gen. Psatos), which on the surface do not appear very "countly." We therefore accept Komes as an undeclined patronymic.

To compound concerns such as these, names in both positions are frequently abbreviated, sometimes but not always when space was a demanding scribal consideration. This makes it difficult to know which case or which declension the writer may have had in mind, challenging standards of editorial imagination and consistency in their resolution. An interesting instance in which the scribe seems to show his own indecision occurs at 8r.11, where he wrote Απολλωστος, appending the genitive ending to the nominative form. Names are also frequently indeclinable, whether biblical (e.g., Ἐνῶχ) or Egyptian (many examples), though examples with final Coptic epsilon are relatively rare (e.g., Λοοϫε, Παρακοτε, Πανε, Πατσοουϩε, Τοοσε; cf. the place name Τβακε (Τβακη at 11r.11) with its Greek and Coptic attestations in Drew-Bear 1979: 270). Various names in final eta (e.g., Βαχη, Σουριχη) also seem to be indeclinable. In the Temseu Skordon pages of the codex (see especially Menas son of Enoch and Menas the meat-cook), the name Menas in first position almost always appears as Μηνᾶ. The alpha is to be treated as the sign of the Greek genitive case for Μηνᾶς rather than a Coptic nominative; this editorial decision is supported by assured examples of Μηνᾶς in first position at 10v.22 and 27r.6. Rarely does the codex provide attested examples of nominative-genitive declension. One is the familiar name Phib, which occurs regularly as Φῖβις in the nominative and Φιβίου (not Φίβιος) in the genitive. This has provided a model for resolving a series of names that are either always abbreviated or never show a nominative or genitive fully written out:

Abraamis. This name, always in first position, is with one exception abbreviated at rho (seven times) or mu (five times). When extended to abbreviation at mu, it appears with single alpha four times, double alpha once (1r.26, in a damaged reading). It is spelled in full at 11r.27 with double alpha and single mu and iota-sigma ending, which we have accepted as the standard for resolving the seven examples abbreviated at beta.

Anouphis. In one lone instance (1v.14) the name is written out in the nominative (Ἀνοῦφις). In all other instances, whether in first position or second, the name is abbreviated at phi.

Iakybis. Frequently abbreviated in short form at kappa (16r.22, 16v.13, 17r.28, etc.), only once at beta (5r.24); when written in full, the name is always spelled out as Ἰακυβίου whether in first or second position.

Iosephis. Whether in first or second position, this name is always abbreviated at phi: Ἰωσηφ/.

Pachymis. This name appears only in second or patronymic position, frequently abbreviated at mu (1r.19, 2r.19, 3v.16, etc.), but also frequently written out in full as Παχυμίου (5v.4, 7r.5, 7v.7, etc.).

Papnouthis. In all its 16 appearances, whether in first or second position, this name is abbreviated at theta.

Ionios (nominative in –ις only at 11r.17) could also belong to this group, but given its Greek character we have left its omicron in place. The names Sarapion (frequent) and Senekion or Sinikion (five instances) end in –ίον, not -ίων; the genitive remains uncertain. At 16r.9 we have resolved the former as Σαραπ(ίωνος), but contrast Σινικίου at 12r.6 in first position, κλ(ηρονόμοι) Σενικίον at 16r.18.

Besides obviously Coptic names, Coptic words also make an appearance in the text. For example, the Greek στρατιώτης is never used, but always (eight times) the Coptic equivalent, ματοι, applied to men named Biktor (five instances) and Tatianos (three). We have accepted the word as meaning soldier, though it could instead be a patronymic. More interesting is the case of two smiths, father and son (see below under Section 10, Occupations). The father is always Banos the smith, χαλκ(εύς)—χαλκ(οτύπος) is also strictly possible; his son Tatianos (16v.7) is with one exception (18r.26) referred as Tatianos φομντ. Why the scribe used the Greek term for the father while preferring the Coptic for the son, we cannot explain. The text contains a single instance of the word Πμασε in the second position (4v.14) following the name Anouph(is). Crum's *Dictionary* 186a s.v. μαcε gives as a meaning "*young animal*, esp. *calf*, *bull*." If such is intended here, one wonders whether the word is to be taken as a calque for the Greek Taurinos; but the codex yields no confirmatory Anouphis son of Taurinos. Cf. also the slightly redundant Κουϊμασε ("little young animal") in *P.Sorb.* II 69.5.11. It does, however, include numerous instances of the mysterious word ϭεc attached to seven different individuals with very popular names, Abraamis, Apollos, Biktor, Ieremias, Ioannes, Tatianos and Phibis. The meaning is unknown; it is treated as an epithet by Crum 1939: 832a, presumably because it always appears in second position in its application to the names just mentioned—apparently a way to distinguish the holders of such common names from their namesakes, an alternative to identification by patronymic. There are five names introduced by the Coptic Κουι = little or small (Crum 1939: 92b–93; see below, Section 12, Onomastics): Κουι Νου, Κουι Σνοβ, Κουι Ϣα, Κουι Σον ("Little Brother," only at Topos Demeou, 25r.6, 27r.18), and, with the most references, Κουι Τικ, or "Little Spark." Let us call them "Koui-names." They always appear just by themselves, apparently as names, never as patronymics. Other meaningful names, though such identifications are always a tricky business, include Πϫαϫ, "the sparrow"—always in second position and attached to the name Phibis—and ϩαμποι, perhaps meaning something like "bench-craftsman."

Two curious cases are provided by the names Moniskos and Tatianos. The former, a diminutive of the name Monis, appears twice in perfectly Greek form as Μονίσκου in first position (11v.23, 29); but in one other instance (5v.20), the name appears as Μονίου κου with the core of the name cast in the genitive and the diminutive apparently positioned as a separable and probably indeclinable suffix, reminiscent of the Coptic κουι. Cf. 20v.16 Πακου. The name Tatianos appears 47 times in the Temseu Skordon pages of the codex, always in first position. It is 35 times abbreviated at nu, but it is written out four times in the nominative, four times in the genitive case. Of interest are those instances where the scribe either corrects Τατιαν- to Τιτιαν- (8r.24, 18r.7), or writes Τιτιαν- in the first place (11v.27), finishing the name off with Coptic epsilon (11v.27, 18r.7 [Τιτιανε], cf. 11v.21 [Τατιανε], 15r.22 [Τιτιανα]).

The word κληρονόμος appears frequently, usually abbreviated at lambda, less commonly after rho. We resolve these abbreviations in Greek in the plural despite one instance of the evidently Coptic singular equivalent κληρε at 12r.8. It is less clear how to categorize 6v.20, 10v.6, 12v.20, 18r.13, and 19r.28, where κληλ is written.

Generalized phonological idiosyncrasies are these three:

1. Simplification of double kappa in ἐκλ(ησίας): Gignac, *Grammar* I 160.

2. Loss of nu before sigma (with two exceptions, 11v.30 and 12r.11) in Κωσταντ(ῖνος). For this loss, particularly in Latin loanwords: Gignac, *Grammar* I 117.

3. Simplification of double beta in Ἄβα (see below; no examples in Gignac, *Grammar*).

More particular are the following, in order as they appear in Gignac's *Grammar*:

Consonants:

Loss of tau in sigma-tau combination at 10v.1, σιπ(πουργῶν) for στιπ-, Gignac, *Grammar* I 66–67.

A one-time substitution (9r.5) of initial kappa for gamma in the name Γερμανός. A more frequent interchange of initial gamma and kappa in the name Γερμιϫου, Κερμιϫου, references in Index II(A), cf. Gignac, *Grammar* I 77–78.

Internal exchange of gamma and kappa, Παργατης (24r.8, cf. 1v.24), Παρκατης (12v.5, 16v.2), Gignac, *Grammar* I 79–80.

One-time intervocalic substitution of delta for tau at 13v.25, σκυδ(έων), Gignac, *Grammar* I 82–83.

Variation between beta and pi in Ἀβα (sic) and Ἀπα, Gignac, *Grammar* I 83–86. The former is consistently applied to Aba Stex, the latter to Apa Hsaias, Apa Ionios, and Apa

Nokis. The division between specific persons in the usage is distinctive, perhaps therefore not just phonological.

One-time substitution of theta for tau in the place-name ʽΑρμότνις at 4v.27 (ʽΑρμόθ/), Gignac, *Grammar* I 87, cf. Drew-Bear 1979: 73–74 for the complications of this place-name.

Intervocalic substitution of medial chi for kappa (Νοχις for Νοκις) at 1v.2 and 12r.20, Gignac, *Grammar* I 92.

Apparent substitution of lambda for rho, κληλ = κληρ (κληρ(ονόμοι)), at 6v.20, 10v.6, 12v.20, 18r.13, and 19r.28, Gignac, *Grammar* I 102–03.

A one-time substitution (11r.3) of kappa-sigma for xi in Ἀβα Στεκς (for the usual Ἀβα Στεξ), Gignac, *Grammar* I 139.

Geminated mu in ʼΑβραμμ/ at 16r.4 and 18r.3, Gignac, *Grammar* I 157–58. Cf. the double mu in φομμητ at 4r.8.

Geminated nu, medial position, in ϩελέννα at 14v.23, Gignac, *Grammar* I 158. See also the variation between single and double nu in the name Πατσαλαμαν(ν)α, single at 8v.8, 13v.7, 14r.11, double at 11v.7, 12r.32. We have treated single nu as the standard, double nu as the variant.

One-time substitution of Coptic fai for Greek beta in Πενοϥ (6v.13); cf. for this phenomenon *P.Bal.* I, pp. 93–94.

One-time substitution of schima for djandja in ϫιϭ (11r.4). Substitution of djandja for schima in Περϫουϣ at 25v.23.

Vowels

Three-time substitution (2v.21, 11r.4, 14r.25) of omicron-upsilon for omega, Κουρ for Κωρ, see Index II(A), Gignac. *Grammar* I 209–11.

Alpha-iota for eta in γυνή. The four times it is spelled out (5r.7, 9v.16, 14r.15, 17), it is written as γυναί, Gignac, *Grammar* I 247–48. (It is more usually, 13 times, abbreviated at nu.)

One-time substitution of accented eta for epsilon in ϩελήνα at 11r.9, Gignac, *Grammar* I 244–47. In the name Σαμεει/Σαμηει, always a patronymic, the spelling with eta outnumbers the spelling with epsilon, 12 to 7 (Index II(A) for references).

Exchange of upsilon for eta, notably Ζυνοδ(ώρου) for Ζηνοδ(ώρου), 13r.16, 14v.29, 16v.21, 18v.5 vs. 9v.26, 10v.12, Gignac, *Grammar* I 262–65.

Consistent substitution of upsilon for epsilon-iota in the word μάγυρ(ος) = μάγειρ(ος), Index V for references, Gignac, *Grammar* I 273.

Interchange of omicron and omega in the name Παρακοτε/Παρακωτε, Gignac, *Grammar* I 275–78. In this case, omicron sets the statistical norm (5v.13, 11r.16, 13v.11, etc.), and omega is the exception (4v.13, 9r.8).

The name Πουη(η)β appears once with single eta (5r.5), three times with eta doubled (9v.34, 11r.29, 18v.11); no examples in Gignac's *Grammar.*

Despite all the indicators, we must leave it to Coptic specialists to speculate upon the dialect underlying the linguistic idiosyncrasies of the codex's Greek as just outlined.

4. Nature of the Document and Analysis of Entries

It was Gascou's identification of the symbols in the codex's third columns as standing for talents and not wheat (Gascou 1989: 84 = 2008: 364) that brought clarity to the nature of the document as a whole. It is a running list of taxes on land, paid in cash. References to κτήτορες (10v.16–17, 27v.2) are especially suggestive.

The standard Temseu Skordon page will have a dated heading with page number, under which runs a straight line across much or all of the page. The slight squiggle occasionally present at the beginning of the line suggests that this line may be intended to represent ο(ὕτως), a normal heading for an itemized list. The cases where this seems clear to us are 7v, 12r, 20v, and 21r, and there we have printed the word accordingly. But similar lines appear in other places as well, where that resolution would not make sense; the line above 10v.16 is an example. And in about three dozen instances we see no sign at all that the line represents ο(ὕτως). We have therefore preferred to print the lines as such in these cases and in doubtful instances rather than resolving them as Greek words (and assigning them their own line numbers).

The body of each page employs a three-columned format. In column 1, the taxpayer or tax-paying institution (primarily the church) will be identified. The majority of the former are presented by name and patronymic, but some will have trade titles, still others will appear with single names; occasionally single-named taxpayers will be identified in pairs. Occasionally, also, it is the "heirs (κλ(ηρονόμοι)) of So-and-So" who are recorded as paying taxes, presumably on parcels of inherited land as yet undivided. This is a phenomenon familiar from contemporary Aphrodito (*P.Aphrod.Reg.*) and from the seventh-century Hermopolite (*P.Sorb.* II 69), though vastly more frequent in both those cases than at Temseu Skordon and Topos Demeou. The same may be said for payments made "through," διά, third parties.

The standard—again, Temseu Skordon—page runs on average to thirty-two lines (including heading and totals; see below for the latter). Against each taxpayer identification a second column records payments in carats, or larger payments in solidi, these then being converted in the third column into talents by a standard scale (with some variant alternatives). The equations between the mutual expectations of figures in columns 2 and 3 occasionally aid and almost always confirm specific decipherments. See the chart below, Section 5.

Centered at the bottoms of most pages, the total in talents from column 3, not always correct, will be recorded. If space at the bottom is lacking, the total can sometimes be found in the right margin toward the bottom of the page (4r, 4v, 5r, 6r, 9v, 12r); we have found one total wedged between columns 1 and 2 (15v). Some page totals (8r, 10r, 10v, 14r, ?16r) are lacking, that is, they were never entered; but if so they can be found in the page-by-page reckonings (*kataselides*): 23r for Temseu Skordon (pages [1]–40 from the beginning of the codex), cf. 22v.1–8 for Topos Demeou (pages 1–6, inward from the codex's end).

Oblique strokes in the left margin against the individual entries seem to be universal, except for canceled entries, visible wherever left margins of pages or parts of pages survive. These are presumably evidence that each page was rechecked in the course of adding up the figures for individual payments per page in advance of their transfer to the relevant *kataselis*. On 1r and 1v the oblique strokes are topped by X-marks. Beginning at 15v.19 down to 19v.2 the majority of entries are followed by such X-marks.

At the ends of lines in a considerable number of cases (see Index VII s.v. for the references), we find an indication ἀγρ( ). We suppose that this is likely to represent some form of ἄγραφος, but at no point is it written in full. Of the forty cases we have observed, 27 have been crossed out. The most likely explanation is that given by Preisigke, *WB* I 11 s.v., "unverbucht," i.e., the transaction in question had not yet been entered in an official register to the credit of the taxpayer; the notation was crossed out after it had been entered. We represent these notations in the translations with the cryptic "unr." (for "unrecorded").

While these page layouts are of interest for diplomatics and for scribal practice, for tax-collecting procedures and pacing this interest is surpassed by the dates given in the text and the number of payments made per date. The relevant information is as follows:

Temseu Skordon

Thoth 29 (= September 26)	
1r	28 payments
1v	26 payments – 1 cancellation = 25
	= 53 payments (+ those from the lost 1st page, folio 0v)
Phaophi 15 (= October 12)	
2r	28
2v	28
3r (a short page)	18
	= 74
Phaophi 24 (= October 21)	
3v	25
4r.1–19	18
	= 43
Hathyr 9 (= November 5)	
4r.20–31	11

4v	31
	= 42
Hathyr 26 (= November 22)	
5r	31 – 1 cancellation = 30
Hathyr 27 (= November 23)	
5v.1–25	24
Choiak 10 (= December 6)	
5v.26–27	1
6r	31 – 1 cancellation = 30
6v	31
7r	28
	= 90
Choiak <1>6 (= December 12)[3]	
7v	30
Choiak 20 (= December 16)	
8r.1–9	8
Tybi 5 (= December 31)	
8r.10–34	24
8v	31
9r	33
9v	34 – 1 cancellation = 33
10r.1–5	4
	= 125
Tybi 9 (= January 4)	
10r.6–31	24
10v.1–15	13
	= 37
Mecheir 4 (= January 29)	
10v.16–31	14

[3] See commentary to page 7v.1-1a.

11r	31
11v	29
12r	34
12v.1–2	1
	= 109

Mecheir 22 (= February 16)

12v.3–32	28
13r	32
13v	31
14r.1–9	8
24r.1–18 ("mikros logos")	17 – 1 cancellation = 16
	= 115

Phamenoth 1 (= February 25)

14r.10–34	24
14v	31
15r	29
15v.1–17	16
	= 100

Phamenoth 17 (= March 13)

15v.18–33	15
16r	29 – 1 cancellation = 28
16v	29 – 1 cancellation = 28
17r	28
17v.1–13	12 – 1 cancellation = 11
24r.19–32 ("mikros logos")	14
	= 124

Pharmouthi 8 (= April 3)

17v.14–28	14
18r	30
18v	31
19r.1–18	17
	= 92

Pharmouthi 11 (= April 6)

19r.19–20	2

Pharmouthi 24 (= April 19)

19r.21–33	12

19v	31 – 1 cancellation = 30
20r	24
	= 66

Pachon 10 (= May 5)	Second *eispraxis*
Fragment lines 1–4	3
Pachon 20 (= May 15)	Second *eispraxis*
20v	30
Thoth 10 (= September 8)	Second *eispraxis*?
Fragment lines 5–8	3

Topos Demeou

(Note: dates duplicating dates on which payments are also made for Temseu Skordon are emboldened. Possible duplication is italicized.)

Mesore 15 (= August 8)	
27v.1–21	19 (minimum)
Phaophi [15/24?] = October 12/21)	
27r.1–21	20
27r.22–33	12
	= 32

(Note: There is a horizontal line between lines 21–22, perhaps signifying the start of a new date, perhaps even separating entries for Phaophi [15 and 24]. See commentary on 22v.3.)

Phaophi or later, but on or before Tybi 5 (between October 21 and January 1?)	
26v.1–9	9
Tybi 5 (= January 1)	
26v.10–34	24
Tybi 15 (= January 10)	
26r.1–8	7
Mecheir 4 (= January 29)	
26r.9–27	17

Mecheir 22 (= February 16)	
25v.1–6	5
Phamenoth 12 (= March 8)	
25v.7–18	11
Pharmouthi 24 (= April 19)	
25v.19–31	12
25r	8
	=20

The Topos Demeou data are obviously sketchy, but they suggest several dates where collections there were coordinated with those being made at Temseu Skordon. Some were days of especially heavy traffic at Temseu Skordon (Tybi 5, Mecheir 4 and 22; Phaophi 15 and 24 if these dates did in fact match). We have failed to find any overarching pattern in the order of payments themselves, as for example in the annual sheep counts at sixteenth-century Morebath as described by Eamon Duffy (*The Voices of Morebath: Reformation and Rebellion in an English Village*, New Haven and London, 2001: 43), where the repeated sequence of taxpayers is linked to a topographically ordered circuit of the parish terrain. Smaller, localized patterns do, however, sometimes emerge from our text.

(1) Payments made "through" (διά) intermediaries, when they do occur, are a few times clustered under the name of the intermediary, who is obviously the one physically present making the recorded payments. Thus, to give the best examples, Ieremias the *protokometes* at 8r.23–26, Pessoous at 8v.19–25, cf. 13v.18–20.

(2) Petros son of Elias makes sixteen payments in the Temseu Skordon pages of the codex; Tatianos son of Elias makes eighteen. On twelve occasions they appear on the same pages (2r, 3r, 3v, 4r, 7r, 12r, 12v, 15v, 16r, 18v, 19v, 20v), and on five occasions they appear in sequence, though in variant order (3v.13–14, 4r.12–13, 7r.19–20, 15v.4–5, 16r.15–16; also close together at 2r.25 and 27). It is hard to resist the conclusion that they are brothers who at times paid one after the other, but dangerous to suggest they are also the heirs of Elias at 9v.27, 17r.8, and 20r.24. Cf., however, Ioannes and Iosephis, heirs of Paulos, at 5v.5–6, presumably brothers.

(3) 27r is the second page of the record for Topos Demeou. There are horizontal strokes between lines 21 and 22, but no indication, except perhaps for these, that payments below the line came at a date later than those above. Twenty taxpayers appear above the line, twelve below. Almost all the below-the-line payers are repeats from the twenty above the demarcation lines. Names and equivalent line numbers are as follows:

Peus	22 = 2
Monis	23 = 3
Anouphis son of Pamites	24 = 4
Elias son of Ionios	25 = 11
Peshoi son of Ionios	26 = 20
Kabios	27 = 13
Hatres, *kephalaiotes*	28 = 5
Enoch son of Horos	29 = 9
Pkylis, baker	30 = ?
Pilatos	31 = 21
Eus daughter of Horos	32 = 10
[Minos] son of Kyra	33 = ?

The first three names come in the same order above and below the line. After that any pattern seems lost. There is no match for [Minos] son of Kyra, but there is above the line a Pkylis son of Victor (line 15), whom, given the prevalence of other duplicates, one might be inclined to identify with Pkylis the baker from line 30. 27r also produces, perhaps unintentionally, an alphabetical string, lines 8–15, from Enoch to Pkylis. See also the family cluster at 16r.9–11, but see especially 25v, the upper and lower halves of which would yield results similar to those presented here for 27r.

The codex pages have other, still smaller signs of patterning: three names followed by ϭες occur in sequence at 2r.10–12; two sequential sons of Kollouthos at 3r.14–15; Lakon paying for himself, then as intermediary for Kor Jij at 8r.13–14. Of special interest is that most of the payers recorded in Temseu Skordon's Mecheir 22 "small account" (24r), some of whom appear twice, are also to be found in the main account's section for the same date (12v.3–14r.9), some of these also occurring twice. Did such a taxpayer pay the various Mecheir 22 installments all at once? If so, why are the payments not recorded in each case back-to-back (main account, "small account"). Or did such a taxpayer make several separate appearances before the tax-collector on the same day—if so, why?

5. Money[4]

On few subjects have so many words been spent, with no sign of an emergent consensus, as the money of Egypt in the fifth and sixth centuries. The detailed monograph of K. Maresch (1994), which remains the fullest treatment, was ignored by J. Banaji (1998) in his important argument for a metrological interpretation of the evidence; Banaji's arguments

[4] The first discussion on the financial accounting of this papyrus is MacCoull 1994.

were in turn dismissed without serious discussion by C. Zuckerman (2004: 57–114 at 78) in the most recent significant treatment of the subject. We shall not attempt a comprehensive approach to this complex matter here; rather, we shall describe the situation in our register and try to position it with respect to these explanations.

As we know from the accounting on 21r.5, the tax collector or official whose assistant presumably drew up these accounts was obliged to deliver a sum of 354 gold solidi, described as "of full weight" (εὔσταθμα), meaning 4 Roman grams each, minted at 72 to the pound since Constantine. These solidi are then translated into the copper currency, in which most of the collection was actually carried out, at a rate of 25,000 talents per solidus, and a sum in talents needing to be collected is given (8,850,000 T. = 354 x 25,000). To this was added 180,000 talents for the collector's "expenses," yielding a total needed collection of 9,030,000 T. The computation in talents would seem to suggest that these solidi would have to be acquired by the tax collector at a rate that is for the purposes of this reckoning set at 25,000 talents, or 3,750 myriads of denarii, each. The relationship of this number to the actual cost of acquiring solidi at the date of the account, however, is not immediately clear. It is a reasonable assumption that this figure provided some margin of safety against fluctuation in the ratio of the solidus against the copper currency.

Solidi actually mentioned in the account, however, are never reckoned at this value. We need, therefore, to find out what we can about the collector's accounting practices. Most actual payments were clearly made in talents, i.e., in the copper currency of the time, as given in the third column of the register. In this respect the situation is entirely different from that proposed by Constantin Zuckerman in analyzing the sixth-century tax register otherwise most similar to that from Temseu Skordon, namely the Aphrodito register published by him in Zuckerman 2004. We may give a brief summary of the situation there as background for the Temseu Skordon codex.

In the Aphrodito register, no fewer than 340 payments are recorded in gold, shown as solidi minus carats. (In 331 cases, the payments are of a single solidus; in 8 cases, of 2 solidi; in one case, of 5 solidi.) These deductions of carats are, except in a single case, always equal to 2 or more carats per solidus (there is only one case where the deduction is 2 carats). Zuckerman points out acutely that a single explanation for the deductions will not suffice: "Étant donné que nos comptes datent d'avant l'introduction, par Justinien, des solidi légers, que l'usure normale d'un solidus en circulation est négligeable et que chaque pièce est certifiée 'de bon poids', la soustraction de plusieurs carats sur chaque solidus encaissé ne peut pas être expliquée par le manque de poids. Par ailleurs, on constate que la soustraction est souvent identique lorsque le même contribuable paie l'impôt en plusieurs versements . . . La nature de l'impôt foncier, impossible à exprimer en solidi ronds, suggère une autre explication: le *boêthos* rend la monnaie. Ce fait est manifeste, mais il n'apporte pour autant qu'une explication partielle des déductions opérées" (Zuckerman 2004: 67). Up to this point, Zuckerman agrees with some of the key points made by previous scholarship, including most recently Banaji (1998), particularly the rejection of either wear on the coins or light-weight coinage as possible explanations of the system in use. By implication, he would also accept Banaji's rejection of the notion that the system was an arbitrary one enforced by the government in defiance of any real monetary facts.

Zuckerman continues to analysis of the minimum 2 car. deduction that is always present as representing a fixed deduction on every solidus paid. This, in his view, officially protects the collector against the gap between the total weight demanded by the government and the actual weight of several pounds' worth of gold coins, even with a seemingly negligible loss of weight for each coin. The 2 carats per solidus rate, however, "dépasse le niveau de précaution raisonnable," and should be taken as a margin retained to cover the costs of collection and unanticipated budgetary needs on the part of the village.[5] He believes that the fact that the discount does not apply to payments in copper (the remainder of the payments in the Aphrodito codex, described in the codex itself as *keratismos*) guarantees the correctness of his view that compensation for the lack of weight is at the origin of the 2-carat charge.

If Zuckerman's explanation of the Aphrodito codex is correct, most payers delivered their taxes in gold and received change in copper; far fewer paid in copper. At Temseu Skordon, by contrast, the overwhelming mass of payments were clearly made in copper, and few in gold. This is true both of payments denominated in carats and of those stated to be solidi. In most cases (nearly 70 instances), a whole solidus is reckoned at 18 carats or 17,000 tal.[6] This is true even in two cases (2v.27, 19r.13), where it is claimed (probably in error) that the payment was made in gold. Payments for whole solidi plus a fraction of a solidus also follow this method of calculation. Thus, 1 ½ solidi are consistently 25,500 tal. Most payments in the account are for less than a solidus, but they use the 17,000 tal. solidus as their basis of computation, so that the carat (1/24 of the solidus) was worth 944 tal., rounded down to 900 for 1 carat, up to 1,900 for 2 carats, and so on. A payment of 2 solidi minus 1 carat in 5v.7 is reckoned at 33,000 tal. (2 x 17,000 – 1,000: a bit of rounding). Similarly, in 24r.10, 1 sol. minus 1/2 carat is reckoned at 16,500 tal. (17,000 – 500, the latter rounded up slightly from 472). These 18-carat solidi *not* claimed to be in gold should, we believe, be taken as units of account rather than representing coins.[7] We provide here a table of the equivalences found in the text:

---

[5] Banaji (1998: 194-95), by contrast, argues that 6.25 percent, or 1.5 carat per solidus, was a normal commission on the use of solidi in large payments. He also suggests (p. 201) that the *rhope* of 0.5 carat per solidus was charged in the case of exchange from copper into solidi.

[6] An exception is the payment of 16,500 tal. for 1 sol. in 10r.10. The reason is not apparent.

[7] Cf. Keenan in *BASP* 42 (2005) 290 and Zuckerman 2004: 78. The account refers at various points to numbers of solidi to be collected in terms of the weight standard of Antinoopolis (2r.13a, 3v.2) and of the village (4r.20, 4v.1). No actual payments are made in these standards, however, and it is not easy to see whether these figures have any specific significance.

In gold	Talents	In gold	Talents	In gold	Talents
0.25 c.	200	5.875	5400	15.0	14,000
0.5	400	6.0	5600	16.0	15,000
0.75	700	6.25	5800	16.75	16,000
1.0	900	6.5	6100	17.0	15,900
1.25	1200	6.75	6300	17.5	16,500
1.5	1400	7.0	6500	1 sol. - .5 c.	16,500
1.75	1600	7.5	7000	17.75 c.	16,600
2.0	1800/1900	7.75	7200	18.0	17,000
2.25	2100	8.0	7500	1 sol.	17,000
2.5	2300	8.25	7700	18.5	17,500
2.67	2500	8.5	7900	19.25	18,100
2.75	2600	9.0	8500	21.0	19,800
2.875	2700	9.25	8600	23.5	22,100
3.0	2800	9.75	9100	1.33 sol.	22,600
3.25	3000	10.0	9300	25.0	23,500
3.5	3300	[10.25]	9600	2 sol. – 1 c.	33,000
3.75	3500	10.75	10,100	36.0	34,000
4.0	3700	11.0	10,200	2 sol.	34,000
4.25	4000	11.25	10,600	3 sol.	51,000
4.5	4200	12.0	11,200	5 sol.	85,000
4.75	4400	12.25	11,400	6 sol.	102,000
5.0	4600	13.0	12,100	7 sol.	119,000
5.25	4900	13.125	12,400	8 sol.	136,000
5.5	5100	13.5	12,400	10 sol.	170,000
5.75	5300	14.0	13,100		

A smaller number of payments, apart from the errors mentioned in the previous paragraph, is said to be in gold. In 15v.17, a payment of 17.25 carats is said to be in gold, and it is equated to 16,300 tal. The carat is thus valued at 944.9275 tal., or the solidus at 22,678. In 19r.15 and 16 we have two payments said to be in gold, of 1 sol. minus 6 ¾ carats and 1 sol. minus 8 carats, equating to 16,100 and 15,000 tal. respectively. The 24-carat solidus, on this reckoning, would come to 22,400 or 22,500 tal. It seems evident from these three payments that the use of a reckoning in solidus minus carats here does not refer to a standardized procedure of valuing solidi at a fixed number of carats less than full weight, as Zuckerman argues for the first 2 carats of deduction in the Aphrodito register. Rather, it appears instead to indicate more precisely situations in which payment was made in gold but change in copper was given, i.e., what Zuckerman argues for the remainder of his deductions. That is, "1 sol. minus 8 carats" means the same as "16 carats" but is expressed in this fashion because the payment was in fact made in gold. John Shelton (*P.Mich.* XI 607.22–23n., cited with disapproval by Carrié 1980: 269) already suggested that "It is possible that 'one solidus less six carats' is nothing more than a linguistic equivalent for '18 carats.'" Zuckerman modifies this view to the extent of the 2-carat deduction described above, but, as indicated, he takes amounts over 2 carats to reflect change given by the collector. In our case, it appears that true payments in gold occur only in these instances with change being made.

In 19r.17, a payment of 2 1/3 solidi is recorded, equated to 51,900 T. That would give us an equivalence of 22,275 tal./sol. This is close to those in the preceding lines, close enough to attribute the difference to rounding somewhere (22,400 x 2.33 = 52,192). The phrase "in gold" does not occur here, but it probably was omitted in error.

How close is the Temseu Skordon codex to the Aphrodito one in practice? The reader familiar with the Aphrodito fiscal register will recognize the significant differences between what we observe in that register and this one. For example, the term εὔσταθμος does not occur in reference to solidi at Aphrodito. And the figures in carats are there not translated into talents. That does not mean they were not collected in talents, only that the collector did not record the equivalences in the register that we have. But these are essentially formal differences, not divergences of substance. The latter are more difficult to see.

The use of an 18-carat solidus in accounting—there is no suggestion that any actual coin is meant—brings us to the question of the "local standards" in sixth-century Egypt. It is well established that in the Hermopolite nome almost all documents after 542 use a solidus minus 6 carats standard (see the table in Maresch 1994: 65–66). It is hard to avoid seeing this as reflecting the same practice as the 18-carat solidus accounting standard in the London codex. Banaji (1998) argued that these local standards reflected the use of pounds of varying weight in different localities. This view is rejected by Zuckerman (2004: 78). Leaving aside the implications in private transactions, about which we have no new evidence to bring to bear, what seems to us clear, and indeed is a tenet shared by Banaji and Zuckerman, is that the system somehow both reflects and helped to manage the basic facts of the situation: that a large part of the tax burden was collected in copper currency but paid to the imperial authorities in gold. Moreover, the system had to allow the collectors to cope with the fact that at any given moment more than one issue of copper currency was in circulation, with weights that varied far more considerably than was the case with the gold solidi. This is the underlying reality that led Banaji to emphasize the critical point, as he puts it, that "the distinctive feature of the late antique monetary system was that it seemed to lack a legal limit between bullion and coin" (1998: 188). That is, in the end it was the weight of gold, not the number of gold coins, that determined the amount collectors had to deliver, and for copper as well, weight, not numbers, determined the value of a payment (1998: 197–98). All the same, the many shifts in the copper currency from its reform by Anastasius to the multiple changes under Justinian show that the weight of individual coins was not a matter of indifference to the authorities. In any event, the solidi of 18 carats used as an accounting standard in the register are an entirely different matter from the physical solidi that the collector had to acquire and deliver.

It is evident that for the collector at Temseu Skordon to succeed in avoiding loss, he must have purchased solidi at a net price, including all exchange charges, lower than the 25,000 that he used to generate the number of talents needed. We can find solidi trading at 25,000 talents or 3,750 myriads of denarii already in the late fourth century (see Bagnall 1985: 62), at roughly similar levels (3,800 to 4,000 myriads) in the undated fifth-century reports in *P.Oxy.* LI 3628–3636, and still at 28,000 talents or 4,200 myriads in the Skar codex (*CPR* V 26), from the mid- to late fifth century. As fluctuation of prices in a 5 percent band is found even within the same four-month period in the Oxyrhynchos reports, we should not push small differentials too far in looking at these prices. At the same time, it seems highly likely that the number of talents with which the collector credited those who paid in gold was lower than the actual value of the solidi, even though the apparent Aphrodito habit of showing a 1/12 discount on solidi was not in use.

We have noted that no amount is paid anywhere in the Temseu Skordon codex that cannot be divided by 100 tal. That may reasonably be guessed, therefore, to be the value of the standard coin in which payment was made; it does not necessarily follow that no smaller coins were available in the money supply at the time, nor that no coins of variant weight were in use. Now the standard coin of the period beginning with Anastasius, the follis, was struck at 18 to the pound of copper from 512 to 538 and then again after 550, but at 15 to the pound between 538 and 550, according to Zuckerman (2004: 83). This follis was denominated as being worth 40 nummi.[8] Zuckerman has argued that a stable ratio of 16 pounds of copper per gold solidus prevailed throughout this period. The 1/15 lb. follis of 538–550, in his scheme, would thus have been 1/240 of the value of a solidus (15 x 16 = 240), or 1/10 of the value of a carat. The solidus will in turn have been worth 9,600 nummi (240 x 40). These relationships strongly suggest, then, that schematically the follis was worth 100 tal., the carat 1,000 tal., and the solidus 24,000 tal., which coincides well with a point around which fluctuations of 5–6 percent would have been normal. The follis of 538–550 is thus the unit used at Temseu Skordon for collection of the tax.

Both the rate at which the solidus is credited at Temseu Skordon and the rate at which the carat is converted into talents show a discount of 6 2/3 percent from this standard, or about 1.6 carats, compared to the 2-carat deduction used in the Aphrodito register, and close to the 6.25 percent or 1.5 carat exchange cost proposed by Banaji. But our collector has created a second type of self-protection here, by using 25,000 instead of 24,000 to generate the number of talents required. In this case the discount to the level at which the currency is actually reckoned (22,400) can be seen as 10.4%, higher than the standard discount at Aphrodito. To put it another way, the collector would in principle need 84,960 (354 x 240) folles to acquire 354 solidi. He sets out to collect instead the equivalent of 88,500 folles (354 x 250). But he values this at 100 talents to the follis, setting a goal of 8,850,000 tal.

---

[8] MacCoull 1994 suggested that the 33-nummi coin minted by Justinian in Alexandria was worth 100 tal.

By crediting the folles actually paid to him at only 93.33 tal. rather than 100 tal., however, he winds up looking to collect 94,825 folles. If he is successful, he receives not only his stated pay of 1,800 folles but another nearly 10,000 in overcharges. Of course, collectors faced real risks and costs in exercising their offices, most of all the possibility that some taxpayers would fail to pay despite all of the collector's best efforts. But the margin is substantial.

Different places, different approaches to accomplishing the same purpose. We may, of course, wonder if the difference actually marks a geographical or instead chronological distinction. The only appropriate 10th indiction during the period when the coinage aligns properly is 546/7, or two decades after the Aphrodito codex. At this time, on Zuckerman's view, the theoretical weight of the follis was 21.64 g. In 546/7, the average observed weight of measured specimens, however, is according to Zuckerman actually lower than that, or 19.5 g, or 90 percent of the nominal weight. That suggests another possible explanation for our collector's procedures: that his folles were not counted when delivered to buy solidi but instead weighed. If he could have collected some of the pre-542 folles, which have been observed to be slightly heavier than the nominal weight, of course, he would have benefited himself considerably. But we must also reckon that payments could have been made in other issues as well, including the 12-nummi pieces of 5.41 g, which would have been overvalued against the follis. A 10.4% overcharge may well thus have been intended to protect himself against a higher percentage of lighter coins, of whatever issue, in the bag. The 354 solidi required, on Zuckerman's computation, 5,664 pounds of copper, or 1,829.5 kg. That would require 93,818 folles of the post-542 weight, or very nearly the target we deduce. No wonder the imperial authorities demanded gold.

6. Chronology

There are only a few elements in the register helpful for determing its date. The most explicit is the 10th indiction mentioned in six places. But this offers us only a choice of one year in every 15-year cycle. The second element is the information on monetary matters described in the preceding section. There we argue that 546/7 is by far the year most suited to the monetary situation in the codex, although the argument may well be deemed to fall short of certainty. The use of solidi minus carats reckoning is not found in the papyri before the middle of the fifth century, with a cluster of early instances beginning in 445 (*SPP* XX 123). Indeed, carats themselves are not found as a unit of currency (as opposed to bullion weight) much before that date (Bagnall 1985: 10).

7. Taxation

The catalyst behind the codex, the tax collector, is known neither by name, nor even by title. The same anonymity is shared by the assistant (βοηθός) whose "expenses," i.e., salary, at Temseu Skordon for the 10th indiction were budgeted at 180,000 talents (21r.6–7). The assistant (see Section 5) is presumably the person who drew up the accounts; the collector himself, or another person working for him, may have been responsible for the various check marks against the individual entries in the course of compiling the *kataselides*, or page-by-page summations (23r [Temseu Skordon]; 22v.1–8 [Topos Demeou]). The unfortunate loss of the codex's first leaf deprives us of what might have been a fuller descriptive heading for the codex as a whole.

By previous "agreement," expressed it seems by the neutral Latin loanword πάκτον (21r.4, cf. *P.Lond.* V 1783, *SPP* III 271 + *BL*, references thanks to Todd Hickey), the collector had to deliver for Temseu Skordon for the 10th indiction 354 solidi (21r.4–5). The tax was the standard δημόσιον (10v.16). The village quota for any given indiction was its μερισμός (20v.1, 22v.1, 23r.1, 24r.1). The act of collecting was expressed by the word εἴσπραξις (20v.1, 21r.9, 23r.42, Frag. 1). The record of payment was, in brief, an ἀπόδοσις (1r.1, 1v.1, 2r.1, etc., but esp. 21v.1 to verify the singular in abbreviated page headings), more fully (3v.2) a λόγ(ος) τῶν ἀποδ(όσεων). That the fiscal payments at Temseu Skordon were in cash has been taken as reflecting "a thoroughly monetized countryside" in sixth-century Egypt (Banaji 2001: 169–70). How much more so for the much less significant Topos Demeou!

As far as the tax-collecting scenario is concerned, we envision the collector (or more likely, his assistant) making a circuit of a certain number of Hermopolite villages, or, more precisely, rural tax units. Temseu Skordon and the much smaller Topos Demeou (apparently a satellite hamlet of Temseu Skordon) contributed to the same *merismos*. They were grouped together for practical purposes of collection, but recorded separately, their totals combined at the end (see below). The assistant, probably accompanied by one or more guards, would seem to have set up his table at one spot and received tax payments for both places, preferably on the same days. On busy days (see Section 4) the number of individual collections ran to 100 or more (Tybi 5, Mecheir 4 and 22, Phamenoth 1 and 17); but there were also days of very limited activity (e.g., only two payments for Temseu Skordon on Pharmouthi 11), perhaps by some kind of special arrangement between taxpayers and tax-collector. Taxpayers paid overwhelmingly in bronze coins (folles, see Section 5); payments in gold were specially marked, but not always accurately (2v.27, 15v.17, 19r.13, 15, 16). Whether the coins of the payments in bronze were counted or weighed is uncertain (see Section 5 at end).

A number of entries, scattered through the codex, are marked at the end as ἀγρ( ), see Index VII for references. A majority of these additional notations were subsequently canceled, but not all. We suppose that some form of ἄγραφος is intended but cannot be confident what it modified (cf. p. 22, where we suggest that these entries indicate payments not yet entered in a master register, crossed out when entries were made later).

Records for both places were maintained in the same codex. The Temseu Skordon entries were written from the front of the codex inwards, the Topos Demeou entries from the back of the codex inwards. The accumulation of information grew over the course of the indictional year, with the Temseu Skordon and Topos Demeou sections of the codex gradually approaching one another, eventually merging and interleaving at 21r–24r:

Fol. 21. This is the inserted leaf, not part of the originally constructed codex (see Section 1).

21r (Plate 3), undated, with only ten short lines, is the final reckoning (λόγος) for Temseu Skordon's first *eispraxis*. It must therefore date after Pharmouthi 24 = April 19, the date of the last page (40 = 20r) in the record of Temseu Skordon payments for the first *eispraxis.* It also must have been written after 23r, the Temseu Skordon *kataselis*, on which 21r's Temseu Skordon total was based.

21v, dated only to Thoth (August 29–September 27), for the 10th indiction, with perhaps a blank left for later insertion of an exact date, records two more payments by known residents of Temseu Skordon (ὑπὲρ) παραλ(λη̣λισμοῦ), which only appear here (see note ad loc.). We suppose that the Thoth payments of 21v were made after the close of the 10th indiction but credited to it. The spread of dates between recto and verso texts cannot be precisely determined; nor can the precise timing and circumstances of the insertion of this leaf into the already-existent codex. See above, Section 1.

Fol. 22

22r is blank.

22v.1–8 contains the *kataselis* for Topos Demeou, followed by crossed-out entries for Temseu Skordon tax payments (date lost).

Fol. 23

23r (Plate 4) is the Temseu Skordon *kataselis* in two columns. It seems to have been written all at once, not, that is, as a gradually accruing set of totals from the Temseu Skordon pages. Of particular interest are lines 42–46, where Temseu Skordon and Topos Demeou totals are given one after the other. 23r.42–43 therefore had to have been written after Pharmouthi 24 = April 19 (20r) but before 21r (the Temseu Skordon *logos*). 23r.44–46 had to have been written after 22v.1–8 (the Topos Demeou *kataselis*).

23v is blank.

Fol. 24

24r is the "small account" from Temseu Skordon, dated Mecheir 22 = February 16.

24v is blank.

The order of the pages from 21r to 24v, including the blanks at 22r, 22v, and 24v, is hard to explain, as are the interleaving of information from the two different places and the chronological sequence of writing on the pages concerned.

Of great interest for the end result of this 10th-indiction tax-collecting process are 21r.1–10, 22v.8, and 23r.42–46. 22v.8 provides the total for the six pages of the Topos Demeou portion of the codex: 516,900. 23r.42–43 adds up the totals from pages [1]–40 (= 20r) of the Temseu Skordon portion of the codex, arriving at a figure of 7,345,300 talents. The Topos Demeou total is then transferred from 22v.8 and entered at 23r.44–45. These two main figures are then added together and the result entered at 23r.46: 7,862,200. The total is correct. This total in turn is entered at 21r.10 as the results of the "first collection" (πρώτη εἴσπραξις). We know from 21r.8 that according to the *pactum* a total of 9,030,000, including a 180,000-talent expense payment for the assistant, was required. The deficit of 1,167,800 talents was presumably to be made up in a supplementary, or second, *eispraxis* whose recording is found in part at 20v (Pachon 20 = May 15), whose surviving and restorable talents amount to 269,100 talents. The unplaced fragment, also from the second *eispraxis*, records payments totalling at least 100 more solidi = 1,700,000 talents, considerably more than needed. They may therefore not be connected with the same operation. Perhaps a continuation can be seen in the crossed-out parts of 22v. Why the three blank pages (22r, 23v, 24v) were not used to complete the recording of the second *eispraxis* is anybody's guess. They should have been just about sufficient for that purpose, but have provided a truly incoherent pagination. It is possible that additional parts of the second collection stood on pages now lost from the end of the codex. In any case, the practices as exemplified in the Temseu Skordon codex, to the extent that they are discoverable, do not seem to fit the system of *katabolai* in effect at contemporary Aphrodito, as described by Zuckerman 2004: esp. 182–84. All the same, it is likely that the taxes were delivered by the responsible official to the government in such installments, even if we cannot recover them from this register.

8. Tabulation of Payments

In the tabulation presented here, we have separated the Temseu Skordon population from that of Topos Demeou. It should be noted, however, that a handful of individuals had holdings in both places. They are not statistically material. In the following tables these are listed separately under Temseu Skordon and Topos Demeou.

The following principles are used in tabulating the payments:

(1) Canceled payments are not included.

(2) Payments by two people ("A and B") are listed under both, but only half of the amount is credited to each person.

(3) Amounts restored on the basis of the number of carats are included.

(4) Where the amount is missing and cannot be restored, it is counted as zero (but the entry is included in the number of payments).
(5) Where neither the person's name nor the patronymic can be recovered, the payment is omitted from the table.
(5) Entries under a name without patronymic are combined with those of an individual of the same name with a patronymic, if there is only one possible candidate. If not, they are kept separate (Iosephis, Kyriakos, Minos, Papnouthis son of Minos [two different grandfathers possible], Psas, Soios). Obviously there is some residual uncertainty about identifications, but they are not material.
(6) Heirs of an individual who also occurs are combined with entries for that individual: Senekion, Tjeer, Theophilos.
(7) NN son of someone and NN heir of the same person are combined: Ieremias of Elias, Ioannes of Paulos, Iosephis of Paulos.
(8) Unnamed sons and daughters of an individual are combined with a sole known son or daughter of that individual: Tatianos son of Banos, Paulos son of Kalatous.
(9) Institutional property (Holy Church and Holy Martyrion) is not included in the table or in the calculations of inequality below, where only individuals are tallied.
(10) The abbreviation "gs." in the table denotes grandson of the person following. It is certain that there are some identifications that we have not made but which could be made with more evidence. The result of this will be to suggest a slightly greater dispersion of ownership and prevalence of very small holdings than was actually the case. We do not believe that this effect is material. In multi-line entries, the name is on the last line.

Temseu Skordon Payments

Name	Patronymic or identifier	Lines	Total	Payments	Sex
Aba Stex		1r.27,1v.26,4v.20,11r.3, 14r.29,16r.4	8,100	6	M
Abraamis	anagnostes	19r.31	7,900	1	M
Abraamis	carpenter	12r.33,14v.3,16v.14	12,100	3	M
Abraamis	from Antinoou	11v.30	5,600	1	M
Abraamis	Pesoous	1r.26,2v.15,12v.8,16r.13, 18r.3	35,300	5	M
Abraamis	qes	9r.9,10r.20,11r.27,16r.4, 18r.6	8,900	5	M
Ailianos	wine producer	1v.17,2r.26,4v.29	4,700	3	M
Akoui	fuller	18r.9	1,900	1	M
Ama Tasous	monazousa	1r.29,5v.7,18r.21,19r.18	73,700	4	F
Annios		1r.17,2r.22,9r.28	4,400	3	M
Anouphis	Aba Stex	6v.15	1,900	1	M
Anouphis	Albios	10v.25	2,800	1	M
Anouphis	Apollos	9r.19,10v.13,14	1,700	3	M

Anouphis	Enoch	9r.4	5,600	1	M
Anouphis	from Tbake	1v.5,3v.23,7r.4,8v.5,11r.11,14v.31,24r.25	9,700	7	M
Anouphis	Iakybis	1v.14,5r.24,6v.28,7v.4,8v.32	5,500	5	M
Anouphis	Konstantinos	1v.15,4r.30,7v.28,8v.30,10r.31,13v.23,15r.10,16v.17,19r.33	39,800	9	M
Anouphis	Kosmas	5r.31	1,900	1	M
Anouphis	mason	8v.9	1,900	1	M
Anouphis	Minos, gs. Dioskoros	11v.20,13v.32,14v.9,15v.29,19v.19,20r.8,20r.25,	15,800	7	M
Anouphis	Pamides	20v.20,25v.4,30,26v.12,26r.19,27r.4,24	39,900	7	M
Anouphis	Pinoution	14r.18	2,800	1	M
Anouphis	Pioul	1r.14,3r.6,6r.21,11r.23,15r.20	19,700	5	M
Anouphis	Pmase	4v.14	1,900	1	M
Anouphis	qes	14v.32	8,500	1	M
Antonios	Apollos	24r.13	900	1	M
Apa Apalo	monazon	7r.26,12v.17,17v.8,19r.18,20r.2	17,200	5	M
Apa Ionios		19r.19	17,900	1	M
Apa Nochis		1v.2,2v.18,8r.21,12r.20,15r.9,17v.2,19v.23	54,900	7	M
Apollos	Anouphis	19r.8	400	1	M
Apollos	diakonos	10r.29,12r.24,19r.10	4,700	3	M
Apollos	Hatres	6v.19,7v.20,9r.24,12v.13,15r.26,18v.19,19v.13	16,000	7	M
Apollos	Ioannes	3r.12,6r.25,7r.22,8r.7,11,23,11r.22,12v.6,15r.27,16v.5,18v.6	78,600	11	M
Apollos	Kasia	4r.16,7v.25,8r.34,9r.16	20,600	4	M
Apollos	Lasouk	1v.16,6r.2,8v.31,11v.8,14r.22,18v.14,19v.10	22,000	7	M
Apollos	Lene	2r.5,5v.2,11v.5	22,900	3	M
Apollos	oilworker	1v.3,2v.9,5r.28,6v.27,12r.35,12v.16,13r.3,15r.29,16r.12,19r.11	40,400	10	M
Apollos	Ophelios	1v.27,6r.18,14v.7,18v.2	5,600	4	M
Apollos	Pachymis	5r.27	2,800	1	M
Apollos	Pioul	9r.6	900	1	M
Apollos	qes	2r.10,4v.10,6r.3,9r.3,9v.30,12r.18,14v.21,17r.13,24r.29	17,900	9	M
Apollos	Zoe	1r.5	5,300	1	M
Apor	via Apollos s. Lasouk or Victor	11v.17,14v.5,17r.25,19v.3,20v.14	18,200	5	M
Banos	smith	8r.8,12v.7,18,15v.3	8,400	4	M
Choor	Anouphis	2r.21,6r.15,9r.7,11v.25,12r.14,13v.14,19r.3,19v.17	42,500	8	M
Choor	Georgios	2r.14	3,700	1	M

Choor	tailor	15r.11	1,900	1	M
Cobblers		8v.13,13v.25,15v.24,24r.15, 32	14,900	5	C
Daughter of Phanoub		20r.15	1,400	1	F
Dioskoros	Horos	19r.32	900	1	M
Elias	Kelele	20v.18	15,000	1	M
Elias	Kollouthos	20r.3	1,400	1	M
Elias	Patsalamanna	18v.3	2,800	1	M
Enoch	fuller	4r.24,8v.10,10v.27,14r.19, 16v.15,17v.23,19v.21,24r.3	26,100	8	M
Enoch	Kollouthos	6v.5,8r.18,10v.30,12r.21, 13v.28,15r.24,17v.22, 18v.16	16,000	8	M
Enoch	Kyriakos	13r.22,17r.9,26v.21	3,700	3	M
Enoch	Lousia	9v.31,12v.15,16v.8,18v.17, 19v.6	11,200	5	M
Enoch	oikonomos	3v.5,6v.21,8r.2,9r.20, 10r.10,11r.31,13r.5,17r.26, 19r.15,24r.24	244,900	10	M
Esaias (Apa)	presbyteros	2r.9,3r.3,5r.20,7v.5,8r.33, 10v.9,12r.4,15v.12,16v.20, 19r.30	41,400	10	M
Eus	Ioannes	1v.13,2v.5,4v.4,5r.15,6v.8, 9r.32,10r.23,11r.19,13r.11, 15v.13,19r.29,20v.12	31,200	12	F
Georgios	meat-cook	1v.7,4r.29,6r.8,11r.28, 13r.32,15r.5,24r.22	55,100	7	M
Georgios	Matheias	20v.6,26v.14	7,500	2	M
Georgios	Phibis	2v.11,5r.4,24r.31	20,000	3	M
Georgios	Taurinos	4v.2,5v.24,12r.17,13r.10, 13r.27,15r.7,16r.23,20r.11, 24r.7	48,900	9	M
Halmios	sometimes via Ioannes pel( )	4v.26,7v.10,10r.15,12r.28, 15v.2,16v.19	10,200	6	M
Hampoi		2v.3,4r.6,8v.4,9v.20,10v.23, 13v.8,14r.28,16r.21,17v.17	44,000	9	M
Hatres	Georgios	1r.18,10v.29	5,800	2	M
Hatres	Hyperechios	2v.28,5v.22,6r.10,7r.18, 9v.25,10v.4,11v.6,13r.9, 14r.5,15r.8,19v.20,20v.10	30,500	12	M
Hatres	Parakote	11r.16,13v.11,16v.16	5,500	3	M
Hatres	Pebos	14v.11,17r.24,17v.16	3,700	3	M
Hatres	Pemen	6r.14,8r.31	2,700	2	M
Hatres	Sameei	3v.22,8v.7,10v.3,11v.10, 14r.26	10,300	5	M
Hatres	tailor	1r.7,6v.24,9v.19,11v.16, 15r.25,17r.29,18r.18,19r.24	15,000	8	M
Heirs of deacon		1v.4,2r.20,4r.2,18,5r.17, 6v.23,7v.17,12v.25,15r.28, 16r.14,18v.7,20r.17	105,900	12	C
Heirs of Elias	son of Pessoous	9v.27,13r.15,17r.8,20r.24	94,500	4	C

Heirs of Kah		6v.20,9v.33,10v.6,12r.8,12v.20,14r.14,16v.24,18r.13,19r.28	11,800	9	C
Heirs of Konstantinos		4r.3,5v.19,27,13v.29	92,500	4	C
Heirs of Poueeb		18v.11	900	1	M
Heirs of Theophilos		3r.4,5v.3,8r.3,15r.30,16v.23,20r.7	63,200	6	C
Helena		2r.6,3v.6,4r.17,5r.16,6r.22,7v.21,9r.15,11r.9,13v.4,14v.23,17r.21,19v.25	103,700	12	F
Hirqosh		4v.12,7r.29	5,600	2	
Horos	Souriche	2r.23,4v.28,8r.15,14r.31,16v.12,17v.21,18r.17	15,700	7	M
Horos	Victor	5r.6,9r.21,13v.6	2,700	3	M
Iakybis	Anoubion	2v.29	14,100	1	M
Iakybis	Ioannes	4v.3	2,800	1	M
Iakybis	Isakis	16r.26	900	1	M
Iakybis	Kollouthos	3r.15,13v.31,16v.13,18r.10	6,000	4	M
Iakybis	smith	15r.13,19v.24,20v.26	7,500	3	M
Ieremias	Elias	2v.13,26,12r.15,13v.18,15r.19,19r.16,20r.19,24r.16,26v.30	169,500	8	M
Ieremias	Halmios	4r.28,8v.27	3,100	2	M
Ieremias	Pane	2r.13,4r.5,5v.18,25,7r.17,9v.29,12r.12,29,12v.23,13v.3,14r.20,17r.17,18v.25,20v.17	63,200	14	M
Ieremias	protokometes	17r.12	1,900	1	M
Ieremias	qes	3r.8,18r.5,20r.6	29,400	3	M
Ioannes	Akoris (Aqor)	4v.8,7r.7,9r.11,11r.6,16v.6	9,700	5	M
Ioannes	Horos	9r.23	5,600	1	M
Ioannes	Iakybis	6v.3,8r.17,10v.24,14r.6,15r.3,17r.28,18v.4	20,400	7	M
Ioannes	Iosephis	3r.10,11r.17	19,700	2	M
Ioannes	laborer	7v.14	1,400	1	M
Ioannes	Lene	13r.29,14r.24	3,700	2	M
Ioannes	Leus	5r.10,6v.18,7r.28,8v.17,11r.21,17r.18,17v.28,18v.12,20v.19	23,600	9	M
Ioannes	oikonomos ekklesias	11r.30	17,000	1	M
Ioannes	Panoube	3r.16,5r.23,7r.27,7v.18,17v.27	7,400	5	M
Ioannes	Pargata (Pargates)	1v.24,24r.8	3,200	2	M
Ioannes	Patsalamanna	18r.19,18v.13	5,100	2	M
Ioannes	Paulos	2v.23,5v.5,8v.22,12r.10,13v.19,14v.26,18r.20	120,200	7	M
Ioannes	Pnahkas	10r.18,12v.14	5,600	2	M
Ioannes	qes	2r.12	1,900	1	M
Ioannes	Sarapion gs. Theonilla	16r.10	900	1	M

Ioannes	Sinouere	11v.11	900	1	M
Ioannes	Zenodoros	9v.26,10v.12,13r.16,14v.29, 16v.21,18v.5	7,900	6	M
Ionios	Anouphis, gs. Iakybis	16r.22	5,600	1	M
Ionios	carpenter	4v.16	2,800	1	M
Ionios	Iosephis	3v.20,7r.12,7v.29,8r.27, 13r.28,14v.25,17v.20, 18v.10,19r.4	72,400	9	M
Ionios	Komes	15v.26,33	1,900	2	M
Iosephis	gramm( )	2v.27,6v.30,17r.4	28,500	3	M
Iosephis	Haroous	1v.6,23,3v.19,6v.6,11v.12, 13r.7	23,800	6	M
Iosephis	Horos	1r.25,2v.19,3v.18,4r.19, 4v.23,5r.25,6r.26,7v.12, 8r.22,10r.27,11v.3,13r.18, 13r.26,13v.12,15r.12,24r.5	69,400	18	M
Iosephis	Nonna	7r.21,25	16,800	2	M
Iosephis	Paulos	5v.6,23,9v.4,12v.28	22,400	4	M
Iosephis	Pinoution	4r.23	2,800	1	M
Iosephis		9r.34	5,600	1	M
Isakis	carpenter	3v.25,6r.11	2,800	2	M
Isakis	cholos	20v.9	1,900	1	M
Isakis	heir of Elias	2r.4,15v.16,20v.21,23, 24r.10,26	62,800	6	M
Isakis	presbyteros	2r.29,2v.7	4,200	2	M
Isidoros	Kale	19r.22	3,700	1	M
Isis	Hermapollon	9r.27	900	1	F
Kajoj		12v.2	1,900	1	
Kapai	Wine producer	18r.24,20v.7	2,300	2	M
Kasia	Pinoution	10r.25,12v.30,13v.21	2,700	3	F
Kasia	Sameei	7v.26	5,600	1	F
Kelele		15v.17	16,300	1	M
Kelle		6r.27,8v.15,10r.22,11r.2, 14r.21,17v.24,19v.29	17,500	7	
Kometa	Sarapion gs. Theonilla	16r.9	1,900	1	M
Konstantinos	doctor	14v.28	17,000	1	M
Konstantinos	Pachymis	1r.19,2r.19,3v.16,6v.32, 7v.7,9r.10,12r.11,15v.11, 18r.25,18v.15,19v.26	118,500	11	M
Kooh(a)		4v.15,6v.7	4,700	2	
Kor Jij		1v.20,2v.21,6v.31,7v.27, 8r.14,9r.25,11r.4,12v.31, 14r.25,16v.3,18r.4,19r.26	32,300	12	M
Koui Nou		4v.7,6v.12,9v.13,18v.21, 20r.14	7,400	5	M
Koui Sha	with Laho	8r.16,17v.18,19r.5	11,600	3	M
Koui Snob		8v.20,12r.16,15v.14,20r.5, 20v.30,24r.2	38,400	6	M

Koui Tik		1r.4,2r.2,3v.10,4v.9,5r.14, 6r.32,7v.2,9v.36,10r.19, 10v.21,12v.10,15v.10, 17r.20,19v.27	80,000	14	M
Kyra	Taurinos	6r.17,9r.30,13v.10,15r.14, 18r.30	5,000	5	F
Kyriakos	Anouphis	4r.9,6r.5,8r.26,11r.32, 11v.22	20,500	5	M
Kyriakos	Germijou	4v.6	1,800	1	M
Kyriakos	Patsoouhe	4r.7,9v.23,12r.31,16r.27, 18r.8	11,200	5	M
Kyriakos		6v.10	1,900	1	M
Kyros	carpenter	9r.29,14r.2	2,800	2	M
Kyros	stonecutter	1r.20,3r.13,8v.14,10r.16, 11v.19,13v.5,14v.30,17r.19	18,600	8	M
Lahe	mason	9v.5,13r.24,15r.21	3,900	3	M
Lahe	Panoube	16r.3	900	1	M
Laho		4r.22,6r.23,8r.16,10v.20, 14r.23,17r.11,19r.5	12,500	7	M
Lakon		3v.8,4r.26,6v.29,8r.13, 10r.14,10v.19,14v.2	7,300	7	M
Looje		2v.20,10r.4,26,11v.18, 17v.25,18r.15	12,300	6	M
Lota		12r.25,13v.16,17r.10	5,600	3	M
Loulous	Ioannes	7r.11,9v.15,11r.25,12r.13, 15v.19,19v.2	7,900	6	M
Loulous	Germanos	9r.5	400	1	M
Lythis	laborer	2r.8,3r.11,4v.31,5v.10, 7v.24,8r.28,12r.3,13r.6, 14v.13,16r.29,18r.23,18v.9	29,700	12	M
Makarios	Germanos	4v.19,8v.24,9r.13,11r.13, 14r.16,17r.14,18r.22	16,700	7	M
Makarios	mason	8v.12,10v.8,11v.28,13r.8, 16r.7,19v.14	13,400	6	M
Makarios	Papnouthis	7r.3,9r.2	3,800	2	M
Makarios	Poueeb	11r.29	1,900	1	M
Maria	Palikous	1r.18,3v.11,6v.4,9v.35,20v.3	8,100	5	F
Maria	Victor	20r.18	4,600	1	F
Mathetes		16v.4	900	1	M
Menas	meat-cook	4r.4,5r.12,6r.7,13v.2,17r.22, 24r.14,19	47,700	7	M
Menas	Enoch	4r.14,6r.19,9r.17,9v.12, 11r.7,13r.33,14r.33,16v.10, 18r.11,19r.7	47,400	10	M
Menas	Peret	8v.26	900	1	M
Menas	Pinoution	10v.22	2,800	1	M
Menas	Thabounos	14v.19,16v.22	1,800	2	M
Minos	anagnostes	15v.7	1,900	1	M
Minos	Anouphis gs. Enoch	3r.5,6v.25,7v.13,8v.29, 11v.24,14r.7,15v.21	17,800	7	M
Minos	Dioskoros	1v.18,2r.24,3r.19,3v.27, 5v.12,10r.28,13r.25,15r.2	28,700	8	M

Minos	Pis	1r.2,2r.16,5v.17,6r.6,8v.16, 11v.15,13r.2,15v.6,19r.27	19,900	9	M
Minos	Timoute	4r.21,4v.17,7v.23,12r.22, 13v.13,26v.18	17,400	6	M
Minos	with Pohe	9r.31	1,400	1	M
Monis	Hermapollon	8v.11,13v.26,16r.2, 24r.12,20	9,100	5	M
Monis	Komes	7r.6,10r.8,13r.19,18r.2, 24r.21,30	9,300	6	M
Monis	Papnouthis	4v.5,6v.16	2,800	2	M
Monis	Paulos	6v.22	17,000	1	M
Monis	Poueeb	5r.5,9v.34	1,800	2	M
Monis	protokometes	12r.9	17,000	1	M
Monis/Moniskos	Aqor (Akoris)	5v.20,11v.23,29,20v.16	28,200	4	M
Moses		9r.14	900	1	M
NN	Enoch	7v.30	3,700	1	?
NN (--om( ))	Apollos	15v.30	4,200	1	M
Nonna	Parsas	8v.19	11,200	1	F
Nonna	Stephanos	17v.6	2,800	1	F
Onnophrios (Onober)	Panoube	14r.27,16v.30	2,800	2	M
Paesis	Nohe	5r.11,6r.12,10r.3,24,14v.18, 17v.11,18r.16,19r.12	11,500	8	M
Panecheutes		12r.5	3,700	1	M
Panejnou	via Ioannes pel( )	7v.10,13r.12,13v.9,17r.23, 18r.27,20r.20,24r.6	15,300	7	M
Papnouthis	Klumax or Klem( )	7v.6,8r.25,11v.13,12v.27, 17r.27,18v.26,20v.8	38,600	7	M
Papnouthis	Minos	19v.22	3,900	1	M
Papnouthis	Minos, gs. Anouphis	14v.8,15v.25	6,800	2	M
Papnouthis	Minos, gs. Dioskoros	13v.22	1,900	1	M
Parakote		4v.13,5v.13,9r.8,10v.11, 15r.6,17v.26,18v.31,20r.12	33,100	8	M
Pastamou		9v.24	700	1	M
Patjits		1v.12,5r.32,17r.16	4,200	3	M
Patoul		17v.9	700	1	M
Patsalamanna	sometimes via Kooha	6v.17,8v.8,11v.7,12r.32, 13v.7,14r.11,20r.13	36,900	7	M
Paulos	Kalatous	16r.25,18v.22,19v.32	7,500	3	M
Pe.e	baker	20v.2	1,200	1	M
Pekysis	carpenter	17r.3	1,900	1	M
Peschal	Makarios	1r.21,3r.9	10,000	2	M
Pessoous		8v.18,14r.3,16r.8	42,400	3	M
Petoueeb		14r.13	1,900	1	M
Petros	Elias	1r.15,2r.27,3r.18,3v.13, 4r.13,5v.14,6r.13,7r.20, 11r.26,12r.7,12v.4,12,15v.4, 16r.15,18v.28,19v.18, 20v.28	147,600	17	M

Peurot	Pachymis	2r.17,5v.4,7r.5,7v.11,8r.30, 10v.18,11v.26,13r.31, 14v.14,15v.20	60,200	10	M
Peurot	Parbas	11r.20	2,800	1	M
Phibis	from Harmotnis	3v.24,4v.27,14r.8,16r.19	13,000	4	M
Phibis	Hatres	4r.10	2,800	1	M
Phibis	Iosephis	2v.6,24,16v.25,19r.2,20r.16	42,800	5	M
Phibis	Lousia	1r.11,3v.9,20v.11	4,100	3	M
Phibis	Phoibammon gs. Toose	3v.4,5r.8,9v.8	93,500	3	M
Phibis	Pjaj	2r.28,3v.15,8r.5,9v.32, 12r.27,20v.27	21,400	6	M
Phibis	qes	5r.3	1,900	1	M
Phibis	Taroou	1r.10,2v.10,5r.9,10r.5,7, 12r.34,12v.24,15r.18,17v.10	133,100	9	M
Phibis	Theophilos	1r.13,2r.3	23,300	2	M
Phibis	Toose	1r.9,2v.12,6v.9,7r.23,8r.6, 11v.3,14r.4,15r.17,17v.3, 18v.29,20r.23	229,300	11	M
Phoibammon	meat-cook	2r.7	5,600	1	M
Phoibammon	Germanos	5v.11	1,800	1	M
Phoibammon	Lota	1v.10,4v.22,7r.10,10v.15, 14v.4	13,000	5	M
Phoibammon	Matrona	3v.12,4v.32,5r.13,6r.16, 7v.22,8v.6,11r.5,13r.30, 14v.12,16v.18,18r.31	95,100	11	M
Phoibammon	Pinoution	1r.16,2v.2,4r.25,5r.26, 8v.21,9v.21,10r.13,10v.28, 13v.20,15v.22,18v.20, 19v.12,20r.22,20v.22	50,600	14	M
Phoibammon	smith	19r.6	1,900	1	M
Phoibammon	wine producer	10r.30,11v.31,12v.32	4500	3	M
Pieous	Sameei	6r.29,17r.5	2,850	2	M
Pioul		8v.2,17v.19	3,800	2	M
Pistos		16r.20	2,800	1	M
Pitechou		6r.28,8v.28,12v.29,14r.12, 17r.6,18r.12	7,350	6	M
Piter	Apollos	13v.15,15v.32	3,300	2	M
Pkylis	Kollouthos	1v.22,2v.16,3r.14,3v.26, 4r.27,4v.11,5v.9,6v.2,9r.12, 10v.7,14v.15	28,400	11	M
Pkylis	Pamiates	14r.30,26v.27	12,100	2	M
Pkylis	Pasothis	18r.28	900	1	M
Pkylis	Petros	20v.15	10,200	1	M
Pkylis	Phoibe (Phybe)	6r.9,10v.26,14v.20,16r.24	15,000	4	M
Plotion (Ploution)		2r.15,5r.21,5v.16,7r.9, 8v.23,9v.10,12r.19,12v.22	14,900	8	M
Pnahkas		7v.3,9v.11	4,300	2	M
Pohe	with Minos	9r.31	1,400	1	M
Psas	Ioannes	8v.3,14r.32	3,800	2	M

Psas	Komes	2v.8,4r.15,5r.19,6v.11, 7v.31,8r.19,11r.24,12r.23, 14r.9,14v.24,16r.17,19r.9, 19v.11,24r.9	52,900	14	M
Psas	with Laho	4r.22	1,400	1	M
Saie	Elias	4v.21	900	1	F
Sanna	Pamides	20v.5	2,800	1	F
Sarapion	Bache	1r.23,2v.4,7v.16,10r.9, 13r.20,17v.7,13,18v.18, 19v.5	26,100	9	M
Sarapion	Iakybis	3r.7,9v.17,11r.15,14v.22, 16v.29,24r.4,18	41,800	7	M
Sarapion	Menas	20r.21	5,600	1	M
Sarapion	Pasothis	6v.26,7r.15,8r.29,11r.14, 15v.23	11,200	5	M
Sarapion	sitometres	1r.24,2r.18,4r.11,4v.18, 7r.13,7v.8,9r.22,10v.31, 13v.17,15r.4,17r.15,19r.17	101,600	12	M
Sarapion	Theonilla	16r.11,19r.25	3,000	2	M
Senekion		2v.25,9v.6,12r.6,16r.18, 20v.25	96,200	5	M
Serenos	Konstantinos	19r.14,20v.25	18,400	2	M
Soios	(w. Pitechou, via Iosephis)	12v.29	2,050	1	M
Soios	Phibis	9v.3,14r.34,17r.5,17v.15	9,350	4	M
Soios	Talaou	1v.8	4,200	1	M
Solomon	Phibis	3v.17,6r.30,7r.8,11r.10, 14v.10,24r.27	4,900	6	M
Son of Parkates		12v.5,16v.2	5,600	2	M
Son of Saul s. Aoug		19v.16	17,000	1	M
Tatianos	baker	24r.28	900	1	M
Tatianos	Banos, smith	3v.7,4r.8,5r.30,6r.20,8r.12, 9v.18,12v.11,15v.15, 16v.7,28,18r.26,19r.13	64,000	12	M
Tatianos	Elias	2r.25,3r.2,3v.14,4r.12,4v.24, 5r.22,7r.19,24,8v.25,12r.30, 12v.21,13r.17,15v.5,16r.16, 18v.32,19v.30,20v.13	159,700	17	M
Tatianos	Parbas	1v.11,9v.2,15r.22,17r.2, 18r.7,24r.23	12,200	6	M
Tatianos	Pessous	1r.12	2,800	1	M
Tatianos	qes	8r.24,11v.20,14v.16	28,200	3	M
Tatianos	soldier	3r.17,5v.15,7v.19	7,500	3	M
Tatianos	tailor	1v.9,8r.9,11v.26,19v.31	7,000	4	M
Teshneene	sometimes via Menas s. Enoch	9v.14,15v.27	2,800	2	F
Theophilos		5r.18,7v.15,12v.9,16v.26	21,600	4	M
Tjeer		10v.10,16r.28,24r.17	4,600	3	F
Trasias	Paulos	6r.4,8r.20,9r.18,10r.17	14,500	4	M
Victor	Apollos	17v.4	1,900	1	M

Victor	baker	1r.8,7r.16,9v.22,10v.5, 11v.9,13v.30,14v.27, 15v.28,18r.29	32,400	9	M
Victor	carpenter	20v.4	2,300	1	M
Victor	Hellos	18v.24	4,600	1	M
Victor	Iouloumenos	1v.25,7r.2,15r.23,15v.31, 18v.8,19v.7	10,500	6	M
Victor	Kermijou	3v.21,4v.25,9r.26,11r.18, 11v.14,13v.24,14v.6, 19v.28,20v.24	30,400	9	M
Victor	qes	2r.11,5v.8,10r.21,13r.23, 14v.17,16v.9,19v.15	17,300	7	M
Victor	Sameei	1r.3,1v.19,2v.22,5r.29, 6r.24,9r.33,10r.2,11r.12, 12v.19,13r.14,15v.9,19v.8,9	103,800	12	M
Victor	soldier	1r.6,4v.30,6v.14,8r.32, 13r.13	24,700	5	M
Wife of	Anouphis s. Iakybis	13v.27,20r.4,20v.31	14,900	3	F
Wife of	Peilish	14r.15,16v.11	3,400	2	F
Wife of	Penob	5r.7,6v.13,9v.16,11r.8, 13r.21,14r.17,17r.7,18r.14, 18v.23,19r.23	24,300	10	F

Topos Demeou Payments

Name	Patronym or identifyer	References	Total	Payments	Gender
Annou (Annios?)	Elias	25v.9	3,700	1	M
Apion	Petros	25v.14,25,26r.23,26v.3,27r.16	8,100	5	M
Elias	Ionios	25v.5,26r.21,26v.13,27r.11,25	28,100	5	M
Elias	Peshoi, gs. of Ionios	25r.4	2,800	1	M
Elias	Pison	25v.3	5,600	1	M
Enoch	Horos	25v.6,20,26r.27,27r.9,29	21,400	5	M
Enoch	Peteneou	25r.3,26r.14,26v.7,27r.8	7,800	4	M
Eus	Horos	25v.17,22,27r.10,32	6,400	4	F
Georgios	Petros	25v.16,28,26r.6,24,26v.8,26,27r.17	6,600	7	M
Hatres	kephalaiotes	26r.12,27r.5,28	6,500	3	M
Hatres	Pamates	26r.11	1,900	1	M
Heirs of Pamides		25v.2	11,200	1	C
Ieremias	Ieremias	25r.8,26v.32	6,500	2	M
Ioannes	Pajeer	25v.29	1,200	1	M
Kabios		25r.5,26v.17,27r.13,27	17,300	4	M
Koinon Epoikioton		25r.9	8,700	1	C
Konta (Kounta)	Apion	26r.4,26v.6	1,800	2	M
Koui Son		25r.6,27r.18	3,300	2	M

Kyriakos	Shnet (Shinetos)	25v.10,26r.2,15,26v.25,27r.12	10,100	5	M
Menas	Ioannes	25v.11	900	1	M
Menas	Pesjal	26r.13,26v.5,20,27r.6	5,600	4	M
Minos	Enoch	26v.1	900	1	M
Minos	Kabios	26r.26	2,800	1	M
Minos	Kyra	25v.15,26r.8,20,26v.22,27r.33	5,000	5	M
Monis		27r.3,23	5,600	2	M
NN	Pamides	26v.28	5,600	1	?
Pachaon		25v.24	2,100	1	M
Paulos	Petros	25v.8,26	13,300	2	M
Peeus		27r.2,22	15,600	2	M
Peroush		25r.2,26r.16	9,400	2	M
Peshoei	Ionios	26r.22,27v.20,26	8,700	3	M
Peteneou		26r.5	900	1	M
Petros	Phibis	25v.18	900	1	M
Phoibammon	Pion	25r.7,25v.21	5,600	2	M
Pilatos		27r.21,31	1,100	2	M
Pkylis	baker	26r.7,26v.24,27r.30	3,100	3	M
Pkylis	Victor	25v.13,27,26r.25,27r.15	5,600	4	M
Pouroush		26r.3,26v.2,19,27r.14	4,600	4	M
Sarapion	NN	26v.9	900	1	M
Taurinos	Pamides	26r.18	14,000	1	M
Wife of	Perjoush (Perqoush)	25v.23,26r.17,26v.4,27r.19	6,700	4	F
Zacharias		25v.12,31,26v.34,27r.7	8,300	4	M

9. Analysis of Distribution of Wealth

A first discussion of the distribution of wealth in the Temseu Skordon register was presented by Bagnall to the Strasbourg Dioskoros colloquium in 2005 and is published as Bagnall 2008. The reader is referred to that article for a comparative discussion and background, putting the Temseu Skordon figures into perspective.

Inequality is normally measured by the Gini index or coefficient. This is in essence a single number measure of the degree of inequality of distribution of anything measurable. In modern societies it is mostly used to describe the degree of inequality in the distribution of income, but for ancient societies we have no data for incomes and mostly find ourselves measuring landed property. It gives a measurement, expressed in a decimal number between 0 and 1, of the proportional relationship between actual inequality in a population and potential inequality. Thus a Gini of 0 would reflect a society in which everyone had exactly the same amount of whatever is being measured, with zero inequality, and a Gini of 1.0 would reflect a society in which one person had all of the item being measured and all other members of society had zero: perfect inequality, if that is not too strong an oxymoron. It should be emphasized that it is in the nature of property registers and of tax registers based on property that those who had no property at all do not appear and thus do not have any impact on the measurement of inequality. This is a serious limitation on the power of the Gini index for describing fully the stratification of any Egyptian communities, but it does not seriously diminish the utility of such figures for comparative study.

In the preliminary study, the computation was based on the aggregate data of the entire register. The Gini computed there was .653. Since it was conducted, the text of the register has been improved significantly, and we have identified a number of taxpayers treated separately at the time of that computation. In addition, the data for Topos Demeou have been separated out here for analysis. The result is a Gini for Temseu Skordon of, remarkably, .653, no different from the figure computed earlier. This is not, however, surprising. The study of the Aphrodito register also showed that changing various assumptions used in the calculations had only a minor impact on the outcome. The basic structures of the distribution of wealth are strongly marked, and marginal changes do not affect them.

In the preliminary article, it was noted that at Temseu Skordon the top 30 percent of the population owned 79.2 percent of the land (now 79.7 percent), with more than half in the hands of the top 10 percent. It is true that the top decile includes the oikonomos, presumably of the church in Hermopolis, but there is no indication that this is institutional property rather than personal. The poorer half of the population at Temseu Skordon owns just 8.7 percent of the land, compared to 19.2 percent at Aphrodito.[9]

There is no indication in the Temseu Skordon register of inclusion of holdings of any person not a resident of the village; no one is identified as a metropolitan resident or Alexandrian. (We do not know if the handful of people identified as "from (place)" are to be taken as outsiders or residents who have relocated to Temseu Skordon.) The one curiosity, again, is the oikonomos, who would be expected to be a metropolitan if his office does in fact refer to the episcopal church of Hermopolis. Women own only 5.4 percent of the land at Temseu Skordon and 5 percent at Topos Demeou.

Although the amount of data for Topos Demeou is far smaller than for Temseu Skordon, it is interesting that the Gini index is just .442, more than 200 points lower than for the larger village and comparable to the figure at Karanis in the fourth century. Undoubtedly there was land at Topos Demeou owned by residents of Temseu Skordon; a handful of such entries have been identified, but the quantity of such land is trivial. Whether there was land at Topos Demeou owned by a major absentee landowner in the metropolis or elsewhere, we cannot say, in the absence of any other information about the place. (It appears, according to Drew-Bear 1979: 90, in only one other text, a list of places in *SPP* X 25 B.10.)

---

[9] Bagnall 2008: 207-08 has, using the data of *P.Col.* IX 247, suggested that Temseu Skordon may have had around 4050 arouras (2.25 percent of the Hermopolite nome), which would mean an average of around 11 arouras per taxpayer.

10. Occupations

Occupations found in the codex were first listed, along with other "descriptive words," by Crum (1905: 450, in Greek type). They occur at times in place of patronymics to serve to identify some taxpayers. Crum's list was reproduced by MacCoull (1987: 104, in Coptic type). Codex occupations were subsequently discussed by Bagnall 2005; he provides (p. 562) a list of occupations with numbers of individuals represented in each as derived from MacCoull's earlier, unpublished transcription. Here Bagnall's categories are retained; differences from his list are due to subsequently improved readings. The principal if not sole concern here is with the numbers of individuals represented for each occupation for the village of Temseu Skordon. For the pages for Topos Demeou yield very little on this topic, only a baker (ἀρτοκόπος) named Pkylis (26r.7, 26v.24, 27r.30). For present purposes, it is assumed that the lower part of 27v concerns Temseu Skordon, not Topos Demeou (despite the heading in line 1), because three tradesmen found in lines 22–32 share names and trades with three individuals well attested in the codex's Temseu Skordon pages. They are an oil-worker (ἐλαιουργός) named Apollos (27v.22), and two meat-cooks (μάγειροι), Menas (Μη]νᾶ, 27v.31) and Georgios (27v.32). See below, and consult Indexes II and V for further verification of what follows.

A. Agriculture and food processing

1. Wine producers (ἀμπελουργοί)[10] 3

   The three, with number of appearances given in parentheses, are named Ailianos (3), Kapai (2, once without trade name), and Phoibammon (3).

2. Baker (ἀρτοκόπος) 1

   His name is Pe . e; he appears only once.

3. Fine bakers (καθαρουργοί)[11] 2

   They are named Victor (9) and Paulos (2).

4. Oil-worker (ἐλαιουργός)[12] 1

   His name is Apollos; he appears eleven times.

5. Meat-cooks (μάγειροι)[13] 3

[10] On the meaning of the term ἀμπελουργός, see *P.Jena* II 30.3n.

[11] The καθαρός in the stem of this term refers to the use of sifted or fine flour in baking, hence the definition in lexica adopted here. It is by no means clear exactly what range of products they baked: white bread, cakes and pastries, or both. There are specialized terms for types of confectioners (like πλακουντᾶς).

[12] See *CPR* XIII, pp. 72-79.

[13] See *CPR* XIII, pp. 123-128. We think that the term μάγειρος denoted men who in modern terms were both butchers and cooks; that is, meat was most typically bought already cooked rather than raw, and functions we distinguish today were not separated. The list of tools and vessels belonging to one in *P.Sijp.* 54 indicates clearly that our distinction is not ancient. We have therefore adopted the somewhat awkward term "meat-cook" to refer to these individuals, for want of a better English equivalent.

Their names are Georgios (8), Menas (8), and Phoibammon (1).

Subtotal 10

B. Construction

1. Masons (οἰκοδόμοι) 3

Their names are Anouphis (1), Lahe (1), and Makarios (6).

2. Stonecutter (λαξόος) 1

His name is Kyros, with eight appearances, always in nominative case. We take the following word to represent his trade, not a patronymic, though it regularly appears in the genitive case (lone exception: 11v.19).[14] See below, under D.1.

3. Carpenters (τέκτονες)[15] 6

At least six, with one name (1r.22) lost. The surviving names are Abraamis (3), Victor (1), Isakis (2), Ionios (1), Kyros (2), and Pekysis (1).

4. Laborers (ἐργάται) 2

A certain Ioannes appears only once (7v.14), but Lythis appears twelve times (once without mention of occupation: 2r.8). Given these appearances and his substantial total payments (32 carats = 29,700 talents), perhaps Lythis was something more specialized than a common laborer; for the latter see Banaji 2001: 181–82; cf. also *CPR* XIII, p. 79. In any case, their presence in the tax codex proves that Lythis, and by extension Ioannes, were not, here at least, the landless laborers Banaji describes.[16]

Subtotal 12

C. Clothing

1. Cobblers (σκυτεῖς) 2+

As indicated by Bagnall (2005: 562 n. 29), the cobblers, whenever they are mentioned (five times in fact, see Index V), appear anonymously and in the plural. It is therefore impossible to count them as individuals. All that can be said is that they were at least two in number (though probably more). Whether they appear in this way because they formed a landowning "guild" cannot be said.[17]

---

[14] This is also, interestingly, the sole instance in which the word is written with a single omicron, λαξός, as is the normal spelling otherwise in the papyri.

[15] It is impossible to say how adequately this usual English rendering of τέκτων covers the actual range of activities of these builders; one can only say that their role is distinguished from that of the masons.

[16] On the complex issue of specialized ἐργάται and their possible roles, see Fikhman 2006: 304-05.

[17] On the economic activities of guilds, see Fikhman 2006: 302-23 (original publication 1994), especially 316 on the scarcity of information about communally-owned property. For a later period (Aphrodito in the early eighth century), Rémondon 1965 discusses collective tax payments by guilds that are clearly based on

2. Tailors (ῥάπται) 3
   They are Hatres (8), Tatianos (4), and Choor (1).
3. Fullers (γναφεῖς)[18]
   They are Akoui (1) and Enoch (8). 2
4. Tow-workers (σιπ(πουργοί)) 2+
   The head of one page (10v.1) refers to an account (*logos*) of σιπ(πουργοί), "tow-workers." No individual is named as such here or elsewhere in the codex, but, as with cobblers (above C.1), this reference seems to establish the existence of at least two persons of this occupation at Temseu Skordon.

Subtotal 9+

D. Crafts

1. Smiths (χαλκεῖς in Greek, φομντ in Coptic) 5
   Three of the five are named Paulos (1), Iakubis (4), and Phoibammon (1)—all of them χαλκεῖς. Besides these, and more important, is a father-and-son team, Banos and Tatianos. References to these two form an interesting complex. Though they can be tracked from Indexes II and V, they are worth deploying here separately for inspection.

3v.7	Tatian(os) φομντS—Phaophi 24
4r.8	Tatian(os) φομμητ (sic)—Phaophi 24
5r.30	Tatian(os) φομντ—Hathyr 26
6r.20	Tatian(os) φομντ—Choiak 10
8r.8	Banos the smith, Βάνου χαλκ(έως)—Choiak 20
8r.12	son of Banos the smith (υἱὸς Βάνου χαλκ(έως))—Tybi 5
9v.18	son of φομντ—Tybi 5
12v.7	Banos the smith, Βάνος χαλκ(εύς)—Mecheir 22
12v.11	son of φομντ—Mecheir 22
12v.18	Banos the smith, Βάνος χαλκ(εύς)—Mecheir 22
15v.3	Banos the smith, Βάνος χαλκ(εύς)—Phamenoth 1
15v.15	son of φομντ—Phamenoth 1
16v.7	Tatian(os) son of Banos the smith, Βάνου χαλκ(έως)—Phamenoth 17
16v.28	son of φομντ—Phamenoth 17
18r.26	Tatian(os) the smith, Τατιαν(ὸς) χαλκ(εύς)—Pharmouthi 8
19r.13	Tatianos φομντ—Pharmouthi 8

landholdings. The fragmentary column X of the Aphrodito register (Zuckerman 2004: 258) also lists payments by various occupational groups that in this context seem likely to be for land.

[18] See *CPR* XIII, pp. 58-65.

As the above references make clear, Banos is regularly (six times) styled a χαλκεύς, Tatianos is regularly (five times) styled a ϥομντ; but he is also clearly the son of Banos (16v.7) and is himself once called a χαλκεύς (18r.26). This is obviously critical to establishing the semantic equivalency of the Greek and Coptic terms. And since ϥομντ never appears in first position in the codex, always in the second slot, we are confident in treating it as the craft title rather than a personal name (though see Crum 1939: 678a–b at end). In this section on Occupations, we have applied the same principle, though with less confidence, to stonecutter (Greek λαξόος, above B.2) and soldier (Coptic ματοι, below, E.4). Whether the "son of ϥομντ" (four references) points to Tatianos as the son of Banos or to a son of Tatianos himself is unclear (the former seems more likely). Why the father should be exclusively referred to by the Greek term (at least when he is named by name) and the son all but once by the Coptic term is even less apparent—scribal playfulness? The doubling of references to these individuals on the same days or pages seems noteworthy.

Subtotal	5

E. Services

1. Scribe or teacher (γραμμ/)	1
His name is Iosephis; appears three times.	
2. Doctor (ἰατρός)[19]	1
His name is Konstantinos; only appears once.	
3. Grain-measurer (σιτομέτρης)	1
His name is Sarapion; twelve appearances.	
4. Soldiers (ματοι in Coptic)	2
They are named Victor (5) and Tatianos (3). This is another word that never appears in the first slot of any entry, always second (but only evidenced by these eight references). Cf. above, D.1.	
Subtotal	5
Total	41 (at least)

The absence of potters at Temseu Skordon is not surprising since the codex is a list of landowners. Interest naturally is drawn to those individuals above who figure prominently in terms of numbers of payments recorded. These are, in ascending order:

Makarios the mason (6)
Georgios the meat-cook (8)
Kyros the stonecutter (8)

[19] See *CPR* XIII, pp. 89-100.

Hatres the tailor (8)
Enoch the fuller (8)
Menas the meat-cook (8)
Victor the baker (9)
Apollos the oil-worker (11)
Lythis the laborer (12)
Sarapion the grain-measurer (12)
Banos and Tatianos (taken together), smiths (16)

11. The Church

Apa Esaias (Isaiah) appears making ten payments; in all but one he is described as *presbyteros*. These total 41,400 tal., placing him near the top of the second decile (from the top), although far from the wealth of the deceased deacon whose heirs appear frequently. An Isakis *presbyteros* also appears, but only twice and for a total of 4,200 tal. or 4.5 car., a figure that places him well below the village median. In neither case are we told of what church the individual was presbyter, but there is no reason to think that it was not one in Temseu Skordon itself.

Two deacons appear in the register. Apollos makes three payments totalling 4,700 tal. or 5 carats. Ammonios appears only once (5v.26) as intermediary for a payment of 41 carats. This is not a regular entry, and its precise nature is not clear. Certainly it cannot be taken to represent taxes on his own property. Apollos's payments are a little below the median and would not have sufficed to support a family. An altogether more substantial figure is the deacon, whose name is never given, whose heirs appear twelve times, always simply as "heirs of deacon". Their payments total 105,900 tal. (1 sol. and 94.75 car.), placing him among the top ten payers. It is possible that "deacon" in this case is actually a personal name Diakonos, but the prominence of other clergy and church institutions in the register makes us think that this is unlikely. It is not indicated of what church this person was deacon. The fact that his wealth greatly exceeds that of the *presbyteros* Apa Isaiah (Esaias) may suggest that he was in fact deacon of the metropolitan church in Hermopolis.

Two holders of the office of *anagnostes* (lector, reader) appear, once each. Abraamis pays 8.5 carats, a middling amount; Minos pays 2 carats, placing him in the ninth decile. It is usually assumed that lower orders of clergy were not paid enough, especially outside the metropolitan episcopal churches, to support them and that they had other sources of income. Neither could have supported a family solely on the landholdings implied by these payments. It is, of course, possible that one or both of them may have had holdings elsewhere than Temseu Skordon, or that they were tenants on lands belonging to others.

The *oikonomos* Enoch, who makes eleven payments, delivers a total of 244,700 tal., or nearly ten full-weight gold solidi, making him the second largest taxpayer in the village. It is never said of what he was *oikonomos*, but it is a reasonable assumption that it was the episcopal church of Hermopolis. No monasteries are mentioned in the register as being landowners in the village, and it seems likely that a monastery elsewhere would be explicitly mentioned in the title. One other person explicitly identified as οἰκονόμ(ος) ἐκλησί(ας), Ioannes, appears a single time (11r.30) with a payment of one (18-carat) solidus. The absence of the adjective ἁγία modifying the church in his title might lead one to think that in his case the church was not that of the metropolis, but this would not be a secure inference.

It is somewhat striking that monastics identified as such are much less common. One woman, Ama Tasous, is identified as *monazousa* in 5v.7 and 19r.18; in two other instances she is not given that descriptor. Her total payments of 67,000 tal. put her in the top decile of the village, and in one instance (1r.29) she pays through Phibis son of Toose, the largest taxpayer in the village. He may well have been a close relative.

Apa Apalo *monazon* appears in 19r.18, again bearing that descriptor only in this instance. But he appears without that title four more times, and his total payments come to 17,200 tal., or about a solidus as reckoned in this register. That puts him at the bottom of the top quartile of the taxpayers.

Another individual with the title Aba, Aba Stex, appears six times paying a total of 8,100 tal. He never is identified with any other monastic title, but it is reasonable to suppose that he was a monk. He must in that case have become one in middle life, because his son Anouphis appears once as a taxpayer also (6v.15, just 2 carats).

Three individuals appear with Ἄπα before their name rather than Ἄβα. This may or may not be significant. (See Derda and Wipszycka 1994 for the complexities of usage.) Apalo mostly has a Coptic form Ἀπε rather than Ἄβα, for reasons we cannot determine, undermining any attempt to distinguish between the significances of these two terms (cf. above, p. 20). The other two are Apa Ionios, paying 19 carats in 19r.19, and Apa Nokis or Nochis, a substantial figure with seven payments totalling 54,900 talents, placing him toward the bottom of the top decile. None of these is explicitly identified as a monk, but all may have been. They do not have any other ecclesiastical title. We thus have two explicitly designated monastics and three possible ones.

Two church institutions appear in their own right. One is "the Holy Church" (ἡ ἁγία ἐκλησία, as our scribe regularly spells it). Thirteen payments are made on its account, totalling 1,275,000 tal. or 75 of the accounting-unit solidi (51 of the 25,000-talent full-weight solidi). It has more than four times the holdings of any individual (or other institution) in the list. The "Holy Church" is the normal designation of the principal church, the seat of the bishop, and that of Hermopolis is well attested (*P.Sorb.* II, p. 72; the term is also used for the principal church of Antinoopolis, with the geographical indication given). The very large amount of property in the hands of this establishment in the register show that this must in fact be the church meant.

The second institution is the Holy Martyrion, paying 119,500 tal. There is no indication of which martyrion is meant by this designation. The amount is very substantial, putting it in sixth place in the village overall if one omits the Holy Church. It is interesting that no martyrion appears in the seventh-century register edited by Gascou (*P.Sorb.* II 69), nor in the Aphrodito register edited by Zuckerman. Papaconstantinou (2001: 274) lists only a small number, including one of Stephanos in the Hermopolite or Antinoite nome.

Zuckerman (2004: 226) has remarked on the "medieval" aspect given to the Aphrodito cadaster and register by the presence of numerous ecclesiastical institutions as landholders. One might in general think that the same is true of the Temseu Skordon register. But in fact the picture is very different from that of Aphrodito. Where monasteries play an important part at Aphrodito, they are absent in Temseu Skordon. The holdings of institutions seem in general to belong to metropolitan institutions, not those of the village. No extra-Hermopolite institutions appear. On the other hand, Zuckerman notes the rarity of monastics as actual landholders at Aphrodito; here they are, if not numerous, also not rare and hold significant amounts of land.

Another interesting body of material for comparison is the entries of *P.Sorb.* II 69. But there we are dealing with a metropolitan setting, and Gascou enumerates (pp. 65 ff.) about fifty members of the clergy or ecclesiastical administration, including bishops.

12. Onomastics

A. Temseu Skordon names

In publishing the early seventh-century Hermopolite codex *P.Sorb.* II 69, Jean Gascou remarked that it presented "un capital onomastique qu'il faudra bien un jour monnayer" (p. 53). Although our codex is not as extensive as the Sorbonne register and is limited to one village and a hamlet, it has many points of interest for names. Moreover, it seems in general to lack the one difficulty that Gascou signalled in his text, namely the presence of tax accounts, *onomata*, referring to persons long dead. It is thus likely to be a good snapshot of the village population at a single point, even taking into account the presence in the register of the names of some recent decedents represented by their heirs. There are, moreover, many points of commonality with the Sorbonne codex, which has (along with Gascou's rich commentary) made it a point of first referral in studying the Temseu Skordon names. As with the Sorbonne codex, again, what we present here is no more than a first approach to this body of information.

Gascou's first point was the strong majority of Christian onomastics, in which he stressed the popularity of New Testament figures and local martyrs. The three commonest names in his register are Phoibammon, Ioannes, and Victor, in that order. All are indeed common in our account, although in the order Ioannes, Victor, Phoibammon. Gascou's second division includes Menas, Theodoros, Georgios, Petros, Serenos, Paulos, and Sarapion. Of these, Temseu Skordon lacks Theodoros but has all the rest with varying frequency. In our view, Gascou may underrate the Old Testament contribution ("le petit nombre des références à l'Ancien Testament," p. 53). We can mention Abraham, Enoch (not in *P.Sorb.*), Elijah, Isaiah, Jacob, Jeremiah, Isaac, Noah (not in *P.Sorb.*), Solomon, and Zoe (= Eve). Zachariah appears at Topos Demeou. Some of these are common (the patriarchs, mainly).

In second place Gascou enumerated names of distinctively Hermopolite flavor. A first group is names ending in –δωρος, common throughout the Thebaid in this period. These are many fewer in Temseu Skordon, with only Zenodoros and Isidoros to be cited. It is possible to wonder if their popularity was particularly characteristic of the cities rather than the villages. As the second group Gascou cites names that are exclusively Hermopolite or Antinoite. From his list of 28 names, we have instances of (Apa) Nokis, Ionios, Lythis, and Toose. His third group comprises 41 names that are characteristic of the region but not unique to the Hermopolite. Of this, we find Ailianos, Banos, Eus, Hermapollon, Hyperechios, Kollouthos, Leus, Loulous, Lousia, Pinoution, Piter(on), Pkylis, Psas, and Taurinos, or 14 in all. We would add Haroous, Lene, Monis, Nonna, Peret, Trasias, and Choor as locally characteristic names, many of them found in the Sorbonne codex.

We give below a list of names, separated by provenance. For each name, the number of identifiable individuals is given, including patronymics and papponymics. References to the Coptic name repertories given below are cited only for names not found in other Greek texts.[20] Only Hasitzka, the most recent of these, is cited except for etymologies. Names not found in either Greek texts (as searched in the Duke Data Bank of Documentary Papyri) or in the repertories listed below are marked with an asterisk.

Ἀβραάμις (6). OT patriarch Abraham. *P.Sorb.* II (7).

Αἰλιανός (1). Roman *Aelianus*. *P.Sorb.* II (5), cf. p. 54 (characteristic of region).

Ἀκουι (1). Hasitzka. Ἀκοῦις, Ἀκούιτος in Greek texts.

Ἀκῶρις (1). = Ἀϭορ. Egyptian *hgr* (*NB Dem.* 766, which lists both forms).

Ἄλβιος (1). Roman *Albius*.

Ἀμμώνιος (1). Greek form from god Amun. Martyrs, including one at Antinoopolis (Papaconstantinou 2001: 47). *P.Sorb.* II (9 + 3 prob.).

Ἄννιος (1). Roman *Annius*. Not in *P.Sorb.* II, but Ἀννία is.

Ἀνουβίων (1). Greek form from god Anubis. *P.Sorb.* II (1).

[20] We do not cite Preisigke, *Namenbuch*, for names listed there only on the basis of the description of the present codex in Crum's catalogue.

Ἀνοῦφις (23). Egyptian form from god Anubis; several saints, including co-founder of Bawit (Papaconstantinou 2001: 51). *P.Sorb.* II (4).

Ἀντώνιος (1). Roman *Antonius*; probably not referring to the famous anchorite (cf. Papaconstantinou 2001: 53). *P.Sorb.* II (6).

Ἀπαλο (1). Hasitzka; a variant of Apollos, or Ἄπα + Λο? in *P.Mon.Apollo* 1.27. Λο without prefix Ἄπα in *P.Sorb.* II (1). We print as a single word because of consistent presence of Ἀπε before it.

Ἀπολλῶς (18). Saint, founder of Bawit (Papaconstantinou 2001: 53–56). *P.Sorb.* II (5).

*Ἀπορ (1).

Ἀροοῦς (1). "Horus the elder" according to M. Chauveau, cf. *BASP* 45 (2008) 52. All Greek examples Hermopolite or Antinoite. *P.Sorb.* II (1).

Ἀτρῆς (9). Egyptian, "twin." Calque of Didymos/Thomas? Cf. Heuser 1929: 8 etc. Monastic saint (Papaconstantinou 2001: 224). *P.Sorb.* II (3).

Ἀϭωρ (1); cf. Ἀκῶρις = Ἀϭορ. "Serpent," cf. Heuser 1929: 34 etc. Gascou suggests alternatively deriving it from Hagar, with the meaning "Arab."

Βάνος (1). Egyptian *bne*, "date-palm" (*NB Dem.* 142), often Βανε in Coptic. *P.Sorb.* II (6), cf. p. 54 (characteristic of region; Bane a revered monk, Papaconstantinou 2001: 61–62).

Βαχη (1). Etymology unknown.

Βίκτωρ (13). Roman "Victor." Martyr (Papaconstantinou 2001: 62–68). *P.Sorb.* II (48).

Γερμανός (3). Roman *Germanus*. *P.Sorb.* II (5)

*Γερμιϫου (1) = Κερμιϫου. Etymology unknown.

Γεώργιος (6). Saint (Papaconstantinou 2001: 69–72). *P.Sorb.* II (15).

Διόσκορος (4). Saints; perhaps the patriarch (Papaconstantinou 2001: 75–76). *P.Sorb.* II (5).

Ἑλένη (as ϩελένα) (1). Greek, but also the name of the mother of Constantine. *P.Sorb.* II (2).

Ἑλλῶς (1). Egyptian ϩλλο, "old man, monk." *P.Sorb.* II (2).

Ἑνῶχ (10). OT patriarch, also saints (Papaconstantinou 2001: 78–79).

Ἑρμαπόλλων (2). Greek name formed from Hermes + Apollo. *P.Sorb.* II (5), cf. p. 54 (characteristic of region).

Εὖς (1). *P.Sorb.* II (2) (feminine in the Hermopolite, see *P.Sorb.* II 69.67.B4n., cf. p. 54 on characteristic use in region).

Ζηνόδωρος (1). Greek, "gift of Zeus."

Ζωή (1). Greek, "life." Alternative name for Eve.

Ἠλίας (9). OT prophet Elijah, also saints (Papaconstantinou 2001: 89–91). *P.Sorb.* II (4).

Ἠσαίας (1). OT prophet Isaiah. *P.Sorb.* II (1).

*Θαβουνος (1). Heuser 1929: 45 takes to be the same name as Θαμοῦνις/Ταμοῦνις. Perhaps more likely to be "the one of the hill," from Greek βουνός. If so, it would be feminine.

Θεόνιλλα (2). Roman diminutive formation on Greek stem.

Θεόφιλος (2). Archbishop of Alexandria. *P.Sorb.* II (2).

Ἰακῦβις (9). OT patriarch Jacob; brother of Jesus; apostle. *P.Sorb.* II (3 + 8 in other spellings).

Ἰερημίας (7). OT prophet Jeremiah; also saint (Papaconstantinou 2001: 103–05). *P.Sorb.* II (4).

*Ἰουλούμενος (1). Etymology unknown.

Ἰουστῖνος (1). Emperor, martyr.

Ἰσάκις, Ἰσάκ (5). OT patriarch Isaac; several saints (Papaconstantinou 20001: 109). *P.Sorb.* II (11).

Ἰσίδωρος (1). Greek, "gift of Isis"; several saints (Papaconstantinou 2001: 110–12). *P.Sorb.* II (7).

Ἶσις (1). The goddess Isis; very rare in the Byzantine period.

Ἰωάννης (28). The Baptist; NT evangelist; various saints (Papaconstantinou 2001: 116–19). *P.Sorb.* II (60).

Ἰώνιος (4). Greek, "Ionian." *P.Sorb.* II (1). Cf. p. 56 (distinctive to region).

Ἰωσῆφις (14). Biblical patriarch or (less likely) father of Jesus (Papaconstantinou 2001: 120). *P.Sorb.* II (12).

Καλατους (2). Attested as a place name in *P.Col.* VII 124.43. Etymology unknown.

Καλη (1). Greek Καλή, "beautiful"? Cf. A. Papathomas, *Tyche* 10 (1995) 145–46. Or Egyptian, "paralyzed"? Cf. *P.Sorb.* II, p. 55.

Καπαι (1). Only in *CPR* V 26 and Coptic (Hasitzka); also found in Greek form Καπαις. A bird, partridge (Crum 1939: 114a) or sand-grouse or pheasant (Vycichl 1983: 84b), both citing this text.

Κασία (3). Roman *Cassia* (F).

Καϩ (1). Hasitzka, from *P.Lond.* IV 1432.26, 1471. Perhaps "earth," cf. Crum 1939: 131b.

Καϫωϫ (1). Hasitzka, from *O.Vindob.Copt.* 315.10.

Κελελε (2). Hasitzka cites Κελεελε from *P.Lond.* IV 1420.168; Καλεελε appears in other passages in this volume. Φανκελελε appears in *P.Sorb.* II 69.15.14 (with note) and 16.47, where it is taken to be a locksmith, derived from Crum 1939: 103b, κλλε, "bolt").

*Κελλη (2). Not attested as name (Greek κέλλη is attested as a noun). Perhaps from ϭαλε, "lame."

*ΚερμιϪου cf. ΓερμιϪου (1). Etymology unknown.

*Κλεμ( ). We cannot identify this name. It is tempting to see it as a misspelling of Κλήμ(ης), Latin Clemens, but because the only individual with this name is a son of Papnouthis, and Κλῦμαξ (spelled in full in one instance) is also the son of Papnouthis, it seems likely that they are the same individual.

*Κλῦμαξ (1). Perhaps take as Κλῖμαξ? Neither attested as name. Cf. Κλεμ( ).

Κολλοῦθος (4). Martyr (Papaconstantinou 2001: 122–28). *P.Sorb.* II (45), cf. p. 56 (characteristic of region).

Κόμες (2). *P.Sorb.* II (1). Also a title ("count"); cf. above, p. 17.

*Κοοϩ (1). Coptic "corner" (Crum 1939: 132a); = next?

*Κοοϩα (1). = preceding?

*Κουι Νου (1). Egyptian "little time." Νου is not found as name by itself.

*Κουι Σνοβ (1). Coptic "little blood" (Crum 1939: 348a–b, citing this text).

*Κουι Τικ (1). MacCoull 1987: 101. "Little spark."

*Κουι Ϣα (1). Coptic "little nose" (Crum 1939: 543b) or "little feast."

Κύρα (3). *P.Sorb.* II (3).

Κυριακός (5). Greek, "of the lord." *P.Sorb.* II (5).

Κῦρος (2). Persian via Greek. Several saints (Papaconstantinou 2001: 135–36). *P.Sorb.* II (2 + 1 Apa Kyros).

*Κωμήτα (1). Hasitzka cites Κωμετε, Κωμετος, Κωμητος from *P.KRU* p. 441, as variants of Κόμες; also Κωμητε from *P.Ryl.Copt.*, index.

Κωνσταντῖνος (5). Emperor Constantine. *P.Sorb.* II (2). Note that the first nu is mostly omitted, as commonly in Coptic.

Κωρ (1). *SB* XII 11251.8, 9.

Λακον (1). Hasitzka cites *P.Herm.Copt.* 32.5 for Λάκων, also found in Greek texts. Preisigke gives Λάκον as a variant, perhaps based on genitive form Λάκου; but this can also derive from Λάκος. Perhaps to be connected with the measure *lakon*; cf. *P.Sorb.* II, p. 55, on names related to measures, and see Hickey and Worp 1997: 92–93, note to line 2. Cf. Λαϩη.

*Λασουκ (1). Λασυγ in 19v.16 is probably a variant.

*Λαϩη (3). Crum 1939: 149a takes as a name derived from the measure of this name, in Greek the knidion. Cf. Λακον.

*Λαϩο (1). Heuser 1929: 22, 68, interprets as "one with a face."

Λένη (1). Greek instances are all Hermopolite. Short from Ἑλένη?

Λεῦς (1). *P.Sorb.* II (2), where noted as specifically Hermopolite (p. 56). Etymology unknown.

*Λοοϫε (1). Heuser 1929: 22 etc.: perhaps "recovery"?

Λουλοῦς (2). Egyptian *llw3*, "youth" (*NB Dem.* 727). *P.Sorb.* II (7), cf. p. 54. This spelling is almost exclusively Hermopolite in Greek.

Λουσία (2). *P.Sorb.* II (1) (F). Strongly Hermopolite in use (*P.Sorb.* II 69.50.C15n. + p. 56).

Λῦθις (1). *P.Sorb.* II (4), where noted (88.A1n.) to be exclusively Hermopolite.

*Λωτα (2). *P.Lond.* IV 1460.126 has Λωτε.

Μαθείας (1). NT Evangelist, Matthew. *P.Sorb.* II (2).

*Μαθητής (1). Greek "student," not otherwise in papyri as personal name.

Μακάριος (5). Saint (Papaconstantinou 2001: 140). *P.Sorb.* II (4).

Μαρία (2). Mother of Jesus. *P.Sorb.* II (6).

Ματρώνα (1). Latin *Matrona*, "matron."

Μηνᾶς (6). Martyr (Papaconstantinou 2001: 146–54). *P.Sorb.* II (27).

Μίνος (11). Greek?[21] *P.Sorb.* II (1 Apa Minos). Preisigke, *NB*; one example in Hasitzka.

Μόνις (7). *P.Sorb.* II (3). For this name, common in the region, see *P.Sorb.* II 69.35.16n.

*Μόνισκος (1). For Μόνις κου as play on words; cf. p. 19.

Νόννα (3). *P.Sorb.* II (1). See *P.Sorb.* II 69.46.C16n. for this name (one of the "Lallnamen"), particularly common in the Hermopolite. Cf. also B. G. Mandilaras, *P.Ath.Xyla*, pp. 67–70, with tabulation of occurrences in the papyri.

Νόχις (1). Variant of Νόκις. *P.Sorb.* II (1 Apa Nokis).

Νωϩε (1). OT patriarch Noah. This Coptic spelling is common (Hasitzka).

Ὀνοβηρ (= Ὀννώφριος?) (1). Cf. on Onnophris Papaconstantinou 2001: 161–62.

Παῆσις (1). Egyptian, "the one of Isis." Saint (Papaconstantinou 2001: 163–64). *P.Sorb.* II (1).

---

[21] It is not obvious whether this is simply an alternate spelling (found in one late source) of Μίνως, the mythic Cretan king, or from another origin altogether.

Πακοῦς (1). Egyptian, etymology unknown.

Παλικοῦς (1). For nominative see *P.Stras.* I 27.39 (Hermopolite). Etymology unknown.

Παμίδης (2). Unknown origin. *P.Par.* 21.26 has another example of the genitive (Panopolite). Preisigke, *NB*, derives nominative from this and the present text.

Πανε (1). Unknown origin; cf. Heuser 1929: 13.

*Πανεχεύτης (1). Unknown origin; whether = Πανεχώτης, Πανεχάτης, etc., is unknown.

*Πανηϫνου (1). Heuser 1929: 24, 70 renders as "the one of the threshing-floor."

Πανουβε (3). Egyptian, "the one of Anubis" (*NB Dem.* 351). No instances in Coptic texts in this spelling recorded by Hasitzka. This Greek form is common at Aphrodito, but declined forms (Πανοῦβις, Πανουβᾶς) are found in Middle and Lower Egypt. Cf. Φανουβ.

Παπνοῦθις (8). Egyptian, "the one of God." Saints (Papaconstantinou 2001: 165–68). *P.Sorb.* II (10).

*Παρακοτε / Παρακωτε (2). Egyptian, "the man of Alexandria."

*Παρβας (1). Etymology unknown.

*Παργατης / Παρκατης (2). Etymology unknown.

Παρσᾶς (1). Παρσᾶτ(ος) appears as the genitive in *SPP* XX 249.13. Etymology unknown.

*Πασταμου (1). Hasitzka records Πασταμων. Etymology unknown.

Πασῶθις (2). *P.Lond.* V 1673 has several instances of the name, which means "the one of the star Sirius": Heuser 1929: 25 etc.

*Πατσαλαμανα (3; twice Πατσαλαμαννα, once Πατσαλαμαντ( )). Unclear if σαλαμανα is to be referred to Solomon or another root.

*Πατσοουϩε (1). From σοουϩε, "egg," Crum 1939: 374a.

*Πατϫῑτ̄ϲ̄ (1). Etymology unknown.

Παῦλος (7). NT apostle. *P.Sorb.* II (14).

Παχῦμις (3). Egyptian "the one of the Falcon" (*NB Dem.* 165).

Πεβο (1). Variant of Πεβω, Πεβῶς, "the dumb person." Heuser 1929: 22, etc.

*Πειλιϣ (1). Etymology unknown.

Πεκῦσις (1). Egyptian, "the Nubian (Kushite)." *P.Sorb.* II (3).

Πεμην (1). An instance in *O.Mich.* IV 1123. Etymology unknown. We are not attracted to taking it as a variant of ποιμήν.

Πενοβ (1). Not in Hasitzka; a couple of instances in Greek.

Περητ (1). "The promised one," Heuser 1929: 11, etc. Hasitzka gives numerous references. *P.Sorb.* II (1). Common (in various forms) in this region; see *BGU* XII 2186.16n. and *P.Sorb.* II 69.88.A3n.

Πεσσοοῦς (4). Egyptian, "the sheep." Heuser 1929: 26, etc.

*Πεσχαλ, Πεσϫαλ (1). (Apparently the second spelling occurs only in the Topos Demeou pages.) Coptic definite article plus ϣϫαλ (Crum 1939: 615b: meaning?; Vycichl 1983: 278: perhaps "bolt").

Πέτρος (1). NT apostle; other saints. *P.Sorb.* II (17).

*Πευροτ (2). "The gladness," Heuser 1929: 27; Crum 1939: 135b.

Πιηοῦς (1). Probably from ϩηυ, "profit, usefulness" (Crum 1939: 729a, with list of names derived from the stem in 729b).

Πινουτίων (5). Greek formation on Egyptian root, "the one belonging to God." *P.Sorb.* II (6), cf. p. 54. Saint (Papaconstantinou 2001: 178–79). Usage is overwhelmingly Hermopolite and Aphrodito.

Πιουλ (3). We find Πιουλ( ) in *SPP* X 74 v i.4 (cf. *BL* 8.454).

Πις (1). Heuser 1929: 37, without etymology; cf. Brunsch 1984: 138.

Πίστος (1). Greek, "faithful."

Πιτερ (1). *P.Sorb.* II (1, marked as hapax, but citing *P.Lond.Copt.* 1077 for an unpublished instance; *P.Sorb.* II 69.83.B22n.).

*Πιτεχου (1). Hasitzka, following Heuser 1929: 37 etc., identifies this name as a form of Πετεχῶνσις, but we do not see any basis for this.

Πκῦλις (4). Egyptian, "the foreigner." *P.Sorb.* II (11), noted (p. 54) as characteristic of the region.

Πλουτίων / Πλωτίων (2). Greek, "belonging to Ploutos."

*Πμασε (1). "The child," Heuser 1929: 15. Cf. above, p. 18.

*Πναϩκας (2). Heuser 1929: 24 renders as "the boneshaker."

Πουηβ / Πουηηβ (2 or 3). "The priest." Other spellings occur, cf. Πουεεϥ in *P.Sorb.* II 69 (see p. 55). There is nothing to indicate that it should be taken as a Coptic equivalent to *presbyteros* rather than a name.

*Πϫαϫ (1). "The sparrow," = Greek Στρουθός, cf. Crum 1939: 798b (citing from this text).

*Σαίη (1). "Beauty," cf. Crum 1939: 315b.

*Σαμηει/Σαμεει (4). Etymology unknown.

Σαννα (1). Apocopation of Susanna, probably. An example in *SB* VI 9595.5.

Σαραπίων (9). Martyr(s) (Papaconstantinou 2001: 183–85). *P.Sorb.* II (13).

Σενεκίων (1). Roman Senecio.

Σερῆνος (2). Roman Serenus. Martyr(s) (Papaconstantinou 2001: 187–88). *P.Sorb.* II (14).

*Σινουερη (1). Heuser 1929: 30 etc. interprets as "son of the great (Isis)."

Σόϊος (3). *P.Sorb.* II (3), cf. p. 54. Attestations (all in Greek) are largely Hermopolite.

Σολομῶν (1). OT king. *P.Sorb.* II (1).

*Σουριχη (1). Etymology unknown.

*Στεξ (1). Etymology unknown.

Στέφανος (1). Saint (first martyr; other homonymous saints) (Papaconstantinou 2001: 192–95). *P.Sorb.* II (7).

*Ταλαοῦς (1). Presumably Ταλαοῦ is the short ßgenitive. Etymology unknown.

Ταροοῦς (1). *SB* XXII 15346 gives a genitive Ταροοῦτος; probably our form in Ταροοῦ is a short genitive of the same nominative.

Τασοῦς (1). Etymology unknown.

Τατιανός (12). Apologist; no saint's cult in Egypt, and probably another source to be sought.

Ταυρῖνος (2). Martyr (Papaconstantinou 2001: 196–97). *P.Sorb.* II (31), cf. p. 54 (characteristic of region).

*Τεϣνεενε (1). "The daughter who has been brought." Heuser 1929: 41; MacCoull 1987: 101.

*Τιμουτη (1). Probably a variant of Τιμόθεος.

Τοοσε (3) Egyptian, "the tamarisk." *P.Sorb.* II 69.36.A1n. (1), cf. p. 53 (distinctive to region).

Τρασίας (1). Cf. Coptic Τραϣε (Hasitzka). See the Hermopolite *CPR* V 26 (multiple instances). Despite the feminine article at the start, this is apparently a masculine name.

*Τϫεερ (1). "The threshing floor," see Crum 1905: 449b, n. 18 and Crum 1939: 782a s.v. ϫηρε for other names from this root.

Ὑπερέχιος (1). *P.Sorb.* II (2), cf. p. 54 (characteristic of region).

Φανουβ (1). Cf. Πανουβε.

Φῖβις (14). Co-founder of Bawit (cf. Apollos). *P.Sorb.* II (6).

Φοιβάμμων (9). Martyrs (Papaconstantinou 2001: 204–14). *P.Sorb.* II (87).

Φοίβη (1). The name appears only as the parent of Pkylis, three times as Φύβης, once as Φύβις (10v.26). It could be a misspelling of Phibis, but the scribe writes that correctly so often that this is an uneconomical hypothesis. The Greek feminine name Phoibe, although rare in the papyri, is more likely.

Χῶλος (1). Greek "lame" (*P.Sorb.* II p. 55); or the adjective as descriptor.

Χωωρ (4). Characteristic of region.

Ψᾶς (3). Cf. martyr Psate (Papaconstantinou 2001: 217–19). *P.Sorb.* II (2), cf. p. 54 (characteristic of region).

Ὧρος (5). The god Horus. Also a saint (Papaconstantinou 2001: 221). *P.Sorb.* II (2).

Ὠφέλιος (1). Greek, "beneficial." Cf. Πιηοῦς.

*ϩάλμιος (2). Preisigke, *NB* 21, lists as a form of Albios, cf. Heuser 1929: 100 etc. More likely is derivation from ϩαλμε, "spring" (Crum 1939: 670b), from which names like Pathalmei are known.

ϩαμποι (1). "Bench-craftsman," see Heuser 1929: 33, 70; cf. Crum 1939: 260b (from this text). Hasitzka cites an instance from Saqqara.

*ϩιρ(ι)ϭωϣ (2). Heuser 1929: 60 gives an etymology as "Horus has poured forth."

*ϫιϫ (1). Etymology unknown.

ϭες. Probably an epithet rather than a name, cf. Crum 1939: 832a, MacCoull 1987: 101–102.

B. Names from Topos Demeou

Only names not represented at Temseu Skordon are listed here.

Ἀπίων (3). Greek, "belonging to Apis." *P.Sorb.* II (3).

Ζαχαρίας (1). OT prophet. *P.Sorb.* II (4).

Κάβις (2). Heuser 1929: 46.

*Κουι Σον (1). Egyptian, "Little brother."

*Κουντα / Κωντα (2). Hasitzka quotes Κουντε. Perhaps another instance of a container-related name (see above on Λακον). Cf. Worp 2004: 568–69 on the container κουνϫου.

*Παχαον (1). Etymology unknown.

*Παϫεερ (1). Probably "the one of (the) threshing-floor," cf. above on Tϫεερ.

Πεεῦς (1). Egyptian, "the dog" (*NB Dem.* 155).

Πεμοῦς (1). Egyptian, "the tomcat" (*NB Dem.* 187).

*Περουϣ (1). Etymology unknown.

Περϭουϣ (ΠερϪουϣ) (1). *P.Sorb.* II (1). Cf. *P.Sorb.* II 69.5.5n. for discussion of this name, which occurs both as personal name and as toponym.

Πετενηου (2). "The one who has come" according to Heuser 1929: 27.

*Πεϣοει (3). Etymology unknown.

Πιλᾶτος (1). Roman, cf. Pontius Pilatus (and referring to him?). Common at Aphrodito.

*Πιον (1). Etymology unknown.

Πισοι (1). Common as Greek Πισόις. Saint.

Πουρουϣ (1). Hasitzka.

*Ϣνητ (1). Presumably from Coptic ϣενητ (Crum 1939: 572b), a fish.

NOTE ON EDITORIAL PROCEDURE

The text in this volume is presented according to the usual papyrological practices. The following signs have their usual meanings:

( )	Resolution of an abbreviation or a symbol
[ ]	Lacuna in the text
< >	Letters omitted by the scribe
{ }	Letters erroneously written by the scribe
⟦ ⟧	Letters written, then canceled, by the scribe
α̣β̣γ̣δ̣ε̣	Letters the reading of which is uncertain or would be uncertain outside the context
. . . . .	Letters of which part or all remain but which have not been read
[± 5]	Approximate number of letters lost in a lacuna and not restored
` ´	Letters inserted above the line by the scribe

In general, abbreviations are resolved in the text. Fractions printed are d = ¼ and L = ½. Egyptian proper names without terminations (i.e., undeclined or not hellenized) are not accented, nor are names with the typical Coptic termination in epsilon, even if the name appears elsewhere in the account in Greek. Greek names and words written in a non-standard spelling are generally accented as if the correct form had been written. In translations, Greek and Egyptian names are transliterated directly; Roman names are given in Latin form.

The fullest possible critical apparatus would have exceeded the space available on the pages and thus have made the presentation of text and translation on facing pages, which we believe will best serve users' needs, impossible. We have thus limited it somewhat. It provides standard spellings of Greek words misspelled in the text. Proper names are corrected only where confusion might arise. "Read" is used only where confusion might arise. Errors of spelling in names are found in profusion throughout, and case endings are erratic (as described in the introduction). Similarly, readers are referred to the digital images for the forms in which abbreviation is indicated in the text; this is not universally reported in the apparatus.

Interlinear lines in the papyrus take a variety of forms—continuous, broken, straight, wavy, and so on. They are all represented here in a single fashion, for the sake of practicality.

TEXT AND TRANSLATION

[Page 1 is lost before the present Folio 1]

Folio 1 recto (= Page 2)

ἀ(πό)δοσ(ις) ὁμοί(ως) Θὼθ κθ β σελ(ίς)

Μίνος Πις	κ(εράτια) γL	(τάλαντα) Γτ
Βίκτωρ Σαμεει	κ(εράτια) θL	(τάλαντα) Ηϡ
Κουι Τικ	κ(εράτια) ϛ	(τάλαντα) Εχ
Ἀπολλῶτος Ζωή	κ(εράτια) εLd	(τάλαντα) Ετ
Βίκτωρ ματοι	κ(εράτια) εL	(τάλαντα) Ερ
Ἀτρῆτος ῥάπτο(υ)	κ(εράτια) β	(τάλαντα) Αϡ
Βίκτωρ καθαρ(ουργός)	κ(εράτια) ϛ	(τάλαντα) Εχ
Φῖβις Τοοσε	νο(μισμάτιον) α	(ταλάντων) (μυριὰς) α Ζ
Φῖβις Ταροοῦ	νο(μισμάτιον) α π/	(ταλάντων) (μυριὰς) α Ζ
Φῖβις Λουσία	κ(εράτια) β	(τάλαντα) Αω
Τατιανοῦ Πεσσοῦ	κ(εράτια) γ	(τάλαντα) Βω
Φῖβις Θεοφίλ(ου)	κ(εράτια) ιδ	(ταλάντων) (μυριὰς) α Γρ
Ἀνοῦφ(ις) Πιουλ	κ(εράτια) δ	(τάλαντα) Γψ
Πέτρ(ος) Ἠλίας	κ(εράτια) ιγd	(ταλάντων) (μυριὰς) α Βυ
Φοιβάμμ(ων) Πινουτ(ίωνος)	κ(εράτια) γ	(τάλαντα) Βω
Ἀνίου	κ(εράτια) β	(τάλαντα) Αω
[Ἀτρῆ]ς Γεωργ(ίου)	κ(εράτια) εd//	(τάλαντα) Δϡ
[Κωσ]ταντ(ῖνος) Παχυμ(ίου)	κ(εράτια) θ	(τάλαντα) Ηφ
[Κῦρο]ς λαξόου	κ(εράτια) δ	(τάλαντα) Γψ
[Πε]σχαλ Μακαρ(ίου)	κ(εράτια) ϛLd	(τάλαντα) Ϛτ
[. . . .]. τέκτων	κ(εράτια) β	(τάλαντα) Αω
[Σαρα]π̣ίον Βαχη	κ(εράτια) β	(τάλαντα) Αϡ
[Σαρα]πίον σιτομέτρ(ης)	κ(εράτια) ϛ	(τάλαντα) Εχ
[Ἰωσ]ῆφ(ις) Ὥρου	κ(εράτια) ιαd	(ταλάντων) (μυριὰς) α´´ χ
[Ἀβρ]α̣άμ(ιος) Πεσσοῦ	κ(εράτια) ζ	(τάλαντα) Ϛφ
[Ἄβ]α̣ Στεξ	κ(εράτια) γL	(τάλαντα) Γσ
[Μαρί]α Παλικοῦ	κ(εράτια) β	(τάλαντα) Αω
[Ἄμα] Τ̣ασοῦ δ(ιὰ) Φῖβις Τοοσε	ν̣[ο(μισμάτιον) α]	(ταλάντων) (μυριὰς) α Ζ

(ταλάντων) (μυριάδες) ιζ Θϡ

4 κουϊ pap. 6 ματοϊ pap. 7 ϡ ex ω 9 νο( ) ex κ( ); α ex β 13 ϊδ pap. 15 ϊγ, Βϋ pap. 18 κ(ερ.) ε d ex corr. (see note) 23, 24 Σαραπίων 24 σιτομετρ/ pap., σι ex corr. 25 ϊα pap. 26 πεσσουS pap. 30 ϊζ pap.

Folio 1 recto (= Page 2)

Payment likewise on Thoth 29. Page 2.

Minos son of Pis	3 ½ car.	3,300 tal.
Victor son of Sameei	9 ½ car.	8,900 tal.
Koui Tik	6 car.	5,600 tal.
Apollos son of Zoe	5 ¾ car.	5,300 tal.
Victor, soldier	5 ½ car.	5,100 tal.
Hatres, tailor	2 car.	1,900 tal.
Victor, baker	6 car.	5,600 tal.
Phibis son of Toose	1 sol.	17,000 tal.
Phibis son of Taroous	1 sol. less	17,000 tal.
Phibis son of Lousia	2 car.	1,800 tal.
Tatianos son of Pessous	3 car.	2,800 tal.
Phibis son of Theophilos	14 car.	13,100 tal.
Anouphis son of Pioul	4 car.	3,700 tal.
Petros son of Elias	13 ¼ car.	12,400 tal.
Phoibammon son of Pinoution	3 car.	2,800 tal.
Anios	2 car.	1,800 tal.
Hatres son of Georgios	5 ¼ car.	4,900 tal.
Konstantinos son of Pachymis	9 car.	8,500 tal.
Kyros, stonecutter	4 car.	3,700 tal.
Peschal son of Makarios	6 ¾ car.	6,300 tal.
NN, carpenter	2 car.	1,800 tal.
Sarapion son of Bache	2 car.	1,900 tal.
Sarapion, grain-measurer	6 car.	5,600 tal.
Iosephis son of Horos	11 ¼ car.	10,600 tal.
Abraamis son of Pessous	7 car.	6,500 tal.
Aba Stex	3 ½ car.	3,200 tal.
Maria daughter of Palikous	2 car.	1,800 tal.
Ama Tasous through Phibis son of Toose	[1] sol.	17,000 tal.

179,900 talents

Folio 1 verso (= Page 3)

[ἀ(πό)]δοσ(ις) ὁμοί(ως) Θὼθ κθ γ σελ(ίς)

Ἄπα Νοχις	κ(εράτια) δ	(τάλαντα) Γψ
Ἀπολλῶς ἐλαιουρ(γός)	κ(εράτια) ς	(τάλαντα) Εχ
κληρ(ονόμοι) διακ(όνου)	κ(εράτια) θd	(τάλαντα) Ηψ
Ἀνοῦφ(ις) ἀπὸ Τβακε	κ(εράτια) β	(τάλαντα) Αω
Ἰωσῆφ(ις) Ἀροοῦ	κ(εράτια) γLd	(τάλαντα) Γυ
Γεώργ(ιος) μάγυρ(ος)	κ(εράτια) ζL	(τάλαντα) Ζ
Σοίου Ταλαοῦ	κ(εράτια) δL	(τάλαντα) Δσ
Τατι<α>νοῦ ῥάπτου	κ(εράτια) β	(τάλαντα) Αϡ
Φοιβάμμ(ων) Λωτα	κ(εράτια) γ	(τάλαντα) Βω
Τατι<α>νοῦ Παρβας	κ(εράτια) γ	(τάλαντα) Βω
Πατϫῑτc̄	κ(εράτια) β	(τάλαντα) Αϡ
Εὖς Ἰωάννου	κ(εράτια) εd	(τάλαντα) Δϡ
Ἀνοῦφις Ἰακυβίου	κ(εράτια) β	(τάλαντα) Αϡ
Ἀνοῦφ(ις) Κωσταντ(ίνου)	κ(εράτια) ς	(τάλαντα) Εχ
Ἀπολλ(ῶς) Λασουκ	κ(εράτια) β	(τάλαντα) Αϡ
Αἰλιανὸς ἀμπελ(ουργός)	κ(εράτια) β	(τάλαντα) Αϡ
Μίνος Διοσκόρ(ου)	κ(εράτια) εLd	(τάλαντα) Ετ
Βίκτωρ Σαμεει	κ(εράτια) ζ	(τάλαντα) Ϛφ
Κωρ ϫιϫ	κ(εράτια) γ	(τάλαντα) Βω
[[Σοίου Ταλαοῦ	κ(εράτια) δL	(τάλαντα) Δσ]]
Πκῦλις Κολλ(ούθου)	κ(εράτια) δ	(τάλαντα) Γψ [[ἀγρ( )]]
Ἰωσῆφ(ις) Ἀροοῦ	κ(εράτια) βd	(τάλαντα) Βρ
Ἰωάνν(ης) Παργατα	κ(εράτια) βL	(τάλαντα) Βτ
Βίκτωρ Ἰουλουμ(ένου)	κ(εράτια) αd	(τάλαντα) Ασ
Ἄβα Στεξ	κ(ερατίου) L	(τάλαντα) υ
Ἀπολλ(ῶς) Ὠφελ̣λ(ίου)	κ(εράτιον) α	(τάλαντα) ϡ

(ταλάντων) (μυριάδες) η Εσ

6, 23 ϊωσηφ/ pap. 7 μάγειρος 8 σοϊου pap. 13 ϊωαννου pap. 14 ϊακυβιο^υ pap.
21 σοϊου pap. 24 ϊωαννS pap. 25 ϊουλομ/ pap. 26 ϋ pap.

Folio 1 verso (= Page 3)

Payment likewise on Thoth 29. Page 3.

Apa Nochis	4 car.	3,700 tal.	
Apollos, oilworker	6 car.	5,600 tal.	
Heirs of the deacon	9 ¼ car.	8,700 tal.	
Anouphis from Tbake	2 car.	1,800 tal.	
Iosephis son of Haroous	3 ¾ car.	3,400 tal.	
Georgios, meat-cook	7 ½ car.	7,000 tal.	
Soios son of Taloous	4 ½ car.	4,200 tal.	
Tatianos, tailor	2 car.	1,900 tal.	
Phoibammon son of Lota	3 car.	2,800 tal.	
Tatianos son of Parbas	3 car.	2,800 tal.	
Patjits	2 car.	1,900 tal.	
Eus daughter of Ioannes	5 ¼ car.	4,900 tal.	
Anouphis son of Iakybis	2 car.	1,900 tal.	
Anouphis son of Konstantinos	6 car.	5,600 tal.	
Apollos son of Lasouk	2 car.	1,900 tal.	
Ailianos, wine producer	2 car.	1,900 tal.	
Minos son of Dioskoros	5 ¾ car.	5,300 tal.	
Victor son of Sameei	7 car.	6,500 tal.	
Kor Jij	3 car.	2,800 tal.	
[[Soios son of Talaous	4 ½ car.	4,200 tal.]]	
Pkylis son of Kollouthos	4 car.	3,700 tal.	~~unr.~~
Iosephis son of Haroous	2 ¼ car.	2,100 tal.	
Ioannes son of Pargata	2 ½ car.	2,300 tal.	
Victor son of Iouloumenos	1 ¼ car.	1,200 tal.	
Aba Stex	½ car.	400 tal.	
Apollos son of Ophelios	1 car.	900 tal.	

85,200 talents

Folio 2 recto (= Page 4)

Φαῶφ(ι) ιε ἀ(πό)δοσ(ις) ὁμοί(ως) δ σελ(ίς)

Κουι Τικ	κ(εράτια) ϛ	(τάλαντα) Εχ
Φῖβις Θεοφίλ(ου)	κ(εράτια) ια	(ταλάντων) (μυριὰς) α σ
Ἰσάκ(ις) κλ(ηρονόμος) Ἠλίας	κ(εράτια) δLd	(τάλαντα) Δτ
Ἀπολλῶτος Λένη	κ(εράτια) θd	(τάλαντα) Ηω
ϩελένα	κ(εράτια) ηd	(τάλαντα) Ζψ
Φ̣ο̣ι̣β̣άμμ(ων) μάγ(υ)ρ(ος)	κ(εράτια) ϛ	(τάλαντα) Εχ
Λυθίου	κ(εράτια) β	(τάλαντα) Αϡ
Ἠ̣σ̣αίας πρεσβύτερ(ος)	κ(εράτια) γL	(τάλαντα) Γτ
Ἀπολλ(ῶς) ϭες	κ(εράτια) δ	(τάλαντα) Γω
Β̣ί̣κτωρ ϭες	κ(εράτια) β	(τάλαντα) Αω
Ἰ̣ω̣άννη̣ς ϭες	κ(εράτια) β	(τάλαντα) Αϡ
Ἰερημίας Πανε	κ(εράτια) ϛ	(τάλαντα) Εχ
————————	ἀπὸ νο(μισματίων) κγL \`ζυγ(ῷ) Ἀντ(ινόου)´	
Χωωρ Γεωρ(γίου)	κ(εράτια) δ	(τάλαντα) Γψ
Πλωτίων	κ(εράτια) β	(τάλαντα) Αϡ
Μίνος Πις	κ(εράτια) βL	(τάλαντα) Βτ
Πευροτ Παχυμ(ίου)	κ(εράτια) γ	(τάλαντα) Βω
Σ̣α̣ρ̣α̣πίον σιτομέτρ(ης)	κ(εράτια) ϛ	(τάλαντα) Εχ
Κωσταντ(ῖνος) Παχυμ(ίου)	[κ(εράτια) ιε]	(ταλάντων) (μυριὰς) α Δρ
κλ(ηρονόμοι) διακ(όνου)	κ(εράτια) ε	(τάλαντα) Δφ
Χωωρ Ἀνουφ(ίου)	κ(εράτια) βd	(τάλαντα) Βσ
Ἀ̣ν̣ν̣ί̣ου̣	κ(εράτια) β	(τάλαντα) Αϡ
Ὧρος Σουριχ(η)	κ(εράτια) β̣	(τάλαντα) Αϡ
Μίνος Διοσκ(όρου)	[κ(εράτια) ϛ]	(τάλαντα) Εχ
Τατιαν(ὸς) Ἠλίας	[κ(εράτια) ιd]	(τάλαντα) Θχ
Α̣ἰλι\`α´ν(ὸς) ἀμ̣π̣ε̣λ̣(ουργός)	κ(εράτια) β	(τάλαντα) Αϡ
Πέτρ(ος) Ἠλίας	κ(εράτια) δL	(τάλαντα) Δσ
Φῖβις Πϫαϫ	κ(εράτια) [ϛ]	(τάλαντα) Εχ
Ἰσακίου πρεσβ(υτέρου)	κ(εράτια) β	(τάλαντα) Αϡ

(ταλάντων) (μυριάδες) ιγ ϛσ

1 φαωφ// ϊε pap. 2 κουϊ pap. 3 ϊα pap. 4 ϊσακ/ pap. 7 μάγειρος 9 ησαϊας pap. 29 ϊσακιου pap.

Folio 2 recto (= Page 4)

Phaophi 15, payment likewise. Page 4.

	Koui Tik	6 car.	5,600 tal.
	Phibis son of Theophilos	11 car.	10,200 tal.
4	Isakis heir of Elias	4 ¾ car.	4,300 tal.
	Apollos son of Lene	9 ¼ car.	8,800 tal.
	Helena	8 ¼ car.	7,700 tal.
	Phoibammon, meat-cook	6 car.	5,600 tal.
8	Lythis	2 car.	1,900 tal.
	Esaias, priest	3 ½ car.	3,300 tal.
	Apollos qes	4 car.	3,800 tal.
	Victor qes	2 car.	1,800 tal.
12	Ioannes qes	2 car.	1,900 tal.
	Ieremias son of Pane	6 car.	5,600 tal.
		From 23 ½ solidi by Antinoite standard	
	Choor son of Georgios	4 car.	3,700 tal.
	Plotion	2 car.	1,900 tal.
16	Minos son of Pis	2 ½ car.	2,300 tal.
	Peurot son of Pachymis	3 car.	2,800 tal.
	Sarapion, grain-measurer	6 car.	5,600 tal.
	Konstantinos son of Pachymis	[15 car.]	14,100 tal.
20	Heirs of the deacon	5 car.	4,500 tal.
	Choor son of Anouphis	2 ¼ car.	2,200 tal.
	Annios	2 car.	1,900 tal.
	Horos son of Souriche	2 car.	1,900 tal.
24	Minos son of Dioskoros	[6 car.]	5,600 tal.
	Tatianos son of Elias	[10 ¼ car.]	9,600 tal.
	Ailianos, wine producer	2 car.	1,900 tal.
	Petros son of Elias	4 ½ car.	4,200 tal.
28	Phibis Pjaj	[6] car.	5,600 tal.
	Isakis, priest	2 car.	1,900 tal.
		136,200 tal.	

Folio 2 verso (= Page 5)

† Φαῶφ(ι) ιε ἀ(πό)δοσ(ις) ὁμοί(ως) ε σελ(ίς)

Φοιβάμ(μων) Πινουτί(ωνος)	κ(εράτια) γ	(τάλαντα) Βω
Ϩαμποι	κ(εράτια) ϛ	(τάλαντα) Εχ
Σαραπίον Βαχη	κ(εράτια) ζ	(τάλαντα) Ϛφ
Εὖς Ἰωάννου	κ(ερατίου) Ld	(τάλαντα) ψ
Φῖβις Ἰωσηφ(ίου)	κ(εράτια) ιβ	(ταλάντων) (μυριὰς) α Ασ
Ἰσακίου πρεσ<β>υτέρ(ου)	κ(εράτια) βL	(τάλαντα) Βτ
Ψᾶτος Κόμες	κ(εράτια) δ	(τάλαντα) Γψ
Ἀπολλ(ῶς) ἐλαιουρ(γός)	κ(εράτια) γ	(τάλαντα) Βω
Φῖβις Ταροοῦ	νο(μισμάτιον) α	(ταλάντων) (μυριὰς) α Ζ
Γεώρ(γιος) Φιβίου	κ(εράτια) θLd	(τάλαντα) Θσ
Φῖβις Τοοσε	νο(μισμάτια) β	(ταλάντων) (μυριάδες) γ Δ
Ἰερημίας Ἠλίας	κ(εράτια) ε	(τάλαντα) Δχ
τοῦ ἁγίου μαρτυρ(ίου)	νο(μισμάτια) β	(ταλάντων) (μυριάδες) γ Δ
Ἀβρ(αάμις) Πεσοοῦτ(ος)	κ(εράτια) εd	(τάλαντα) Δϡ
Πκῦλ(ις) Κολλ(ούθου)	κ(εράτια) γL	(τάλαντα) Γτ
τῆς ἁγίας ἐκλ(ησίας)	νο(μισμάτια) ε	(ταλάντων) (μυριάδες) η Ε
Ἄπα Νοκις	κ(εράτια) β	(τάλαντα) Αϡ
Ἰωσῆφ(ις) Ὥρου	κ(εράτια) ζ	(τάλαντα) Ϛφ
ΛοοⲬε	κ(εράτια) β	(τάλαντα) Αϡ
Κουρ ⲬιⲬ	κ(εράτια) γ [[βLd]]	(τάλαντα) Βω
Βίκτωρ Σαμεει	κ(εράτια) αL	(τάλαντα) Αυ
Ἰωάννης Παύλ(ου)	νο(μισμάτια) αγʾ	(ταλάντων) (μυριάδες) β Βχ
Φῖβις Ἰωσηφ(ίου) ὁμοί(ως)	κ(εράτια) ϛ	(τάλαντα) Εχ
Σινικίον	νο(μισμάτια) β	(ταλάντων) (μυριάδες) γ Δ
Ἰερημίας Ἠλίας	νο(μισμάτιον) α	(ταλάντων) (μυριὰς) α Ζ
Ἰωσῆφ(ις) γραμμ(ατ-)	νο(μισμάτιον) α	(ταλ.) (μυριάδες) α Ζ ἐν χρυσῷ
Ἀτρῆτος Ὑπερεχίου	κ(εράτια) γ	(τάλαντα) Βω
Ἰακυβίου Ἀνουβίων(ος)	κ(εράτια) ιε	(ταλάντων) (μυριὰς) α Δρ
	(ταλάντων) (μυριάδες) λε Δϡ	

1 φαῶφ// ϊε pap. 3 ϩαμποϊ pap. 4 Σαραπίων; numerals all ex corr. 5 ϊωαννο^υ pap. 6 ϊωσηφ//, ϊβ pap. 7 ϊσακιο̄ pap.? 13 ϊερημιας pap. 17 ἐκκλ(ησίας) 19 ϊωσηφ/ pap. 22 Αϋ pap. 23 ϊωαννης pap. 25 Σενεκίων 26 ϊερημιας pap. 27 ϊωσηφ/ pap. 29 ϊακυβιο^υ, ϊε pap.

Folio 2 verso (= Page 5)

† Phaophi 15, payment likewise. Page 5.

Phoibammon son of Pinoution	3 car.	2,800 tal.
Hampoi	6 car.	5,600 tal.
Sarapion son of Bache	7 car.	6,500 tal.
Eus daughter of Ioannes	¾ car.	700 tal.
Phibis son of Iosephis	12 car.	11,200 tal.
Isakis, priest	2 ½ car.	2,300 tal.
Psas son of Komes	4 car.	3,700 tal.
Apollos, oilworker	3 car.	2,800 tal.
Phibis son of Taroous	1 sol.	17,000 tal.
Georgios son of Phibis	9 ¾ car.	9,200 tal.
Phibis son of Toose	2 sol.	34,000 tal.
Ieremias son of Elias	5 car.	4,600 tal.
The Holy Martyrion	2 sol.	34,000 tal.
Abraamis son of Pesoous	5 ¼ car.	4,900 tal.
Pkylis son of Kollouthos	3 ½ car.	3,300 tal.
The Holy Church	5 sol.	85,000 tal.
Apa Nokis	2 car.	1,900 tal.
Iosephis son of Horos	7 car.	6,500 tal.
Looje	2 car.	1,900 tal.
Kour Jij	3 [[2 7/8]] car.	2,800 tal.
Victor son of Sameei	1 ½ car.	1,400 tal.
Ioannes son of Paulos	1 1/3 sol.	22,600 tal.
Phibis son of Iosephis, likewise	6 car.	5,600 tal.
Senecio	2 sol.	34,000 tal.
Ieremias son of Elias	1 sol.	17,000 tal.
Iosephis gramm( )	1 sol.	17,000 tal. in gold
Hatres son of Hyperechios	3 car.	2,800 tal.
Iakybis son of Anoubion	15 car.	14,100 tal.
	354,900 tal.	

Folio 3 recto (= Page 6)

Φαῶφ(ι) ιε ὁμοί(ως) ϛ σελ(ίς)

Τατιαν(ὸς) Ἡλίας	κ(εράτια) δd	(τάλαντα) Γϡ
Ἠσαίας πρεσβύτερ(ος)	κ(εράτια) αL	(τάλαντα) Αυ
κλ(ηρονόμοι) Θεοφίλ(ου)	κ(εράτια) β	(τάλαντα) Αϡ
Μίνου Ἀνουφ(ίου)	κ(εράτια) β	(τάλαντα) Αϡ
Ἀνοῦφ(ις) Πιουλ	κ(εράτια) β	(τάλαντα) Αϡ
Σαραπίον Ἰακυβίου	νο(μισμάτιον) α	(ταλάντων) (μυριὰς) Α Ζ
Ἰερημίας ϭες	κ(εράτια) γ	(τάλαντα) Βω [[ἀγρ( )]]
Πεσχαλ Μακαρ(ίου)	κ(εράτια) δ	(τάλαντα) Γψ
Ἰωνίου Ἰωσηφ(ίου)	κ(εράτια) θ	(τάλαντα) Ηφ
Λυθίου ἐργάτ(ου)	κ(εράτια) β	(τάλαντα) Αϡ
Ἀπολλ(ῶς) Ἰωάνν(ου)	κ(εράτια) αd	(τάλαντα) Αρ
Κῦρος λαξόου	κ(εράτια) β	(τάλαντα) Αϡ
Πκῦλ(ις) Κολ(λού)θ(ου)	κ(εράτια) β	(τάλαντα) Αϡ
Ἰακυβίου Κολ(λούθου)	κ(εράτιον) α	(τάλαντα) ϡ
Ἰωάνν(ης) Πανουβε	κ(εράτιον) α	(τάλαντα) ϡ
Τατιανοῦ ματοι	κ(εράτια) δ	(τάλαντα) Γψ
Πέτρ(ος) Ἡλίας	κ(εράτια) ϛ	(τάλαντα) Εχ
Μίνου Διοσκ(όρου)	κ(εράτια) β	(τάλαντα) Αϡ
	(ταλάντων) (μυριάδες) ϛ Βω	

3 ησαϊας, Αϋ pap. 7 Σαραπίων, ϊακυβιο^{υ} pap.; ν(ομ.) ex κ(ερ.) 8 ϊερημιας pap. 10 ϊωνιου, ϊωσηφ/ pap. 12 ϊωαννS pap. 17 ματοϊ pap.

Folio 3 recto (= p. 6)

	Phaophi 15, likewise.	Page 6.		
	Tatianos son of Elias	4 ¼ car.	3,900 tal.	
	Esaias, priest	1 ½ car.	1,400 tal.	
4	Heirs of Theophilos	2 car.	1,900 tal.	
	Minos son of Anouphis	2 car.	1,900 tal.	
	Anouphis son of Pioul	2 car.	1,900 tal.	
	Sarapion son of Iakybis	1 sol.	17,000 tal.	
8	Ieremias qes	3 car.	2,800 tal.	~~unr.~~
	Peschal son of Makarios	4 car.	3,700 tal.	
	Ionios son of Iosephis	9 car.	8,500 tal.	
	Lythis, laborer	2 car.	1,900 tal.	
12	Apollos son of Ioannes	1 ¼ car.	1,100 tal.	
	Kyros, stonecutter	2 car.	1,900 tal.	
	Pkylis son of Kollouthos	2 car.	1,900 tal.	
	Iakybis son of Kollouthos	1 car.	900 tal.	
16	Ioannes son of Panoube	1 car.	900 tal.	
	Tatianos, soldier	4 car.	3,700 tal.	
	Petros son of Elias	6 car.	5,600 tal.	
	Minos son of Dioskoros	2 car.	1,900 tal.	
20		62,800 tal.		

Folio 3 verso (= Page 7)

Φαῶφ(ι) κδ   ζ σελ(ίς)

λόγ(ος) τῶν ἀποδ(όσεων) ὁμοί(ως) νο(μισμάτια) ιη εὔσ(ταθμα) ζυγ(ῷ)
Ἀντ(ινόου)

τῆς ἁγίας ἐκλ(ησίας)	νο(μισμάτια) ε	(ταλάντων) (μυριάδες) η Ε
Φῖβις Φοι(βάμμωνος) Τοοσε	νο(μισμάτια) αL	(ταλάντων) (μυριάδες) β Εφ
Ἐνῶχ οἰκονό(μος)	νο(μισμάτια) αL	(ταλάντων) (μυριάδες) β Εφ
Ϩελένα	κ(εράτια) ς	(τάλαντα) Εχ
Τατιαν(ὸς) φομντ	κ(εράτια) ς	(τάλαντα) Εχ
Λακον	κ(εράτιον) α	(τάλαντα) ϡ
Φῖβις Λουσία	κ(εράτιον) α	(τάλαντα) ϡ
Κουι Τι{τ}κ	κ(εράτια) ς	(τάλαντα) Εχ
Μαρία Παλικοῦ	κ(εράτια) β	(τάλαντα) Αϡ
Φοιβάμ(μων) Ματρώνα	κ(εράτια) ς	(τάλαντα) Εχ
Πέτρ(ος) Ἠλίας	κ(εράτια) γLd	(τάλαντα) Γφ
Τατιαν(ὸς) Ἠλίας	κ(εράτια) ςL	(τάλαντα) Ϛρ
Φῖβις Π⌧α⌧	κ(εράτια) γ	(τάλαντα) Βω
Κωσταντ(ῖνος) Παχυμ(ίου)	κ(εράτια) ςd	(τάλαντα) Εω
Σολομ(ῶν) Φιβίου	κ̣(εράτιον) α̣	(τάλαντα) ϡ
Ἰωσῆφ(ις) Ὥρου	κ(εράτια) βL	(τάλαντα) Βτ
Ἰωσῆφ(ις) Ἀροοῦ	κ(εράτια) ς [[L]]	(τάλαντα) Εχ
Ἰωνίου Ἰωσηφ(ίου)	κ(εράτια) θ	(τάλαντα) Ηφ
Βίκτωρ Κερμι⌧ου	κ(εράτια) δL	(τάλαντα) Δρ
Ἀτρῆτος Σαμηει	κ(εράτια) β	(τάλαντα) Αϡ
Ἀνοῦφ(ις) ἀπὸ Τβακε	κ(εράτιον) α	(τάλαντα) ϡ
Φῖβις ἀπὸ Ἁρμότ(νεως)	κ(εράτια) ς	(τάλαντα) Εχ
Ἰσάκ(ις) τέκτων	κ(εράτιον) α	(τάλαντα) ϡ
Πκῦλ(ις) Κολ(λού)θ(ου)	κ(εράτια) β	(τάλαντα) Αω
Μίνου Διοσκ(όρου)	κ(εράτια) δ	(τάλαντα) Γψ

(ταλάντων) (μυριάδες) κα ςφ

3 ἐκκλ(ησίας)   4 Εφ, Ε ex Ϛ (?)   7 φομντS pap., ομν corrected   10 κουϊ pap.   18,19 ϊωσηφ/ pap.   19 Εχ ex Ϛρ   20 ϊωνιο^{υ}, ϊωσηφ/ pap.   25 ϊσακ/ pap.

Folio 3 verso (= Page 7)

Phaophi 24. Page 7.

<u>Account of payments,</u> likewise, 18 full-weight solidi by the weight of Antinoopolis.

The Holy Church	5 sol.	85,000 tal.
Phibis son of Phoibammon, grandson of Toose	1 ½ sol.	25,500 tal.
Enoch, oikonomos	1 ½ sol.	25,500 tal.
Helena	6 car.	5,600 tal.
Tatianos, the smith	6 car.	5,600 tal.
Lakon	1 car.	900 tal.
Phibis son of Lousia	1 car.	900 tal.
Koui Tik	6 car.	5,600 tal.
Maria daughter of Palikous	2 car.	1,900 tal.
Phoibammon son of Matrona	6 car.	5,600 tal.
Petros son of Elias	3 ¾ car.	3,500 tal.
Tatianos son of Elias	6 ½ car.	6,100 tal.
Phibis Pjaj	3 car.	2,800 tal.
Konstantinos son of Pachymis	6 ¼ car.	5,800 tal.
Solomon son of Phibis	1 car.	900 tal.
Iosephis son of Horos	2 ½ car.	2,300 tal.
Iosephis son of Haroous	6 [[½]] car.	5,600 tal.
Ionios son of Iosephis	9 car.	8,500 tal.
Victor son of Kermijou	4 ½ car.	4,100 tal.
Hatres son of Sameei	2 car.	1,900 tal.
Anouphis from Tbake	1 car.	900 tal.
Phibis from Harmotnis	6 car.	5,600 tal.
Isakis, carpenter	1 car.	900 tal.
Pkylis son of Kollouthos	2 car.	1,800 tal.
Minos son of Dioskoros	4 car.	3,700 tal.

216,500 tal.

Folio 4 recto (= Page 8)

Φαῶφ(ι) κδ ὁμοί(ως) η σελ(ίς)

κλ(ηρονόμοι) διακ(όνου)	κ(εράτια) γL	(τάλαντα) Γτ
κλ(ηρονόμοι) Κωσταντ(ίνου)	[ν]ο̣(μισμάτιον) α	(ταλάντων) (μυριὰς) α Ζ
Μηνᾶ μάγυρ(ος)	κ(εράτια) θ	(τάλαντα) Ηφ
Ἰερημίας Πανε	κ(εράτια) δ	(τάλαντα) Γψ
Ϩαμποι	κ(εράτια) ϛ	(τάλαντα) Εχ
Κυριακὸς Πατσοουϩε	κ(εράτια) β	(τάλαντα) Αϡ
Τατιαν(ὸς) φομμητ	κ(εράτια) γ	(τάλαντα) Βω
Κυρ<ι>ακὸς Ἀνουφ(ίου)	κ(εράτια) δ	(τάλαντα) Γψ
Φῖβις Ἀτρῆτος	κ(εράτια) γ	(τάλαντα) Βω
Σαραπίον σιτομέτρ(ης)	κ(εράτια) ϛ	(τάλαντα) Εχ
Τατιαν(ὸς) Ἠλίας	κ(εράτια) ϛ	(τάλαντα) Εχ
Πέτρ(ος) Ἠλίας	κ(εράτια) δLd	(τάλαντα) Δυ
Μηνᾶ Ἐνῶχ	κ(εράτια) εLd	(τάλαντα) Ετ
Ψᾶτος Κόμες	κ(εράτια) δL	(τάλαντα) Δσ
Ἀπολλ(ῶς) Κασία	κ(εράτια) ϛ	(τάλαντα) Εχ
Ϩελένα	κ(εράτια) ϛ	(τάλαντα) Εχ
κλ(ηρονόμοι) διακ(όνου)	κ(εράτια) εL	(τάλαντα) Εσ
Ἰωσῆφ(ις) Ὥρου	κ(εράτια) εd	(τάλαντα) Δϡ

Ἀθὺρ θ

λόγ(ος) τῶν νο(μισματίων) ζ` ζυγ(ῷ) τῆς κώμ(ης) (ὑπὲρ) παλαιοῦ λόγου
δ(ιὰ) Τατιαν(οῦ)

Μίνος Τιμουτη	κ(εράτια) ϛL	(τάλαντα) Ϛ
Ψᾶς καὶ Λαϩο	κ(εράτια) γ	(τάλαντα) Βω
Ἰωσῆφ(ις) Πινουτ(ίωνος)	κ(εράτια) γ	(τάλαντα) Βω
Ἐνῶχ γναφεύ(ς)	κ(εράτια) β	(τάλαντα) Αϡ
Φοιβάμμ(ων) Πινουτ(ίωνος)	κ(εράτια) βd	(τάλαντα) Βρ
Λακον	κ(εράτιον) α	(τάλαντα) ϡ
Πκῦλ(ις) Κολλούθ(ου)	κ(εράτια) γ	(τάλαντα) Βω
Ἰερημίας Ϩαλμίου	κ(εράτια) βL	(τάλαντα) Βσ
Γεώρ(γιος) μάγυρ(ος)	κ(εράτια) θ	(τάλαντα) Ηφ
Ἀνοῦφ(ις) Κωσταντ(ίνου)	κ(εράτια) δ	(τάλαντα) Γψ

traces of another line (hidden by binding)

(in margin between lines 24 and 25) (ταλάντων) (μυριάδες) ι Γα

4, 29 μάγειρος 5, 28 ϊερημιας pap. 6 ϩαμποϊ pap. 11 Σαραπίων 19, 23 ϊωσηφ/ pap.

Folio 4 recto (= Page 8)

Phaophi 24, likewise. Page 8.

Heirs of the deacon	3 ½ car.	3,300 tal.
Heirs of Konstantinos	1 sol.	17,000 tal.
Menas, meat-cook	9 car.	8,500 tal.
Ieremias son of Pane	4 car.	3,700 tal.
Hampoi	6 car.	5,600 tal.
Kyriakos son of Patsoouhe	2 car.	1,900 tal.
Tatianos, smith	3 car.	2,800 tal.
Kyriakos son of Anouphis	4 car.	3,700 tal.
Phibis son of Hatres	3 car.	2,800 tal.
Sarapion, grain-measurer	6 car.	5,600 tal.
Tatianos son of Elias	6 car.	5,600 tal.
Petros son of Elias	4 ¾ car.	4,400 tal.
Menas son of Enoch	5 ¾ car.	5,300 tal.
Psas son of Komes	4 ½ car.	4,200 tal.
Apollos son of Kasia	6 car.	5,600 tal.
Helena	6 car.	5,600 tal.
Heirs of the deacon	5 ½ car.	5,200 tal.
Iosephis son of Horos	5 ¼ car.	4,900 tal.

Hathyr 9

Account of 7 solidi on the village (weight) standard, for the old account, through Tatianos.

Minos son of Timoute	6 ½ car.	6,000 tal.
Psas and Laho	3 car.	2,800 tal.
Iosephis son of Pinoution	3 car.	2,800 tal.
Enoch, fuller	2 car.	1,900 tal.
Phoibammon son of Pinoution	2 ¼ car.	2,100 tal.
Lakon	1 car.	900 tal.
Pkylis son of Kollouthos	3 car.	2,800 tal.
Ieremias son of Halmios	2 ½ car.	2,200 tal.
Georgios, meat-cook	9 car.	8,500 tal.
Anouphis son of Konstantinos	4 car.	3,700 tal.
traces of another line (hidden by binding)		
(in margin between lines 24 and 25)		131,000 tal.

Folio 4 verso (= Page 9)

† ὁμο(ίως) τοῦ αὐτοῦ τῶν νο(μισματίων) ζʼ ζυγ(ῷ) τῆς κώμ(ης). θ σελ(ίς)

Γεώργ(ιος) Ταυρ(ίνου)	κ(εράτια) ϛ	(τάλαντα) Εχ
Ἰακυβίου Ἰωάνν(ου)	κ(εράτια) γ	(τάλαντα) Βω
Εὖς Ἰωάνν(ου)	κ(εράτια) γL	(τάλαντα) Γτ
Μονίου Παπνουθ(ίου)	κ(εράτιον) α	(τάλαντα) ϡ
Κυριακὸς Γερμιϫου	κ(εράτια) β	(τάλαντα) Αω
Κουι Νου	κ(εράτια) β	(τάλαντα) Αω
Ἰωάνν(ης) Ἀκωρ(ίου)	κ(ερατίου) L	(τάλαντα) υ ἀγρ( )
Κουι Τικ	κ(εράτια) γ	(τάλαντα) Βω
Ἀπολ(λῶς) ϭεc	κ(εράτια) β	(τάλαντα) Αω
Πκῦλ(ις) Κολ(λούθου)	κ(εράτια) γ	(τάλαντα) Βω
Ϩιρϭωϣ	κ(εράτια) γLd	(τάλαντα) Γφ
Παρακωτε	κ(εράτια) βLd	(τάλαντα) Βυ
Ἀνοῦφ(ις) Πμασε	κ(εράτια) β	(τάλαντα) Αϡ
Κοοϩ	κ(εράτια) β	(τάλαντα) Αϡ
Ἰωνίου τέκτ(ονος)	κ(εράτια) γ	(τάλαντα) Βω
Μίνου Τιμουτη δ(ιὰ) Χωωρ	κ(εράτια) β	(τάλαντα) Αω
Σαραπίον σιτομέτρ(ης)	κ(εράτια) εLd	(τάλαντα) Ετ
Μακαρίου Γερμανοῦ	κ(εράτια) β	(τάλαντα) Αω
Ἄβα Στεξ	κ(εράτια) β	(τάλαντα) Αω
Σαίη Ἠλίας	κ(εράτιον) α	(τάλαντα) ϡ
Φοιβάμ(μων) Λωτα	κ(εράτια) β	(τάλαντα) Αω
Ἰωσῆφ(ις) Ὥρου	κ(εράτια) δ̣d	(τάλαντα) Δρ
Τατιαν(ὸς) Ἠλίας	κ(εράτια) γ	(τάλαντα) Βω
Βίκτωρ Γερμιϫου	κ(εράτια) αL	(τάλαντα) Αυ
Ϩαλμίου	κ(εράτια) αL	(τάλαντα) Ατ
Φῖβις ἀπὸ Ἀρμόθ(νεως)	κ(εράτια) γ	(τάλαντα) Βω
Ὧρ Σουριχη	κ(εράτια) β	(τάλαντα) Αω
Αἰλιανοῦ ἀμπελ(ουργοῦ)	κ(εράτιον) α	(τάλαντα) ϡ
Βίκτωρ ματοι	κ(εράτια) ϛ	(τάλαντα) Εχ
Λῦθις ἐργ(άτης)	κ(εράτια) β	(τάλαντα) Αω
Φοιβάμ(μων) Ματρώνα	κ̣(εράτια) θ̣	[(τάλαντα) Η]φ̣

(in margin of line 27) (ταλάντων) (μυριάδες) η ϡ

3 ϊακυβιο^υ, ϊωαννS pap. 7, 9 κουϊ pap. 13 Βϋ pap. 18 Σαραπίων 19 Μακαρίου, ι ex ο 21 σαϊη pap. 23 ϊωσηφ/ pap.

Folio 4 verso (= Page 9)

† Likewise for the same, of 7 solidi by the (weight) standard of the village. Page 9.

Georgios son of Taurinos	6 car.	5,600 tal.	
Iakybis son of Ioannes	3 car.	2,800 tal.	
Eus daughter of Ioannes	3 ½ car.	3,300 tal.	
Monis son of Papnouthis	1 car.	900 tal.	
Kyriakos son of Germijou	2 car.	1,800 tal.	
Koui Nou	2 car.	1,800 tal.	
Ioannes son of Akoris	½ car.	400 tal.	unr.
Koui Tik	3 car.	2,800 tal.	
Apollos qes	2 car.	1,800 tal.	
Pkylis son of Kollouthos	3 car.	2,800 tal.	
Hirqosh	3 ¾ car.	3,500 tal.	
Parakote	2 ¾ car.	2,400 tal.	
Anouphios (son of?) Pmase	2 car.	1,900 tal.	
Kooh	2 car.	1,900 tal.	
Ionios, carpenter	3 car.	2,800 tal.	
Minos son of Timoute, through Choor	2 car.	1,800 tal.	
Sarapion, grain-measurer	5 ¾ car.	5,300 tal.	
Makarios son of Germanos	2 car.	1,800 tal.	
Aba Stex	2 car.	1,800 tal.	
Saie son (?) of Elias	1 car.	900 tal.	
Phoibammon son of Lota	2 car.	1,800 tal.	
Iosephis son of Horos	4 ¼ car.	4,100 tal.	
Tatianos son of Elias	3 car.	2,800 tal.	
Victor son of Germijou	1 ½ car.	1,400 tal.	
Halmios	1 ½ car.	1,300 tal.	
Phibis from Harmothnis	3 car.	2,800 tal.	
Hor son of Souriche	2 car.	1,800 tal.	
Ailianos, wine producer	1 car.	900 tal.	
Victor, soldier	6 car.	5,600 tal.	
Lythis, laborer	2 car.	1,800 tal.	
Phoibammon son of Matrona	9 car.	[8,]500 [tal.]	

(in margin of line 27) 80,900 tal.

Folio 5 recto (= Page 10)

† Ἀθὺρ κς ὁμο(ίως). ι σελ(ίς)

[[Φῖβις Φοιβάμ(μωνος) Τοοσε	κ(εράτια) θ	(τάλαντα) Ηφ]]
Φῖβις ϭεc	κ(εράτια) β	(τάλαντα) Αϡ
Γεώρ(γιος) Φιβίου	κ(εράτια) θ	(τάλαντα) Ηφ
Μονίου Πουηβ	κ(εράτιον) α	(τάλαντα) ϡ
Ὧρ Βίκτωρ	κ(εράτιον) α	(τάλαντα) ϡ
γ̣υ̣ναὶ Πενοβ	κ(εράτια) δL	(τάλαντα) Δρ
Φῖβις Φοι(βάμμωνος) Τοοσε	νο(μισμάτια) β	(ταλάντων) (μυριάδες) γ Δ
Φῖβις Ταροοῦ	νο(μισμάτιον) α	(ταλάντων) (μυριὰς) α Ζ
Ἰωάννης Λεῦτος	κ(εράτια) δ	(τάλαντα) Γω
Παῆσις Νωϩε	κ(εράτια) β	(τάλαντα) Αω
Μηνᾶ μάγυρ(ος)	κ(εράτια) θ	(τάλαντα) Ηφ
Φοιβάμ(μων) Ματρών(ας)	κ(εράτια) θ	(τάλαντα) Ηφ
Κουι Τικ	κ(εράτια) γ	(τάλαντα) Βω
Εὗς Ἰωάνν(ου)	κ(εράτια) βL	(τάλαντα) Βσ
ϩελένα	κ(εράτια) ς	(τάλαντα) Εχ
κλ(ηρονόμοι) διακ(όνου)	κ(εράτια) ιβ	(ταλάντων) (μυριὰς) α Ασ
Θεόφιλ(ος)	κ(εράτια) ς	(τάλαντα) Εχ
Ψᾶτος Κόμες	κ(εράτια) γ	(τάλαντα) Βω
Ἠσαίας πρεσβύτ(ερος)	κ(εράτια) β	(τάλαντα) Αϡ
Πλωτίων	κ(εράτια) β	(τάλαντα) Αϡ
Τατιαν(ὸς) Ἡλίας	κ(εράτια) [β]	(τάλαντα) Αω
Ἰωάννης Πανου̣β̣ε	[κ(εράτια) β]	(τάλαντα) Αϡ
Ἀνοῦφ(ις) Ἰακυβ(ίου)	[κ(εράτιον) α]	(τάλαντα) ϡ
Ἰωσῆφ(ις) Ὥρ̣ου	[κ(εράτια) δ]d	(τάλαντα) Γϡ
Φοιβάμ(μων) Πινο[υτ(ίωνος)	κ(εράτια)] γLd	(τάλαντα) Γφ
Ἀπολλ(ῶς) Λασου[κ]	κ(εράτια) γ	(τάλαντα) Βω
Ἀπολλ(ῶς) ἐλα̣ι̣ου[ρ(γός)]	κ(εράτια) γ	(τάλαντα) Βω
Β̣ίκτωρ Σαμ̣η[ει]	κ(εράτια) ιβ	(ταλάντων) μυριὰς) α Ασ
Τ̣ατιαν(ὸς) φομ̣ν̣[τ]	κ(εράτια) ς	(τάλαντα) Εχ
Ἀνοῦφ(ις) Κωστα̣ν̣τ̣(ίνου)	κ(εράτια) β	(τάλαντα) Αϡ
Πατϫιτc	κ(εράτια) αL	(τάλαντα) Αυ
(in margin of line 24)	(ταλάντων) (μυριάδες) ις Ασ	

7 γυνή 12 μάγειρος 33 ῒς pap.

Folio 5 recto (= Page 10)

† Hathyr 26, likewise. Page 10.

[[Phibis son of Phoibammon, grandson of Toose	9 car.	8,500 tal.]]
Phibis qes	2 car.	1,900 tal.
Georgios son of Phibis	9 car.	8,500 tal.
Monis son of Poueb	1 car.	900 tal.
Hor son of Victor	1 car.	900 tal.
The wife of Penob	4 ½ car.	4,100 tal.
Phibis son of Phoibammon, grandson of Toose	2 sol.	34,000 tal.
Phibis son of Taroous	1 sol.	17,000 tal.
Ioannes son of Leus	4 car.	3,800 tal.
Paesis son of Nohe	2 car.	1,800 tal.
Menas, meat-cook	9 car.	8,500 tal.
Phoibammon son of Matrona	9 car.	8,500 tal.
Koui Tik	3 car.	2,800 tal.
Eus daughter of Ioannes	2 ½ car.	2,200 tal.
Helena	6 car.	5,600 tal.
Heirs of the deacon	12 car.	11,200 tal.
Theophilos	6 car.	5,600 tal.
Psas son of Komes	3 car.	2,800 tal.
Esaias, priest	2 car.	1,900 tal.
Plotion	2 car.	1,900 tal.
Tatianos son of Elias	[2] car.	1,800 tal.
Ioannes son of Panoube	[2 car.]	1,900 tal.
Anouphis son of Iakybis	[1 car.]	900 tal.
Iosephis son of Horos	[4] ¼ [car.]	3,900 tal.
Phoibammon son of Pinoution	3 ¾ [car.]	3,500 tal.
Apollos son of Lasouk	3 car.	2,800 tal.
Apollos, oilworker	3 car.	2,800 tal.
Victor son of Sameei	12 car.	11,200 tal.
Tatianos, smith	6 car.	5,600 tal.
Anouphis son of Konstantinos	2 car.	1,900 tal.
Patjits	1 ½ car.	1,400 tal.

(in margin) 161,200 tal.

Folio 5 verso (= Page 11)

† Ἀθὺρ κζ ὁμο(ίως). ια σελ(ίς)

Ἀπολλῶτος Λένη	κ(εράτια) ϛ	(τάλαντα) Εχ
κλ(ηρονόμοι) Θεοφίλ(ου)	κ(εράτια) γ	(τάλαντα) Βω
Πευρο<τ> Παχυμίου	κ(εράτια) ϛ	(τάλαντα) Εχ
Ἰωάννης κλ(ηρονόμος) Παύλου	κ(εράτια) ιγ	(ταλάντων) (μυριὰς) α Βρ
Ἰωσῆφ(ις) κλ(ηρονόμος) Παύλ(ου)	κ(εράτια) ϛ	(τάλαντα) Εχ
Ἄμα Τασοῦ μονάζ(ουσα)	νο(μισμάτια) β π(αρὰ) α	(ταλάντων) (μυριάδες) γ Γ
Βίκτωρ ϭεc	κ(ερατίου) L	(τάλαντα) υ
Πκῦλ(ις) Κολλ(ούθου)	κ(εράτια) δ	(τάλαντα) Γψ
Λῦθις ἐργ(άτης)	κ(εράτια) δ	(τάλαντα) Γψ
Φοιβάμ(μων) Γερμανοῦ	κ(εράτια) β	(τάλαντα) Αω
Μίνου Διοσκ(όρου)	κ(εράτια) εL	(τάλαντα) Ερ
Παρακοτε	κ(εράτια) γd	(τάλαντα) Γ
Πέτρ(ος) Ἠλίας	κ(εράτια) ϛ	(τάλαντα) Εχ
Τατιαν(ὸς) ματοι	κ(εράτια) βLd	(τάλαντα) Βυ
Πλωτίων	κ(εράτια) β	(τάλαντα) Αω
Μίνου Πις	κ(εράτια) β	(τάλαντα) Αω
Ἰερημίας Πανε	κ(εράτια) ε	(τάλαντα) Δχ
κλ(ηρονόμοι) Κω̣σταντ(ίνου)	νο(μισμάτια) β	(ταλάντων) (μυριάδες) γ Δ
Μονίου κου	κ(εράτια) ϛ	(τάλαντα) Εχ
τῆς ἁγίας ἐκλ(ησίας)	νο(μισμάτια) η	(ταλάντων) (μυριάδες) ιγ ϛ
Ἀτρῆτος Ὑπερεχ(ίου)	κ(εράτια) γ	(τάλαντα) Βω [[ἀγρ( )]]
Ἰωσῆφ(ις) κλ(ηρονόμος) Παύλ(ου)	κ(εράτια) ϛ	(τάλαντα) Εχ [[ἀγρ( )]]
Γεώρ(γιος) Ταυρ(ίνου)	κ(εράτια) ϛ	(τάλαντα) Εχ
Ἰερημίας Πανε	κ(εράτια) βLd	(τάλαντα) Βφ

(2 H.) Χοίακ ι δ(ιὰ) Ἀμμ(ωνίου) διακ(όνου) κ(εράτια) μα ἀποδομ( ) κ(εράτια) μα †

κλ(ηρονόμοι) Κωσταντ(ίνου) κ(εράτια) μα (ταλάντων) (μυριάδες) γ̣ Ηψ

(ταλάντων) (μυριάδες) λβ Θυ

5 ϊωαννης, ϊγ pap. 6 ϊωσηφ/ pap. 7 π(αρά): π with stroke through 8 (τάλ.) ϋ pap. 15 ματοϊ, Βϋ pap. 17 Αω, ω corr. (ex ⲗ ?) 18 ϊερημιας pap. 21 ἐκκλ(ησίας); (μυρ.) ϊ pap. 22 Β ex corr.

Folio 5 verso (= Page 11)

† Hathyr 27, likewise. Page 11.

Apollos son of Lene	6 car.	5,600 tal.	
Heirs of Theophilos	3 car.	2,800 tal.	
Peurot son of Pachymis	6 car.	5,600 tal.	
Ioannes heir of Paulos	13 car.	12,100 tal.	
Iosephis heir of Paulos	6 car.	5,600 tal.	
Ama Tasous, nun	2 sol. less 1 (car.)	33,000 tal.	
Victor qes	½ car.	400 tal.	
Pkylis son of Kollouthos	4 car.	3,700 tal.	
Lythis, laborer	4 car.	3,700 tal.	
Phoibammon son of Germanos	2 car	1,800 tal.	
Minos son of Dioskoros	5 ½ car.	5,100 tal.	
Parakote	3 ¼ car.	3,000 tal.	
Petros son of Elias	6 car.	5,600 tal.	
Tatianos, soldier	2 ¾ car.	2,400 tal.	
Plotion	2 car.	1,800 tal.	
Minos son of Pis	2 car.	1,800 tal.	
Ieremias son of Pane	5 car.	4,600 tal.	
Heirs of Konstantinos	2 sol.	34,000 tal.	
Monis kou	6 car.	5,600 tal.	
The Holy Church	8 sol.	136,000 tal.	
Hatres son of Hyperechios	3 car.	2,800 tal.	~~unr.~~
Iosephis heir of Paulos	6 car.	5,600 tal.	~~unr.~~
Georgios son of Taurinos	6 car.	5,600 tal.	
Ieremias son of Pane	2 ¾ car.	2,500 tal.	

Choiak 10 through Ammonis, deacon, 41 car. . . . 41 car. †

Heirs of Konstantinos	41 car.	38,700 tal.
	329,400 tal.	

Folio 6 recto (= Page 12)

Χοίακ ι ὁμο(ίως). ιβ σελ(ίς)

Ἀπολ(λῶς) Λασουκ	κ(εράτια) ς	(τάλαντα) Εχ
Ἀπολλῶς ϭες	κ(εράτια) γ	(τάλαντα) Βω
Τρασίας Παύλου	κ(εράτια) γd	(τάλαντα) Γ
Κυριακὸς Ἀνουφ(ίου)	κ(εράτια) ς	(τάλαντα) Εχ
Μίνος Πις	κ(εράτια) β	(τάλαντα) Α⅄
Μηνᾶ μάγυρ(ος)	νο(μισμάτιον) α	(ταλάντων) (μυριὰς) α Ζ
Γεώρ(γιος) μάγυρ(ος)	νο(μισμάτιον) α π/	(ταλάντων) (μυριὰς) α Ζ
Πκῦλ(ις) Φύβης	κ(εράτια) γ	(τάλαντα) Βω
Ἀτρῆτος Ὑπερεχ(ίου)	κ(εράτια) β	(τάλαντα) Α⅄
Ἰσακίου τέκ(τονος)	κ(εράτια) β	(τάλαντα) Α⅄
Παῆσις Νωϩε	κ(εράτιον) α	(τάλαντα) ⅄
Πέτρ(ος) Ἠλίας	κ(εράτια) ιβ	(ταλάντων) (μυριὰς) α Ασ
Ἀτρῆτος Πεμην	κ(εράτια) β	(τάλαντα) Αω
Χωωρ Ἀνουφ(ίου)	κ(εράτια) εLd	(τάλαντα) Ετ
Φοιβάμμ(ων) Ματρών(ας)	νο(μισμάτιον) α	(ταλάντων) (μυριὰς) α Ζ
Κύρα Ταυρίνου	κ(εράτια) β	(τάλαντα) Α⅄
Ἀπολλ(ῶς) Ὠφελ(ίου)	κ(εράτια) β	(τάλαντα) Α⅄
Μηνᾶ Ἐνῶχ	κ(εράτια) ς	(τάλαντα) Εχ
Τατιαν(ὸς) φομντ	κ(εράτια) ς	(τάλαντα) Εχ
Ἀνοῦφ(ις) Πιουλ	κ(εράτια) γ	(τάλαντα) Βω
ϩελένα	κ(εράτια) θ	(τάλαντα) Ηφ
Λαϩο	κ(εράτια) αL	(τάλαντα) Αυ
Βίκτωρ Σαμηει	κ(εράτια) ιβ	(ταλάντων) (μυριὰς) α Ασ
Ἀπολλ(ῶς) Ἰωάνν(ου)	κ(εράτια) ς	(τάλαντα) Εχ
Ἰωσῆφ(ις) Ὥρου	κ(εράτια) ς	(τάλαντα) Εχ ἀγρ( )
Κελλη	κ(εράτια) γḶd	(τάλαντα) [Γτ ?]
Πιτεχου	κ(εράτια) β	(τάλαντα) Α⅄
Πιηοῦτος Σαμεει	κ(εράτια) β	(τάλαντα) Α⅄
Σολομ(ῶν) Φιβίου	κ(εράτια) αL	(τάλαντα) Αυ
[[[Ἰ̣ωσ̣ῆφ(ις) Ὥρου	κ(εράτια) αLd	(τάλαντα) *vacat*?]]
Κουι Τικ	κ(εράτια) δLd	(τάλαντα) Δυ

(in margin between lines 29 and 30) (ταλάντων) (μυριάδες) ιε Ηψ

7, 8 μάγειρος 9 Φοίβης 11 ϊσακιου pap. 13 ϊβ pap. 32 κουϊ pap. 33 ϊε pap.

Folio 6 recto (= Page 12)

	Choiak 10, likewise.	Page 12.		
	Apollos son of Lasouk	6 car.	5,600 tal.	
	Apollos qes	3 car.	2,800 tal.	
4	Trasias son of Paulos	3 ¼ car.	3,000 tal.	
	Kyriakos son of Anouphis	6 car.	5,600 tal.	
	Minos son of Pis	2 car.	1,900 tal.	
	Menas, meat-cook	1 sol.	17,000 tal.	
8	Georgios, meat-cook	1 sol. less	17,000 tal.	
	Pkylis son of Phoibe	3 car.	2,800 tal.	
	Hatres son of Hyperechios	2 car.	1,900 tal.	
	Isakis, carpenter	2 car.	1,900 tal.	
12	Paesis son of Nohe	1 car.	900 tal.	
	Petros son of Elias	12 car.	11,200 tal.	
	Hatres son of Pemen	2 car.	1,800 tal.	
	Choor son of Anouphis	5 ¾ sol.	5,300 tal.	
16	Phoibammon son of Matrona	1 sol.	17,000 tal.	
	Kyra daughter of Taurinos	2 car.	1,900 tal.	
	Apollos son of Ophelios	2 car.	1,900 tal.	
	Menas son of Enoch	6 car.	5,600 tal.	
20	Tatianos, smith	6 car.	5,600 tal.	
	Anouphis son of Pioul	3 car.	2,800 tal.	
	Helena	9 car.	8,500 tal.	
	Laho	1 ½ car.	1,400 tal.	
24	Victor son of Sameei	12 car.	11,200 tal.	
	Apollos son of Ioannes	6 car.	5,600 tal.	
	Iosephis son of Horos	6 car.	5,600 tal.	unr.
	Kelle	3 ¾ car.	[3,300?] tal.	
28	Pitechou	2 car.	1,900 tal.	
	Pieous son of Sameei	2 car.	1,900 tal.	
	Solomon son of Phibis	1 ½ car.	1,400 tal.	
	[[Iosephis son of Horos	1 ¾ car.	blank ? tal.]]	
32	Koui Tik	4 ¾ car.	4,400 tal.	
	(in margin)	158,700 tal.		

Folio 6 verso (= Page 13)

Χοίακ ι ὁμο(ίως). ιγ σελ(ίς)

Πκῦλ(ις) Κολλούθ(ου)	κ(εράτια) γL	(τάλαντα) Γσ
Ἰωάννης Ἰακυβίου	κ(εράτια) γ	(τάλαντα) Βω
Μαρία Παλικοῦ	κ(εράτια) β	(τάλαντα) Αϡ
Ἐνῶχ Κολλούθ(ου)	κ(εράτια) γ	(τάλαντα) Βω
Ἰωσῆφ(ις) Ἀροοῦ	κ(εράτια) δLd	(τάλαντα) Δτ
Κοοϩα	κ(εράτια) γ	(τάλαντα) Βω
Εὖς Ἰωάν(νου)	κ(εράτια) βd	(τάλαντα) Βρ
Φῖβις Τοοσε	νο(μισμάτια) αL	(ταλάντων) (μυριάδες) β Εφ
Κυριακός	κ(εράτια) β	(τάλαντα) Αϡ
Ψᾶτος Κόμες	κ(εράτια) ϛ	(τάλαντα) Εχ
Κουι Νου	κ(εράτια) αL	(τάλαντα) Αυ
γυν(ὴ) Πενοϥ	κ(εράτια) δL	(τάλαντα) Δρ
Βίκτωρ ματοι	κ(εράτια) ε	(τάλαντα) Δψ
Ἀνοῦφ(ις) Ἄβα Στεξ	κ(εράτια) β	(τάλαντα) Αϡ
Μονίου Παπνουθ(ίου)	κ(εράτια) β	(τάλαντα) Αϡ
Πατσαλαμαντ( )	κ(εράτια) ιβ	(ταλάντων) (μυριὰς) α Ασ
Ἰωάννης Λεῦτος	κ(εράτια) β	(τάλαντα) Αϡ
Ἀπολλ(ῶς) Ἀτρῆτος	κ(εράτια) β	(τάλαντα) Αϡ [[ἀγρ( )]]
κληλ Καϩ	κ(εράτια) βL	(τάλαντα) Βσ
Ἐνῶχ οἰκονόμ(ος)	νο(μισμάτια) β	(ταλάντων) (μυριάδες) γ Δ
Μονίου Παύλ(ου)	νο(μισμάτιον) α	(ταλάντων) (μυριὰς) α Ζ
κλ(ηρονόμοι) διακ(όνου)	νο(μισμάτιον) α π/	(ταλάντων) (μυριὰς) α Ζ
Ἀτρῆτος ῥάπτου	κ(εράτια) γ	(τάλαντα) Βω
Μίνου Ἀνουφ(ίου)	κ(εράτια) γ	(τάλαντα) Βω
Σαραπίον Πασωθ(ίου)	κ(εράτια) γ	(τάλαντα) Βω
Ἀπολ(λῶς) ἐλαιουρ(γός)	κ(εράτια) ϛ	(τάλαντα) Εχ [[ἀγρ( )]]
Ἀνοῦφ(ις) Ἰακυβίου	κ(εράτια) αL	(τάλαντα) Αυ
Λακον	κ(εράτια) αd	(τάλαντα) Αρ
Ἰωσῆφ(ις) γραμμ(ατ--)	κ(εράτια) θ	(τάλαντα) Ηφ [[ἀγρ( )]]
Κωρ ΧιΧ	κ(εράτια) δ	(τάλαντα) Γψ
Κωσταντ(ῖνος) Παχυμ(ίου)	κ(εράτια) ιβ	(ταλάντων) *vacat*
(in margin of line 31)	(ταλάντων) (μυριάδες) ιθ Β	

3 ϊωαννης, ϊακυβιο^υ pap. 6 ϊωσηφ/ pap.? 8 ϊωανν$ pap. 12 κουϊ pap. 13 Πενοϥ, ο ex corr. 14 ματοϊ pap. 18 ϊωαννης pap. 20 κληλ = κληρ(ονόμοι) 28 ϊακυβιο^υ pap. 30 ϊωσηφ/ pap. 32 ϊβ pap. 33 ϊθ pap.

Folio 6 verso (Page 13)

Choiak 10, likewise.	Page 13.		
Pkylis son of Kollouthos	3 ½ car.	3,200 tal.	
Ioannes son of Iakybis	3 car.	2,800 tal.	
Maria daughter of Palikous	2 car.	1,900 tal.	
Enoch son of Kollouthos	3 car.	2,800 tal.	
Iosephis son of Haroous	4 ¾ car.	4,300 tal.	
Kooha	3 car.	2,800 tal.	
Eus daughter of Ioannes	2 ¼ car.	2,100 tal.	
Phibis son of Toose	1 ½ sol.	25,500 tal.	
Kyriakos	2 car.	1,900 tal.	
Psas son of Komes	6 car.	5,600 tal.	
Koui Nou	1 ½ car.	1,400 tal.	
Wife of Penof	4 ½ car.	4,100 tal.	
Victor, soldier	5 car.	4,700 tal.	
Anouphis son of Aba Stex	2 car.	1,900 tal.	
Monis son of Papnouthis	2 car.	1,900 tal.	
Patsalamant( )	12 car.	11,200 tal.	
Ioannes son of Leus	2 car.	1,900 tal.	
Apollos son of Hatres	2 car.	1,900 tal.	~~unr.~~
Heirs of Kah	2 ½ car.	2,200 tal.	
Enoch, oikonomos	2 sol.	34,000 tal.	
Monis son of Paulos	1 sol.	17,000 tal.	
Heirs of the deacon	1 sol. less	17,000 tal.	
Hatres, tailor	3 car.	2,800 tal.	
Minos son of Anouphis	3 car.	2,800 tal.	
Sarapion son of Pasothis	3 car.	2,800 tal.	
Apollos, oil-worker	6 car.	5,600 tal.	~~unr.~~
Anouphis son of Iakybis	1 ½ car.	1,400 tal.	
Lakon	1 ¼ car.	1,100 tal.	
Iosephis, gramm( )	9 car.	8,500 tal.	~~unr.~~
Kor Jij	4 car.	3,700 tal.	
Konstantinos son of Pachymis	12 car.	*vacat* tal.	

(in margin, line 31) 192,000 tal.

Folio 7 recto (= Page 14)

† Χοίακ ι// ιδ σελ(ίς)

Βίκτωρ Ἰουλούμενος	κ(εράτια) γ	(τάλαντα) Βω
Μακάρ(ιος) Παπνουθ(ίου)	κ(εράτια) β	(τάλαντα) Αϡ
Ἀνοῦφ(ις) ἀπὸ Τβακε	κ(εράτια) β	(τάλαντα) Αϡ
Πευροτ Παχυμίου	κ(εράτια) ι	(τάλαντα) Θσ
Μόνις Κόμες	κ(εράτια) β	(τάλαντα) Αϡ
Ἰωάννης Ἀκωρ(ίου)	κ(εράτια) γ	(τάλαντα) Βω
Σολομῶν Φιβίου	κ(ερατίου) L	(τάλαντα) υ
Πλουτίων	κ(εράτιον) α	(τάλαντα) ϡ
Φοιβάμμ(ων) Λωτα	κ(εράτια) γ	(τάλαντα) Βω
Λουλοῦ[[λ]]\`τος´ Ἰωάνν(ου)	κ(εράτια) β	(τάλαντα) Αϡ ἀγρ( )
Ἰωνίου Ἰωσηφ(ίου)	νο(μισμάτιον) α	(ταλάντων) (μυριὰς) α Ζ [[ἀγρ( )]]
Σαραπίον σιτομέτρ(ης)	κ(εράτια) εL	(τάλαντα) Ερ [[ἀγρ( )]]
τῆς ἁγίας ἐκλ(ησίας)	νο(μισμάτια) η	(ταλάντων) (μυριάδες) ιγ Ϛ
Σαραπίον Πασωθ(ίου)	κ(εράτιον) α	(τάλαντα) ϡ
Βίκτωρ καθαρ(ουργός)	κ(εράτια) γd	(τάλαντα) Γ
Ἰερημίας Πανε	κ(εράτια) ε	(τάλαντα) Δψ
Ἄτρῆτος Ὑπερεχ(ίου)	κ(εράτια) αL	(τάλαντα) Αυ [[ἀγρ( )]]
Τατιαν(ὸς) Ἠλίας	κ(εράτια) δ	(τάλαντα) Γψ [[ἀγρ( )]]
Πέτρ(ος) Ἠλίας	κ(εράτια) ς	(τάλαντα) Εχ [[ἀγρ( )]]
Ἰωσῆφ(ις) Νόννα	κ(εράτια) ς	(τάλαντα) Εχ [[ἀγρ( )]]
Ἀπολλ(ῶς) Ἰωάν(νου)	κ(εράτια) ς	(τάλαντα) Εχ [[ἀγρ( )]]
Φῖβις Τοοσε ὁμοί(ως)	κ(εράτια) θ	(τάλαντα) Ηφ
Τατιαν(ὸς) Ἠλίας	κ(εράτια) ι	(τάλαντα) Θτ
Ἰωσῆφ(ις) Νόννα	κ(εράτια) ιβ	(ταλάντων) (μυριὰς) α Ασ
Ἄπε Ἀπαλο	κ(εράτια) γ	(τάλαντα) Βω
Ἰωάνν(ης) Πανουβε	κ(εράτια) β	(τάλαντα) Αω [[ἀγρ( )]] δι(ὰ) Τατιανοῦ Ἑρμ( )
Ἰωάννης Λεῦτος	κ(εράτια) β	(τάλαντα) Αω
Ϩιριϭωϣ	κ(εράτια) βd	(τάλαντα) Βρ

(ταλάντων) (μυριάδες) κε Βχ

2 ϊουλουμενος pap., read -μένου 5 ϊ pap. 7 ϊωαννης pap. 8 (τάλ.) ϋ pap. 11 ϊωαννS pap. 12 ϊωνιου, ϊωσηφ/ pap. 13, 15 Σαραπίων 14 ἐκκλ(ησίας) 17 ϊερημιας pap. 21, 25 ϊωσηφ/ pap. 27 ϊωανν(ης) pap. 28 ϊωαννης pap.

Folio 7 recto (= Page 14)

† Choiak 10. Page 14.

Victor son of Iouloumenos	3 car.	2,800 tal.	
Makarios son of Papnouthis	2 car.	1,900 tal.	
Anouphis from Tbake	2 car.	1,900 tal.	
Peurot son of Pachymis	10 car.	9,200 tal.	
Monis son of Komes	2 car.	1,900 tal.	
Ioannes son of Akoris	3 car.	2,800 tal.	
Solomon son of Phibis	½ car.	400 tal.	
Ploution	1 car.	900 tal.	
Phoibammon son of Lota	3 car.	2,800 tal.	
Loulous son of Ioannes	2 car.	1,900 tal.	unr.
Ionios son of Iosephis	1 sol.	17,000 tal.	~~unr.~~
Sarapion, grain-measurer	5 ½ car.	5,100 tal.	~~unr.~~
The Holy Church	8 sol.	136,000 tal.	
Sarapion son of Pasothis	1 car.	900 tal.	
Victor, baker	3 ¼ car.	3,000 tal.	
Ieremias son of Pane	5 car.	4,700 tal.	
Hatres son of Hyperechios	1 ½ car.	1,400 tal.	~~unr.~~
Tatianos son of Elias	4 car.	3,700 tal.	~~unr.~~
Petros son of Elias	6 car.	5,600 tal.	~~unr.~~
Iosephis son of Nonna	6 car.	5,600 tal.	~~unr.~~
Apollos son of Ioannes	6 car.	5,600 tal.	~~unr.~~
Phibis son of Toose, likewise	9 car.	8,500 tal.	
Tatianos son of Elias	10 car.	9,300 tal.	
Iosephis son of Nonna	12 car.	11,200 tal.	
Ape Apalo	3 car.	2,800 tal.	
Ioannes son of Panoube	2 car.	1,800 tal.	~~unr.~~ through Tatianos son of Herm( )
Ioannes son of Leus	2 car.	1,800 tal.	
Hiriqosh	2 ¼ car.	2,100 tal.	

252,600 tal.

Folio 7 verso (= Page 15)

	Χοίακ <ι>ς	ιε σελ(ίς)	
1a	ο(ὕτως)		
	Κουι Τικ	κ(εράτια) βLd	(τάλαντα) Βφ
	Πναϩκας	κ(εράτια) αLd	(τάλαντα) Αφ
4	Ἀνοῦφ(ις) Ἰακυβίου	κ(ερατίου) L	(τάλαντα) υ
	Ἠσαίας πρεσβύτερ(ος)	κ(εράτια) γ	(τάλαντα) Βω
	Παπνοῦθ(ις) Κλεμ( )	κ(εράτια) βL	(τάλαντα) Βτ
	Κωσταντ(ῖνος) Παχυμίου	κ(εράτια) ιβ	(ταλάντων) (μυριὰς) α Ασ
8	Σαραπίον σιτομέτρ(ης)		
	δ(ιὰ) Ἰωάν(νου) Πελ(ουλ)	κ(εράτια) ς	(τάλαντα) Εχ
	ΠανηϪνου δ(ιὰ) Ἰωάν(νου) Πελ(ουλ)	κ(εράτια) ς	(τάλαντα) Εχ ἀγ̣ρ( )
	ϩαλμίου δ(ιὰ) Ἰωάν(νου) Πελ(ουλ)	κ(εράτια) β	(τάλαντα) Αω
	Πευροτ Παχυμίου	κ(εράτια) ιβ	(ταλάντων) (μυριὰς) α Ασ
12	Ἰωσῆφ(ις) Ὥρου	κ(εράτια) ςd	(τάλαντα) Εω
	Μίνου Ἀνουφ(ίου)	κ(εράτια) εLd	(τάλαντα) Ετ
	Ἰωάνν(ης) ἐργ(άτης)	κ(εράτια) αL	(τάλαντα) Αυ
	Θεόφιλ(ος)	κ(εράτια) ε	(τάλαντα) Δψ
16	Σαραπίον Βαχη	κ(εράτια) ς	(τάλαντα) Εχ
	κλ(ηρονόμοι) διακ(όνου)	κ(εράτια) δL	(τάλαντα) Δσ̣
	[Ἰ]ωάννης Πανουβε	κ(εράτιον) α	(τάλαντα) ϡ
	[Τ]ατιαν(ὸς) ματοι	κ(εράτια) αL	(τάλαντα) Αυ
20	Ἀπο̣λ̣(λῶς) Ἀτρῆτος	κ(εράτιον) α	(τάλαντα) ϡ
	ϩελένα	κ(εράτια) θ	(τάλαντα) Ηφ
	Φοιβ(άμμων) Ματρώνα	κ(εράτια) ς	(τάλαντα) Εχ
	Μίνου Τιμουτη	κ(εράτια) δd	(τάλαντα) Γϡ
24	Λῦθις ἐργάτης	κ(εράτια) δL	(τάλαντα) Δρ
	Ἀπολλ(ῶς) Κασίας	κ(εράτια) γ̣L	(τάλαντα) Γσ
	Κασίας Σαμηε̣ι	κ(εράτια) ς	(τάλαντα) Εχ
	Κωρ ϪιϪο̣	κ(εράτια) β	(τάλαντα) Αω
28	[Ἀ]νοῦφ(ις) Κωσταν̣τ(ίνου)	κ(εράτια) ς	(τάλαντα) Εχ
	[Ἰω]νίου Ἰωσηφ(ίου)	κ(εράτια) ς	(τάλαντα) Εχ
	. . . . Ἀπολ(λῶτος)	κ(εράτια) δ	(τάλαντα) Γψ̣
	[Ψ]ᾶ̣τος Κόμες	κ(εράτιον) α	(τάλαντα) ϡ
32		(ταλάντων) (μυριάδες) ιβ Γφ	

4 ϊακυβιο^υ, (τάλ.) ϋ pap. 5 ησαϊας pap. 7 ϊβ pap. 8, 9, 10 ϊωαννS pap.
8, 16 Σαραπίων 11 ϊβ pap. 14 Αϋ pap. 28 Κωσταντ/, *ν* ex corr. 29 ϊωσηφ/ pap.

Folio 7 verso (= Page 15).

	Choiak <1>6.	Page 15		
1a	As follows:			
	Koui Tik	2 ¾ car.	2,500 tal.	
	Pnahkas	1 ¾ car.	1,500 tal.	
4	Anouphis son of Iakybis	½ car.	400 tal.	
	Esaias, priest	3 car.	2,800 tal.	
	Papnouthis son of Klem( )	2 ½ car.	2,300 tal.	
	Konstantinos son of Pachymis	12 car.	11,200 tal.	
8	Sarapion, grain-measurer, through Ioannes son of Peloul	6 car.	5,600 tal.	
	Panejnou through Ioannes son of Peloul	6 car.	5,600 tal.	unr.
	Halmios through Ioannes son of Peloul	2 car.	1,800 tal.	
	Peurot son of Pachymis	12 car.	11,200 tal.	
12	Iosephis son of Horos	6 ¼ car.	5,800 tal.	
	Minos son of Anouphis	5 ¾ car.	5,300 tal.	
	Ioannes, laborer	1 ½ car.	1,400 tal.	
	Theophilos	5 car.	4,700 tal.	
16	Sarapion son of Bache	6 car.	5,600 tal.	
	Heirs of the deacon	4 ½ car.	4,200 tal.	
	Ioannes son of Panoube	1 car.	900 tal.	
	Tatianos, soldier	1 ½ car.	1,400 tal.	
20	Apollos son of Hatres	1 car.	900 tal.	
	Helena	9 car.	8,500 tal.	
	Phoibammon son of Matrona	6 car.	5,600 tal.	
	Minos son of Timoute	4 ¼ car.	3,900 tal.	
24	Lythis, laborer	4 ½ car.	4,100 tal.	
	Apollos son of Kasia	3 ½ car.	3,200 tal.	
	Kasia daughter of Sameei	6 car.	5,600 tal.	
	Kor Jijo	2 car.	1,800 tal.	
28	Anouphis son of Konstantinos	6 car.	5,600 tal.	
	Ionios son of Iosephis	6 car.	5,600 tal.	
	. . . . son of Apollos	4 car.	3,700 tal.	
	Psas son of Komes	1 car.	900 tal.	
32		123,500 tal.		

Folio 8 recto (= Page 16)

† Χοίακ κ̣ ὁμοί(ως).	ις σελ(ίς)	
Ἐνῶχ οἰκονόμ(ος)	νο(μισμάτια) β	(ταλάντων) (μυριάδες) γ Δ
κλ(ηρονόμοι) Θεοφίλ(ου)	κ(εράτια) ιϛL	(ταλάντων) (μυριὰς) α Ϛ
τῆς ἁγίας ἐκλ(ησίας)	νο(μισμάτια) δ	(ταλάντων) (μυριάδες) ϛ Η
Φῖβις ΠϪαϪ	κ(εράτια) γd	(τάλαντα) Γ
Φῖβις Τοοσε	νο(μισμάτια) αL	(ταλάντων) (μυριάδες) β Εφ
Ἀπολλ(ῶς) Ἰωάνν(ου)	κ(εράτια) ϛ	(τάλαντα) Εχ
Βάνου χαλκ(έως)	κ(εράτια) γ	(τάλαντα) Βω
Τατιαν(οῦ) ῥάπτου	κ(εράτια) γ	(τάλαντα) Βω
Τῦβι// ε		
Ἀπολλῶ{σ}τος Ἰωάννου	κ(εράτια) θ	(τάλαντα) Ηφ
υἱὸς Βάνου χαλκ(έως) δ(ιὰ)		
Ἀπολ(λῶτος) Ἰωάν(νου)	κ(εράτιον) α	(τάλαντα) ϡ
Λακον	κ(εράτιον) α	(τάλαντα) ϡ
Κωρ ϪιϪ δ(ιὰ) Λακον	κ(εράτια) β	(τάλαντα) Αϡ
Ὥρου Σουριχη	κ(εράτιον) α	(τάλαντα) ϡ
Κουι Ϣα καὶ Λαϩο	κ(εράτια) β	(τάλαντα) Αϡ
Ἰωάννης Ἰακυβίου	κ(εράτια) γ	(τάλαντα) Βω
Ἐνῶχ Κολλούθ(ου)	κ(εράτια) γ	(τάλαντα) Βω
Ψᾶτος Κόμες	κ(εράτια) ϛ	(τάλαντα) Εχ
Τρασίας Παύλου	κ(εράτια) β	(τάλαντα) Αϡ
Ἄπα Νοκις [[ιγL]]	κ(εράτια) ιζ	(ταλάντων) (μυριὰς) α Εϡ
Ἰωσῆφ(ις) Ὥρου	κ(εράτια) γLd	(τάλαντα) Γυ
Ἀπολλ(ῶς) Ἰωσηφ(ίου) δ(ιὰ)		
Ἰερημί(ου) πρωτοκ(ωμήτου)	κ(εράτια) ιζL	(ταλάντων) (μυριὰς) α Ϛφ
Τ[[α]]ιτιαν(ὸς) ϭεc δ(ιὰ) τοῦ αὐτοῦ	κ(εράτια) θ	(τάλαντα) Ηφ
Παπνοῦθ(ις) Κλεμ( ) δ(ιὰ) τοῦ αὐτοῦ	κ(εράτια) ϛL	(τάλαντα) Ϛ
Κυριακὸς Ἀνουφ(ίου) δ(ιὰ) τοῦ αὐτοῦ	κ(εράτια) γ	(τάλαντα) Βω
Ἰωνίου Ἰωσηφ(ίου)	κ(εράτια) θ	(τάλαντα) Ηφ
Λῦθις ἐργάτης δ(ιὰ) τοῦ αὐτοῦ	κ(εράτια) γ	(τάλαντα) Βω
Σαραπίων Πασωθ(ίου)	κ(εράτια) β	(τάλαντα) Αϡ
Πευροτ Παχυμίου	κ(εράτια) ϛ	(τάλαντα) Εχ
Ἀτρῆτος Πεμ̣η̣ν̣	κ(εράτιον) α	(τάλαντα) ϡ
Βίκτωρ μ̣[α]τοι	κ(εράτια) δ	(τάλαντα) Γψ
Ἠσαίας πρ[εσβ]ύτε(ρος)	κ(εράτια) γ	(τάλαντα) Βω
Ἀπολλῶ[ς Κ]ασίας	κ(εράτια) ιLd	[(ταλάντων) (μυριὰς) α]

3 ιϛL: ι ex corr. At end: Ϛ ex Ζ   4 ἐκκλ(ησίας)   7 ϊωαννS pap.   10 ε ex ϛ   11 ϊωαννο[υ] pap.   12 υϊος, ϊωανS pap.   16 ΚουϊϢα pap.   17 ϊωαννης ϊακυβιο[υ] pap., γ ex β   18 Βω, Β ex corr. or rewritten
21 ϊζ pap.   22 ϊωσηφ/ pap.   23 ϊωανS pap.   24 Τατιαν(ός)   27 ϊωνιου, ϊωσηφ/ pap.   33 ησαϊας pap.

Folio 8 recto (= Page 16)

† Choiak 20, likewise.	Page 16.	
Enoch, oikonomos	2 sol.	34,000 tal.
Heirs of Theophilos	16 ½ car.	16,000 tal.
The Holy Church	4 sol.	68,000 tal.
Phibis (son of?) Pjaj	3 ¼ car.	3,000 tal.
Phibis son of Toose	1 ½ sol.	25,500 tal.
Apollos son of Ioannes	6 car.	5,600 tal.
Banos, smith	3 car.	2,800 tal.
Tatianos, tailor	3 car.	2,800 tal.
Tybi 5		
Apollos son of Ioannes	9 car.	8,500 tal.
son of Banos the smith, through Apollos son of Ioannes	1 car.	900 tal.
Lakon	1 car.	900 tal.
Kor Jij through Lakon	2 car.	1,900 tal.
Horos son of Souriche	1 car.	900 tal.
Koui Sha and Laho	2 car.	1,900 tal.
Ioannes son of Iakybis	3 car.	2,800 tal.
Enoch son of Kollouthos	3 car.	2,800 tal.
Psas son of Komes	6 car.	5,600 tal.
Trasias son of Paulos	2 car.	1,900 tal.
Apa Nokis [[13 ½]]	17 car.	15,900 tal.
Iosephis son of Horos	3 ¾ car.	3,400 tal.
Apollos son of Iosephis through Ieremias, protokometes	17 ½ car.	16,500 tal.
Tatianos qes through the same	9 car.	8,500 tal.
Papnouthis son of Klem( ) through the same	6 ½ car.	6,000 tal.
Kyriakos son of Anouphis through the same	3 car.	2,800 tal.
Ionios son of Iosephis	9 car.	8,500 tal.
Lythis, laborer, through the same	3 car.	2,800 tal.
Sarapion son of Pasothis	2 car.	1,900 tal.
Peurot son of Pachymis	6 car.	5,600 tal.
Hatres son of Pemen	1 car.	900 tal.
Victor, soldier	4 car.	3,700 tal.
Esaias, priest	3 car.	2,800 tal.
Apollos son of Kasia	10 ¾ car.	[10,000 tal.]

Folio 8 verso (= Page 17)

† Τῦβι ε ὁμοί(ως) ιζ σελ(ίς)

Πιουλ	κ(εράτια) β	(τάλαντα) Αϡ
Ψάτος Ἰωάννου	κ(εράτια) β	(τάλαντα) Αϡ
Ϩαμποι	κ(εράτια) ϛ	(τάλαντα) Εχ
Ἀνοῦφ(ις) ἀπὸ Τβακε	κ(εράτιον) α	(τάλαντα) ϡ
Φοιβάμμ(ων) Ματρώνα	κ(εράτια) θ	(τάλαντα) Ηφ
Ἀτρῆτος Σαμηει	κ(εράτιον) α	(τάλαντα) ϡ
Πατσαλαμανα δ(ιὰ) Κοοϩα	κ(εράτια) ϛ	(τάλαντα) Εχ
Ἀνοῦφ(ις) οἰκοδ(όμος)	κ(εράτια) β	(τάλαντα) Αϡ
Ἐνῶχ γναφεύ<ς>	κ(εράτιον) α	(τάλαντα) ϡ
Μονίου Ἑρμαπόλ(λωνος)	κ(εράτια) β	(τάλαντα) Αϡ
Μακάρ(ιος) οἰκοδόμ(ος)	κ(εράτια) β	(τάλαντα) Αω
τῶν σκυτέων	κ(εράτια) β	(τάλαντα) Αϡ
Κῦρος λαξόου	κ(εράτια) γ	(τάλαντα) Βω
Κελλη	κ(εράτια) β	(τάλαντα) Αϡ
Μίνος Πις	κ(εράτιον) α	(τάλαντα) ϡ
Ἰωάνν(ης) Λεῦτος	κ(εράτια) β	(τάλαντα) Αϡ
Πεσσοοῦ	νο(μισμάτιον) α	(ταλάντων) (μυριὰς) α Ζ
Νόννα Παρσας δ(ιὰ) τοῦ αὐτοῦ	κ(εράτια) ιβ	(ταλάντων) (μυριὰς) α Ασ
Κουι Σνοβ δ(ιὰ) τοῦ αὐτοῦ	κ(εράτια) ϛ	(τάλαντα) Εχ
Φοιβάμ(μων) Πινουτ(ίωνος)		
δ(ιὰ) τοῦ αὐτοῦ	κ(εράτια) ϛ	(τάλαντα) Εχ
Ἰωάννης Παύλου δ(ιὰ) τοῦ αὐτοῦ	κ(εράτια) ιβ	(ταλάντων) (μυριὰς) α Ασ
Πλωτίων δ(ιὰ) τοῦ αὐτοῦ	κ(εράτια) γ	(τάλαντα) Βω
Μακαρίου Γερμαν(οῦ) δ(ιὰ) τοῦ αὐτοῦ	κ(εράτια) δ	(τάλαντα) Γψ
Τατιαν(ὸς) Ἠλίας δ(ιὰ) τοῦ αὐτοῦ	κ(εράτια) δ	(τάλαντα) Γψ
Μηνᾶ Περητ	κ(εράτιον) α	(τάλαντα) ϡ
Ἰερημίας Ϩαλμίου	κ(εράτιον) α	(τάλαντα) ϡ
Πιτεχου	κ(εράτιον) α	(τάλαντα) ϡ
Μίνου Ἀνουφ(ίου)	κ(εράτια) βLd	(τάλαντα) Βφ
Ἀνοῦφ(ις) Κωσταντ(ίνου)	κ(εράτια) ϛ	(τάλαντα) Εχ
Ἀπολλ(ῶς) Λασουκ	κ(εράτια) β	(τάλαντα) αϡ
Ἀνοῦφ(ις) Ἰακυβίου	κ(εράτιον) α	(τάλαντα) ϡ
	(ταλάντων) (μυριάδες) ια Εχ	

3, 17, 22 ϊωανν- pap. 4 ϩαμποϊ pap. 7 α ex β, ϡ ex Αϡ 19 ϊβ pap. 20 κουϊ pap. 27 ϊερημιας pap. 32 ϊακυβιου pap. 33 ϊα pap.

Folio 8 verso (= Page 17)

† Tybi 5 likewise. Page 17.

	Pioul	2 car.	1,900 tal.
	Psas son of Ioannes	2 car.	1,900 tal.
4	Hampoi	6 car.	5,600 tal.
	Anouphis from Tbake	1 car.	900 tal.
	Phoibammon son of Matrona	9 car.	8,500 tal.
	Hatres son of Sameei	1 car.	900 tal.
8	Patsalamana through Kooha	6 car.	5,600 tal.
	Anouphis, mason	2 car.	1,900 tal.
	Enoch, fuller	1 car.	900 tal.
	Monis son of Hermapollon	2 car.	1,900 tal.
12	Makarios, mason	2 car.	1,800 tal.
	The cobblers	2 car.	1,900 tal.
	Kyros, stonecutter	3 car.	2,800 tal.
	Kelle	2 car.	1,900 tal.
16	Minos son of Pis	1 car.	900 tal.
	Ioannes son of Leus	2 car.	1,900 tal.
	Pessoous	1 sol.	17,000 tal.
	Nonna daughter of Parsas through the same	12 car.	11,200 tal.
20	Koui Snob through the same	6 car.	5,600 tal.
	Phoibammon son of Pinoution through the same	6 car.	5,600 tal.
	Ioannes son of Paulos through the same	12 car.	11,200 tal.
	Plotion through the same	3 car.	2,800 tal.
24	Makarios son of Germanos through the same	4 car.	3,700 tal.
	Tatianos son of Elias through the same	4 car.	3,700 tal.
	Menas son of Peret	1 car.	900 tal.
	Ieremias son of Halmios	1 car.	900 tal.
28	Pitechou	1 car.	900 tal.
	Minos son of Anouphis	2 ¾ car.	2,500 tal.
	Anouphis son of Konstantinos	6 car.	5,600 tal.
	Apollos son of Lasouk	2 car.	1,900 tal.
32	Anouphis son of Iakybis	1 car.	900 tal.
		115,600 tal.	

Folio 9 recto (= Page 18)

† Τῦβι ẹ ὁμο(ίως)   ιη σελ(ίς)

Μακάριος Παπνουθ(ίου)	κ(εράτια) β	(τάλαντα) Αϡ
Ἀπολλῶς ϭεc	κ(εράτιον) α	(τάλαντα) ϡ
Ἀνοῦφ(ις) Ἀπ̣ολλ(ῶτος)	κ(εράτια) ϛ	(τάλαντα) Εχ
Λουλοῦτος Κερμα(νοῦ)	κ(ερατίου) L	(τάλαντα) υ
Ἀπολλῶτ̣ο̣ς Πτουλ	κ(εράτιον) α	(τάλαντα) ϡ
Χωωρ Ἀνουφ(ίου)	κ(εράτια) δ	(τάλαντα) Γψ
Παρακωτε	κ(εράτια) δ	(τάλαντα) Γψ
Ἀβρ(αάμις) ϭεc	κ(εράτια) β	(τάλαντα) Αϡ
Κωσταντ(ῖνος) Παχυμίου	κ(εράτια) θ	(τάλαντα) Ηφ
Ἰωάννης Ἀκωρίου	κ(εράτια) β	(τάλαντα) Αϡ
Πκῦλ(ις) Κολ(λού)θ(ου)	κ(εράτια) β	(τάλαντα) Αϡ
Μακαρίου Γερμαν(οῦ)	κ(εράτια) β	(τάλαντα) Αϡ
Ἄβα Στεξ	κ(εράτιον) α	(τάλαντα) ϡ
Ϩελένα [[ϛ]]	κ(εράτια) ϛ	(τάλαντα) Εχ [[ἀγ̣ρ( )]]
Ἀπολλῶτος Κασία	κ(εράτια) β	(τάλαντα) Αω
Μ̣η̣ν̣ᾶ̣ Ἐνῶχ ϛ	κ(εράτια) *vac*	(τάλαντα) Εχ [[ἀγ̣ρ( )]]
Τ̣ρ̣α̣σ̣ί̣α̣ς Παύλου	κ(εράτια) θ	(τάλαντα) Ηφ
Ἀνοῦφ(ις) Ἀπολ(λῶτος)	κ(ερατίου) L	(τάλαντα) υ [[ἀγ̣ρ( )]]
Ἐνῶχ οἰκονόμ(ος)	νο(μισμάτια) β	(ταλάντων) (μυριάδες) γ Δ
Ὥρου Βικτωρῖν̣ο̣ς	κ(εράτιον) α	(τάλαντα) ϡ
Σαραπίον σιτομέτρ(ης)	κ(εράτια) [[ε]] ϛ	(τάλαντα) Εχ
[Ἰ]ωσῆφ(ις) Ὥρου	κ(εράτια) ϛ	(τάλαντα) Εχ
Ἀπολλῶτος Ἀτρῆτος	κ(εράτιον) α	(τάλαντα) ϡ
Κωρ ϫιϫ δ(ιὰ) Ἀπολ(λῶτος) Κασία [[α]]	κ(εράτιον) α	(τάλαντα) ϡ
Βίκτωρ Κερμ(ιϫου) [[. . .]]	κ(εράτια) δL	(τάλαντα) Δρ
Ἴσιτο̣ς Ἑρμαπόλ(λωνος)	κ(εράτιον) α	(τάλαντα) ϡ
Ἀνν̣ίου [[. .]]	κ(ερατίου) Ld	(τάλαντα) ψ
Κῦρ(ος) τέκτ(ων)	κ(εράτια) β	(τάλαντα) Αϡ
Κύ[ρ]α̣ Ταυρίνου	κ(εράτιον) α	(τάλαντα) ϡ
Παπνοῦθ(ις) Μίν(ου)	κ(εράτια) γ	(τάλαντα) Βω
Εὖς Ἰωάννου	κ(εράτια) γ	(τάλαντα) Βω
Βίκτωρ Σαμε̣ε̣ι̣	κ(εράτια) ϛ	(τάλαντα) Εχ
Ἰωσῆφ(ις) Πα̣ύ̣λ̣ου	κ(εράτια) ϛ	(τάλαντα) Εχ
	(ταλάντων) (μυριάδες) ι̣β̣ Θ̣σ̣	

5 Γερμα(νοῦ)   5, 19 (τάλ.) ϋ pap.   6 Πιουλ   11 ϊωαννης pap.   22 Εχ ex Δψ   27 ϊσιτος pap.

Folio 9 recto (= Page 18)

† Tybi 5 likewise. Page 18.

Makarios son of Papnouthis	2 car.	1,900 tal.	
Apollos qes	1 car.	900 tal.	
Anouphis son of Apollos	6 car.	5,600 tal.	
Loulous son of Germanos	½ car.	400 tal.	
Apollos son of Ptoul (*sic*)	1 car.	900 tal.	
Choor son of Anouphis	4 car.	3,700 tal.	
Parakote	4 car.	3,700 tal.	
Abraamis qes	2 car.	1,900 tal.	
Konstantinos son of Pachymis	9 car.	8,500 tal.	
Ioannes son of Akoris	2 car.	1,900 tal.	
Pkylis son of Kollouthos	2 car.	1,900 tal.	
Makarios son of Germanos	2 car.	1,900 tal.	
Aba Stex	1 car.	900 tal.	
Helena	6 car.	5,600 tal.	~~unr.~~
Apollos son of Kasia	2 car.	1,800 tal.	
Menas son of Enoch	6 car.	5,600 tal.	~~unr.~~
Trasias son of Paulos	9 car.	8,500 tal.	
Anouphis son of Apollos	½ car.	400 tal.	~~unr.~~
Enoch, oikonomos	2 sol.	34,000 tal.	
Horos son of Victorinus	1 car.	900 tal.	
Sarapion, grain-measurer	6 car.	5,600 tal.	
Iosephis son of Horos	6 car.	5,600 tal.	
Apollos son of Hatres	1 car.	900 tal.	
Kor Jij through Apollos son of Kasia	1 car.	900 tal.	
Victor son of Kermijou	4 ½ car.	4,100 tal.	
Isis daughter of Hermapollon	1 car.	900 tal.	
Annios	¾ car.	700 tal.	
Kyros, carpenter	2 car.	1,900 tal.	
Kyra daughter of Taurinos	1 car.	900 tal.	
Papnouthis son of Minos	3 car.	2,800 tal.	
Eus daughter of Ioannes	3 car.	2,800 tal.	
Victor son of Sameei	6 car.	5,600 tal.	
Iosephis son of Paulos	6 car.	5,600 tal.	

129,200 tal.

Folio 9 verso (= Page 19) Plate 1

† Τῦβι ε ὁμο(ίως) ιθ σελ(ίς)		
Τατι\`α´ν(ὸς) Παρβας	κ(εράτια) β	(τάλαντα) Αϡ
Σοίου Φιβίου	κ(εράτια) β	(τάλαντα) Αϡ
Ἰωσῆφ(ις) Παύλου	κ(εράτια) ϛ	(τάλαντα) Ε̣χ
Λαϩη οἰκοδόμ(ος)	κ(εράτιον) α	(τάλαντα) ϡ
Σενικίον	νο(μισμάτιον) α	(ταλάντων) (μυριὰς) α Ζ
Ἰωάνν(ης) τῆς ἁγίας ἐκλ(ησίας)	νο(μισμάτια) ϛ	(ταλάντων) (μυριάδες) ι// Β
Φῖβις Φοιβάμ(μωνος) Τοοσε	νο(μισμάτια) β	(ταλάντων) (μυριάδες) γ Δ
[[κλ(ηρονόμοι) Θεοφ(ίλου) ὁμο(ίως) δ(ιὰ) Ἀπολλ(ῶτος) Λένη κ(εράτια) δ (τάλαντα) Γψ]]		
Πλωτίων	κ(εράτια) β	(τάλαντα) Αϡ
Πναϩκας	κ(εράτια) γ	(τάλαντα) Βω [[ἀ̣γ̣ρ̣( )]]
Μηνᾶ Ἐνῶχ	κ(εράτια) δ	(τάλαντα) Γω
Κουι Νου	κ(εράτιον) α	(τάλαντα) ϡ
Τεϣνεενε δ(ιὰ) Μηνᾶ Ἐνῶχ	κ(εράτια) β	(τάλαντα) Αϡ
Λουλοῦτος Ἰωάνν(ου)	κ(εράτια) β	(τάλαντα) Αϡ
γυναὶ Πενοβ	κ(εράτια) γ	(τάλαντα) Βω
Σαραπίον Ἰακυβίου	κ(εράτια) β	(τάλαντα) Αϡ
υἱὸς φομντ	κ(εράτια) ϛ	(τάλαντα) Εχ
Ἀτρῆτος ῥάπτου	κ(εράτια) αL	(τάλαντα) Α[υ]
ϩαμποι	κ(εράτια) γ	(τάλαντα) Βω
Φοιβάμ(μων) Πινουτ(ίωνος)	κ(εράτια) γd	(τάλαντα) Γ [[ἀγρ( )]]
Βίκτωρ καθαρ(ουργός)	κ(εράτια) δL	(τάλαντα) Δρ
Κυριακὸς Πατσοουϩε	κ(εράτιον) α	(τάλαντα) ϡ
Πασταμου	κ(ερατίου) Ld	(τάλαντα) ψ
Ἀτρῆτος Ὑπερεχ(ίου)	κ(εράτια) β	(τάλαντα) Αϡ
Ἰωάννης Ζηνοδ(ώρου)	κ(εράτιον) α	(τάλαντα) ϡ
κλ(ηρονόμοι) Ἠλίας	νο(μισμάτια) γ	(ταλάντων) (μυριάδες) ε Α
λόγ(ος) Τατι<α>ν(οῦ) Ἑρμ( ) τημ\`αμ´ κ(εράτια) λδLd		
Ἰερημίας Πανε	κ(εράτια) δ	(τάλαντα) Γψ
Ἀπολ(λῶς) ϭες	κ(εράτιον) α	(τάλαντα) ϡ
Ἐνῶχ Λουσία	κ(εράτιον) α	(τάλαντα) ϡ
Φῖβις ΠϪαϪ	κ(εράτια) γLd	(τάλαντα) Γ̣φ
κλ(ηρονόμοι) Καϩ	κ(εράτιον) α	(τάλαντα) ϡ (ταλ.) (μυρ.) κη Θρ
Μονίου Πουηηβ	κ(εράτιον) α	(τάλαντα) ϡ
Μαρία Παλικοῦ	κ(εράτιον) α	(τάλαντα) ϡ
Κουι Τικ	[ν]ο̣(μ.) α̣ κ̣(ερ.) γ̣L	(ταλάντων) (μυριάδες) [β σ]

3 σοϊου pap. 4 ϊωσηφ/ pap. 7 ϊωαννS pap.; read ἐκκλ(ησίας) 13 κουϊ pap. 15 ϊωαννS pap.
16 γυνή 17 ϊακυβιου pap. 18 υϊος pap. 20 ϩαμποϊ pap. 26 Ζηνοδ(ώρου), η ex υ 36 κουϊ pap.

Folio 9 verso (= Page 19)

	† Tybi 5 likewise. Page 19.			
	Tatianos son of Parbas	2 car.	1,900 tal.	
	Soios son of Phibis	2 car.	1,900 tal.	
4	Iosephis son of Paulos	6 car.	5,600 tal.	
	Lahe, mason	1 car.	900 tal.	
	Senecio	1 sol.	17,000 tal.	
	Ioannes for the Holy Church	6 sol.	102,000 tal.	
8	Phibis son of Phoibammon, grandson of Toose	2 sol.	34,000 tal.	
	[[Heirs of Theophilos, likewise through Apollos son of Lene	4 car.	3,700 tal.]]	
	Plotion	2 car.	1,900 tal.	
	Pnahkas	3 car.	2,800 tal.	~~unr.~~
12	Menas son of Enoch	4 car.	3,800 tal.	
	Koui Nou	1 car.	900 tal.	
	Teshneene through Menas son of Enoch	2 car.	1,900 tal.	
	Loulous son of Ioannes	2 car.	1,900 tal.	
16	Wife of Penob	3 car.	2,800 tal.	
	Sarapion son of Iakybis	2 car.	1,900 tal.	
	Son of the carpenter	6 car.	5,600 tal.	
	Hatres, tailor	1 ½ car.	1,[400] tal.	
20	Hampoi	3 car.	2,800 tal.	
	Phoibammon son of Pinoution	3 ¼ car.	3,000 tal.	~~unr.~~
	Victor, baker	4 ½ car.	4,100 tal.	
	Kyriakos son of Patsoouhe	1 car.	900 tal.	
24	Pastamou	¾ car.	700 tal.	
	Hatres son of Hyperechios	2 car.	1,900 tal.	
	Ioannes son of Zenodoros	1 car.	900 tal.	
	Heirs of Elias	3 sol.	51,000 tal.	
28	Account of Tatianos son of Herm( ) . . .	34 ¾ car.		
	Ieremias son of Pane	4 car.	3,700 tal.	
	Apollos qes	1 car.	900 tal.	
	Enoch son of Lousia	1 car.	900 tal.	
32	Phibis (son of?) Pjaj	3 ¾ car.	3,500 tal.	
	Heirs of Kah	1 car.	900 tal.	289,100 tal.
	Monis son of Poueeb	1 car.	900 tal.	
	Maria daughter of Palikous	1 car.	900 tal.	
36	Koui Tik	1 sol. 3 ½ ker.	[20,200] tal.	

Folio 10 recto (= Page 20)

† Τῦβι ε δ(ιὰ) τῶν πραγμ(ατευτῶν)		κ σελ(ίς)
Βίκτωρ Σαμηει	κ(εράτια) γ	(τάλαντα) Βω
Παῆσ{ησ}ις Νωϩε	κ(εράτιον) α	(τάλαντα) ϡ
Λοοϫε	κ(εράτια) β	(τάλαντα) Αω
Φῖβις Ταροοῦ	νο(μισμάτιον) α	(ταλάντων) (μυριὰς) α Ζ
Τῦβι θ		
Φῖβις Ταροοῦ ὁμοί(ως)	νο(μισμάτιον) α	(ταλάντων) (μυριὰς) α Ζ
Μονίου Κόμες	κ(εράτια) β	(τάλαντα) Αϡ
Σαραπίον Βαχ(η)	κ(εράτια) γ	(τάλαντα) Βω
Ἐνῶχ οἰκ(ονόμος) δ(ιὰ) Σαραπίον πρωτ(οκωμήτου)		
	νο(μισμάτιον) α	(ταλάντων) (μυριὰς) α Ϛφ
λόγ(ος) Βίκ(τορος) γνωστῆρ(ος) (ὑπὲρ) σιπ(πίου) τοῦ οἴκ(ου) Ἠλίας		
Τῦβι// θ ἀπὸ νο(μισματίων) δ κ(ερατίων) εLd		
Φοι(βάμμων) Πινουτ(ίωνος) δ(ιὰ) Πανηϫνου		
	κ(εράτια) εLd	(τάλαντα) Ετ [[ἀγρ( )]]
Λακον	κ(ερατίου) Ld	(τάλαντα) ψ
Ϩα̣λ̣μίου	κ(ερατίου) Ld	(τάλαντα) χ
Κ[ῦ]ρος λαξόου	κ(εράτια) γ	(τάλαντα) Βω
Τ[ρα]σίας Παύλου	κ(εράτια) αd	(τάλαντα) Αρ
Ἰωάννης Πναϩκας	κ(εράτια) δd	(τάλαντα) Γψ
Κουι Τικ	κ(εράτια) αL	(τάλαντα) Αυ [[ἀγρ( )]]
Ἀβρ(αάμις) ϭες	κ(εράτιον) [[.]] α	(τάλαντα) ϡ
Βίκτωρ ϭες	κ(εράτια) β	(τάλαντα) Αϡ
Κελλη	κ(ερατίου) Ld	(τάλαντα) ψ
Εὖς Ἰωάννου	κ(εράτια) βd	(τάλαντα) Β
Παῆσις Νωϩε	κ(εράτιον) α	(τάλαντα) ϡ
Κασίας Πινουτ(ίωνος)	κ(εράτιον) α	(τάλαντα) ϡ
Λοοϫε	κ(εράτια) β	(τάλαντα) Αω
Ἰωσῆφ(ις) Ὥρου	κ(εράτια) ε	(τάλαντα) Δψ
Μίνου Διοσκόρ(ου)	κ(εράτια) γ	(τάλαντα) Βω
Ἀπολ(λῶς) διακόνου	κ(εράτια) β	(τάλαντα) Αϡ
Φοι(βάμμων) ἀμπελουργ(ός)	κ(εράτια) γ	(τάλαντα) Βω
Ἀνοῦφ(ις) Μίνου	κ(εράτια) ϛ	(τάλαντα) Εχ [[ἀγρ( )]]

9 Σαραπίων 10 Σαραπίωνος 12 εLd, ε remade? 18 ϊωαννης pap. 19 κουϊ, Αϋ pap.
23 ϊωαννου pap. 27 ϊωσηφ/ pap. 29 διάκονος

Folio 10 recto (= Page 20)

† Tybi 5 through the pragmateutai. Page 20.

Victor son of Sameei	3 car.	2,800 tal.	
Paesis son of Nohe	1 car.	900 tal.	
Looje	2 car.	1,800 tal.	
Phibis son of Taroous	1 sol.	17,000 tal.	
<u>Tybi 9</u>			
Phibis son of Taroous, likewise	1 sol.	17,000 tal.	
Monis son of Komes	2 car.	1,900 tal.	
Sarapion son of Bache	3 car.	2,800 tal.	
Enoch, oikonomos, through Sarapion protokometes			
	1 sol.	16,500 tal.	
Account of Victor, gnoster, for tow of the house of Elias			
Tybi 9 from 4 sol. 5 ¾ car.			

Phoibammon son of Pinoution through Panejnou			
	5 ¾ car.	5,300 tal.	~~unr.~~
Lakon	¾ car.	700 tal.	
Halmios	¾ car.	600 tal.	
Kyros, stonecutter	3 car.	2,800 tal.	
Trasias son of Paulos	1 ¼ car.	1,100 tal.	
Ioannes son of Pnahkas	4 ¼ car.	3,700 tal.	
Koui Tik	1 ½ car.	1,400 tal.	~~unr.~~
Abraamis Qes	1 car.	900 tal.	
Victor Qes	2 car.	1,900 tal.	
Kelle	¾ car.	700 tal.	
Eus daughter of Ioannes	2 ¼ car.	2,000 tal.	
Paesis son of Nohe	1 car.	900 tal.	
Kasia daughter of Pinoution	1 car.	900 tal.	
Looje	2 car.	1,800 tal.	
Iosephis son of Horos	5 car.	4,700 tal.	
Minos son of Dioskoros	3 car.	2,800 tal.	
Apollos, deacon	2 car.	1,900 tal.	
Phoibammon, wine producer	3 car.	2,800 tal.	
Anouphis son of Minos	6 car.	5,600 tal.	~~unr.~~

Folio 10 verso

† λόγ(ος) τῶν σιπ(πουργῶν) δ(ιὰ) Βίκ(τορος) γνωστῆρ(ος) Τῦβι θ
ὁμο(ίως) κα (σελίς)

Ἀτρῆτος Σαμηει	κ(εράτια) γ	(τάλαντα) Βω
Ἀτρῆτος Ὑπερεχ(ίου)	κ(εράτιον) α	(τάλαντα) ϡ
Βίκτωρ καθαρ(ουργός)	κ(εράτια) βLd	(τάλαντα) Βχ
κληλ Καϩ	κ(εράτια) α[d]	(τάλαντα) Αρ
Πκῦλ(ις) Κολλούθ(ου)	κ(εράτια) αL	(τάλαντα) Αυ
Μακαρίου οἰκοδόμ(ου)	κ(εράτια) βL	(τάλαντα) Βτ
Ἠσαίας πρεσβύτερ(ος)	κ(εράτια) γ	(τάλαντα) Βω
Τ⌧εερ	κ(εράτια) γ	(τάλαντα) Βω
Παρακοτε	κ(εράτια) δ	(τάλαντα) Γψ
Ἰωάννης Ζηνοδώρ(ου)	κ(εράτια) β	(τάλαντα) Αϡ
Ἀνοῦφ(ις) Ἀπολ(λῶτος)	κ(ερατίου) L	(τάλαντα) υ
ὁμοί(ως) δ(ιὰ) Λαϩο	κ(εράτιον) α	(τάλαντα) ϡ
Φοι(βάμμων) Λωτα	κ(εράτια) γ	(τάλαντα) Βω̣

λόγ(ος) ἀπὸ τοῦ δημοσί(ου) Μεχεὶρ δ ὑ(πὲρ) διαφ(όρων)
κτητόρ(ων) δ(ιὰ) Ἰωάνν(ου) πραγμ(ατευτοῦ) νο(μισμάτια) λ εὔστ(αθμα)

Πευροτ Παχυμίου	κ(εράτια) ϛ	(τάλαντα) Εχ
Λακον	κ(εράτιον) α	(τάλαντα) ϡ
Λαϩο	κ(εράτιον) α	(τάλαντα) ϡ [[ἀγρ( )]]
Κουι Τικ	κ(εράτια) δ	(τάλαντα) Γψ̣
[[Μηνᾶς]] Μίνου Ἀνουφ(ίου)	κ(εράτια) γ	(τάλαντα) Βω
ϩαμποει	κ(εράτια) θ	(τάλαντα) Ηφ
Ἰωάνν(ης) Ἰακυβίου	κ(εράτια) δ	(τάλαντα) Γψ ἀ̣γ̣ρ( )
Ἀνοῦφ(ις) Ἀλβίου	κ(εράτια) γ	(τάλαντα) Βω
Πκῦλις Φύβις	κ(εράτια) θ	(τάλαντα) Ηφ
Ἐνῶχ γναφ(εύς)	κ(εράτια) η	(τάλαντα) Ζφ
Φοι(βάμμων) Πινουτί(ωνος)	κ(εράτια) ϛ	(τάλαντα) Εχ
Ἀτρῆτος Γεωρ(γίου)	κ(εράτιον) α	(τάλαντα) ϡ
Ἐνῶχ Κολλ(ούθου)	[κ(εράτια) .]	[(τάλαντα) . .]
Σαραπίον σιτ̣ο̣μ̣έ̣τρ(ης)	[κ(εράτια) .]	[(τάλαντα) . .]

4 ϋπερεχS pap. 6 κληλ = κληρ(ονόμοι) 7 Αϋ pap. 8 μακαριō pap. 9 ησαϊας pap. 12 ϊωαννης pap. 13 (τάλ.) ϋ 21 Γψ, Γ ex corr. 23 ϩαμποεϊ pap., read ϩαμποι 24 ϊωαννS, ϊακυβιου pap. 26 φϋβις pap.; read Φοίβης 32 line perhaps hidden by binding?

Folio 10 verso (= Page 21)

† Account of the tow-workers through Victor, gnoster, Tybi 9.
Likewise Page 21.

Hatres son of Sameei	3 car.	2,800 tal.	
Hatres son of Hyperechios	1 car.	900 tal.	
Victor, baker	2 ¾ car.	2,600 tal.	
Heirs of Kah	1 [¼] car.	1,100 tal.	
Pkylis son of Kollouthos	1 ½ car.	1,400 tal.	
Makarios, mason	2 ½ car.	2,300 tal.	
Esaias, priest	3 car.	2,800 tal.	
Tjeer	3 car.	2,800 tal.	
Parakote	4 car.	3,700 tal.	
Ioannes son of Zenodoros	2 car.	1,900 tal.	
Anouphis son of Apollos	½ car.	400 tal.	
Likewise through Laho	1 car.	900 tal.	
Phoibammon son of Lota	3 car.	2,800 tal.	

Account from the tax on Mecheir 4 on behalf of various landowners through Ioannes, pragmateutes, 30 full-weight solidi.

Peurot son of Pachymis	6 car.	5,600 tal.	
Lakon	1 car.	900 tal.	
Laho	1 car.	900 tal.	~~unr.~~
Koui Tik	4 car.	3,700 tal.	
[[Menas]] Minos son of Anouphis	3 car.	2,800 tal.	
Hampoi	9 car.	8,500 tal.	
Ioannes son of Iakybis	4 car.	3,700 tal.	unr.
Anouphis son of Albios	3 car.	2,800 tal.	
Pkylis son of Phoibe	9 car.	8,500 tal.	
Enoch, fuller	8 car.	7,500 tal.	
Phoibammon son of Pinoution	6 car.	5,600 tal.	
Hatres son of Georgios	1 car.	900 tal.	
Enoch son of Kollouthos	[x car.]	[x tal.]	
Sarapion, grain-measurer	[x car.]	[x tal.]	

Folio 11 recto (= Page 22)

† Μεχεὶρ δ ὁμο(ίως)	κβ σελ(ίς)	
Κελλη	κ(εράτια) δ	(τάλαντα) Γψ
Ἀββα Στεκ̅ς̅	κ(εράτιον) α	(τάλαντα) ϡ
Κουρ Ϫιϭ	κ(εράτια) γ	(τάλαντα) Βω
Φοι(βάμμων) Ματρώνα	κ(εράτια) ιη	(ταλάντων) (μυριὰς) α Ζ
Ἰωάνν(ης) Ἀϭορ	κ(εράτια) β	(τάλαντα) Αω ἀγρ( )
Μηνᾶ Ἐνῶχ	κ(εράτια) ς	(τάλαντα) Εχ
γυν(ὴ) Πενοβ	κ(εράτια) βLd	(τάλαντα) Βφ
Ϩελήνα	κ(εράτια) θ	(τάλαντα) Ηφ
Σολομ(ῶν) Φιβίου	κ(εράτιον) α	(τάλαντα) ϡ
Ἀ̣ν̣ο̣ῦ̣φ(ις) ἀπὸ Τβακη	κ(εράτια) β	(τάλαντα) Αϡ
[Βί]κτορ(ος) Σαμεει	κ(εράτια) ιαd	(ταλάντων) (μυριὰς) α υ
[Μα]κάριος Γερμανός	κ(εράτιον) α	(τάλαντα) ϡ
[Σαρ]απίον Πασωθίου	κ(εράτια) γ	(τάλαντα) Βω
Σαραπίον Ἰακυβίου	κ(εράτια) θ	(τάλαντα) Ηφ [[ἀ̣γ̣ρ̣( )]]
Ἀτρῆτος Παρακοτε	κ(εράτια) δ	(τάλαντα) Γψ
Ἰώνις Ἰωσηφ(ίου)	κ(εράτια) ιβ	(ταλάντων) (μυριὰς) α Ασ
Βίκτ(ωρ) ΚερμιϪου δ(ιὰ) Ἰων(ίου) Ἰωσηφ(ίου)		
	κ(εράτια) γL	(τάλαντα) Γτ
Εὖς Ἰωάννου	κ(εράτια) γL	(τάλαντα) Γσ
Πευροτ Παρβας	κ(εράτια) γ	(τάλαντα) Βω
Ἰωάνν(ης) Λεῦτος	κ(εράτια) δ	(τάλαντα) Γψ
Ἀπολλῶτος Ἰωάννου	κ(εράτια) βLd	(τάλαντα) Β̣[φ?]
Ἀνοῦφ(ις) Πιουλ	κ(εράτια) θ	(τάλαντα) Η[φ]
Ψᾶτος Κόμες	κ(εράτια) γLd	(τάλαντα) Γχ
Λουλοῦτος Ἰωάννου	κ(εράτιον) α	(τάλαντα) ϡ
Πέτρος Ἠλίας	κ(εράτια) θ	(τάλαντα) Ηφ
Ἀβραάμις ϭες	κ(εράτια) β	(τάλαντα) Αϡ
Γεώργιος μάγευρ(ος)	κ(εράτια) θ	(τάλαντα) Ηφ
κληρ(ονόμοι) Πουηηβ	κ(εράτια) β	[(τάλαντα) Αϡ]
Ἰωάνν(ης) οἰκονόμ(ος) ἐκλησί(ας) νο(μισμάτιον) α		(ταλάντων) (μυριὰς) α Ζ
Ἐνῶχ οἰκονόμ(ος)	νο(μισμάτια) β	(ταλάντων) (μυριάδες) γ Δ
Κυριακὸς Ἀνουφ(ίου)	κ(εράτια) ς	(τάλαντα) Εχ
	(ταλάντων) (μυριάδες) κζ Γχ	

2 δ ex β 12 ϊα pap. 13 Γερμανοῦ 14-15 Σαραπίων 22 β ex corr. or remade 28 μάγειρος
30 ἐκκλησί(ας)

Folio 11 recto (= Page 22)

† Mecheir 4 likewise. Page 22.

Kelle	4 car.	3,700 tal.	
Abba Steks	1 car.	900 tal.	
Kour Jiq	3 car.	2,800 tal.	
Phoibammon son of Matrona	18 car.	17,000 tal.	
Ioannes son of Aqor	2 car.	1,800 tal.	unr.
Menas son of Enoch	6 car.	5,600 tal.	
Wife of Penob	2 ¾ car.	2,500 tal.	
Helena	9 car.	8,500 tal.	
Solomon son of Phibis	1 car.	900 tal.	
Anouphis from Tbake	2 car.	1,900 tal.	
Victor son of Sameei	11 ¼ car.	10,400 tal.	
Makarios son of Germanos	1 car.	900 tal.	
Sarapion son of Pasothis	3 car.	2,800 tal.	
Sarapion son of Iakybis	9 car.	8,500 tal.	~~unr.~~
Hatres son of Parakote	4 car.	3,700 tal.	
Ionios son of Iosephis	12 car.	11,200 tal.	
Victor son of Kermijou through Ionios son of Iosephis	3 ½ car.	3,300 tal.	
Eus daughter of Ioannes	3 ½ car.	3,200 tal.	
Peurot son of Parbas	3 car.	2,800 tal.	
Ioannes son of Leus	4 car.	3,700 tal.	
Apollos son of Ioannes	2 ¾ car.	2,[500?] tal.	
Anouphis son of Pioul	9 car.	8,[500] tal.	
Psas son of Komes	3 ¾ car.	3,600 tal.	
Loulous son of Ioannes	1 car.	900 tal.	
Petros son of Elias	9 car.	8,500 tal.	
Abraamis qes	2 car.	1,900 tal.	
Georgios, meat-cook	9 tal.	8,500 tal.	
Heirs of Poueeb	2 car.	[1,900 tal.]	
Ioannes, oikonomos of the church	1 sol.	17,000 tal.	
Enoch, oikonomos	2 sol.	34,000 tal.	
Kyriakos son of Anouphis	6 car.	5,600 tal.	

273,600 tal.

Folio 11 verso (= Page 23)

Μεχεὶρ δ ὁμο(ίως) κγ σελ(ίς)

——

ο(ὕτως)

Ἰωσῆφ(ις) Ὥρου	κ(εράτια) ϛ	(τάλαντα) Εχ
Φῖβις Τοοσε	νο(μισμάτια) β	(ταλάντων) (μυριάδες) γ Δ
Ἀπολλ(ῶς) Λένη	κ(εράτια) θ	(τάλαντα) Ηφ
Ἁτρῆτος Ὑπερεχεί(ου)	κ(εράτια) γ	(τάλαντα) Βω
Πατσαλαμαννα	κ(εράτια) βLd	(τάλαντα) Βω
Ἀπολλ(ῶς) Λασουκ	κ(εράτια) γ	(τάλαντα) Βω
Βίκτορος καθαρουργ(οῦ)	κ(εράτια) δL	(τάλαντα) Δρ
Ἁτρῆτος Σαμεει	κ(εράτια) β	(τάλαντα) Αϡ
Ἰωάνν(ης) Σινουερη	κ(εράτια) α	(τάλαντα) ϡ
Ἰωσῆφ(ις) Ἀροοῦτος	κ(εράτια) ζ	(τάλαντα) Ϛφ
Παπνοῦθ(ις) Κλῦμαξ δ(ιὰ) Ἰωάν(νου) Πελουλ		
	κ(εράτια) ιζ	(ταλάντων) (μυριὰς) α Ϛ
Βίκτορος Κερμιϫου	κ(εράτιον) α	(τάλαντα) ϡ
Μίνου Πις	κ(εράτιον) α	(τάλαντα) ϡ
Ἁτρῆτος ῥάπτου	κ(εράτια) αL	(τάλαντα) Αυ
Ἀπορ δ(ιὰ) Ἀπολλ(ῶτος) Λασουκ κ(εράτια) γ		(τάλαντα) Βω
Λοοϫε	κ(εράτια) β	(τάλαντα) Αϡ
Κῦρος λαξός	κ(εράτια) γ	(τάλαντα) Βω
Ἀνοῦφ(ις) Μίνος Διοσκόρ(ου) κ(εράτια) γ		(τάλαντα) Βω
Τατιανε ϭες δ(ιὰ) Ἀνουφ(ίου)	κ(εράτια) ιβ	(ταλάντων) (μυριὰς) α Ασ
Κυριακ(ὸς) Ἀνουφ(ίου) δ(ιὰ) Ἰερημ(ίου) κ(εράτια) γ		(τάλαντα) Βω
Μονίσκου	κ(εράτια) δ	(τάλαντα) Γψ
Μίνος Ἀνουφ(ίου) Ἐνῶχ	κ(εράτια) αLd	(τάλαντα) Αχ
Χωωρ Ἀνουφ(ίου)	κ(εράτια) γ	(τάλαντα) Βω
Πευροτ Παχυμίου	κ(εράτια) ϛ	(τάλαντα) Εχ
Τιτιανε ῥάπτου	κ(εράτια) αL	(τάλαντα) Αυ
Μακάριος οἰκοδ(όμος)	κ(εράτια) γ	(τάλαντα) Βω
Μονίσκου Ἀϭωρ	κ(εράτια) β	(τάλαντα) Αϡ
Ἀν̣[οῦ]φ̣(ις) [Κω]ν̣σταντί(νου)	κ(εράτια) ϛ	(τάλαντα) Εχ
Φοι(βάμμων) ἀμπελ(ουργός)	κ(εράτια) α̣Ld	(τάλαντα) Αφ
(τάλαντα) (μυριάδες) traces		

7 Βω corrected? 11 Ιωάννης, ι ex corr.? 16 Αϋ pap. 17 λασουκ/ pap. 20 Μίνου 27 Αϋ pap.

Folio 11 verso (= Page 23)

	Mecheir 4 likewise.	Page 23.	
	——		
	As follows:		
	Iosephis son of Horos	6 car.	5,600 tal.
4	Phibis son of Toose	2 sol.	34,000 tal.
	Apollos son of Lene	9 car.	8,500 tal.
	Hatres son of Hyperechios	3 car.	2,800 tal.
	Patsalamanna	2 ¾ car.	2,800 tal.
8	Apollos son of Lasouk	3 car.	2,800 tal.
	Victor, baker	4 ½ car.	4,100 tal.
	Hatres son of Sameei	2 car.	1,900 tal.
	Ioannes son of Sinouere	1 car.	900 tal.
12	Iosephis son of Haroous	7 car.	6,500 tal.
	Papnouthis son of Klymax through Ioannes son of Peloul		
		17 car.	16,000 tal.
	Victor son of Kermijou	1 car.	900 tal.
	Minos son of Pis	1 car.	900 tal.
16	Hatres, tailor	1 ½ car.	1,400 tal.
	Apor through Apollos son of Lasouk	3 car.	2,800 tal.
	Looje	2 car.	1,900 tal.
	Kyros, stonecutter	3 car.	2,800 tal.
20	Anouphis son of Minos, grandson of Dioskoros		
		3 car.	2,800 tal.
	Tatiane qes through Anouphis	12 car.	11,200 tal.
	Kyriakos son of Anouphis through Ieremias		
		3 car.	2,800 tal.
	Moniskos	4 car.	3,700 tal.
24	Minos son of Anouphis, grandson of Enoch		
		1 ¾ car.	1,600 tal.
	Choor son of Anouphis	3 car.	2,800 tal.
	Peurot son of Pachymis	6 car.	5,600 tal.
	Titiane, tailor	1 ½ car.	1,400 tal.
28	Makarios, mason	3 car.	2,800 tal.
	Moniskos son of Aqor	2 car.	1,900 tal.
	Anouphis son of Konstantinos	6 car.	5,600 tal.
	Phoibammon, wine producer	1 ¾ car.	1,500 tal.
32	- - - tal.		

Folio 12 recto (= Page 24) Plate 2

† Μεχεὶρ δ ὁμο(ίως) κδ σελ(ίς)		
ο(ὕτως)		
Λῦθις ἐργάτ(ης)	κ(εράτια) βL	(τάλαντα) Βτ
Ἠσαί(ας) πρε(σβύτερος)	κ(εράτια) ϛd	(τάλαντα) Εω
Πανεχεύτ(ης)	κ(εράτια) δ	(τάλαντα) Γψ
Σινικίου	κ(εράτια) ιβ	(ταλάντων) (μυριὰς) α Ασ
Πέτρ(ος) Ἠλίας ὁμοί(ως)	κ(εράτια) γ	(τάλαντα) Βω
κληρε Καϩ	κ(εράτια) αd	(τάλαντα) Αρ
Μόνις πρωτοκ(ωμήτης)	νο(μισμάτιον) α	(ταλάντων) (μυριὰς) α Ζ
Ἰωάνν(ης) Παύλου	κ(εράτια) ιβ	(ταλάντων) (μυριὰς) α Ασ
Κωνσταντῖ(νος) Παχυμίου	νο(μισμάτιον) α	(ταλάντων) (μυριὰς) α Ζ
Ἱερημίας Πανε δ(ιὰ) Παύλ(ου) χαλκ(έως)	κ(εράτια) β	(τάλαντα) Α̣ϡ
Λουλοῦτος Ἰωάννου ὁμοί(ως)	κ(εράτιον) α	(τάλαντα) ϡ
Χωωρ Ἀνουφ(ίου) ὁμοί(ως)	κ(εράτια) γ	(τάλαντα) Βω
Ἱερημ(ίας) Ἠλίας δ(ιὰ) Ἱερημ(ίου) πρωτ(οκωμήτου)		
	νο(μισμάτιον) α	(ταλάντων) (μυριὰς) α Ζ
Κουι Σνοβ	κ(εράτια) ϛ	(τάλαντα) Εχ
Γεώργ(ιος) Ταυρ(ίνου)	κ(εράτια) ϛ	(τάλαντα) Εχ
Ἀπολλ(ῶς) ϭες	κ(εράτια) β	(τάλαντα) Αϡ
Πλωτίων δ(ιὰ) Ἱερημ(ίου) πρωτ(οκωμήτου)	κ(εράτια) γ	(τάλαντα) Βω
Ἄπα Νοχις	κ(εράτια) ιζLd	(ταλάντων) (μυριὰς) α ϛχ
Ἐνῶχ Κολλοῦθος ὁμοί(ως)	κ(εράτιον) α	(τάλαντα) ϡ
Μίνος Τιμουτη	κ(εράτια) βLd	(τάλαντα) Βφ
Ψᾶτος Κόμις	κ(εράτια) β	(τάλαντα) Αϡ
Ἀπολλ(ῶς) διάκ(ονος)	κ(εράτια) β	(τάλαντα) Αϡ
Λωτα	κ(εράτια) γ	(τάλαντα) Βω
Μεχεὶρ κβ λόγ(ος) Τατιαν(οῦ) Ἑρμ( )		
Φῖβις ΠϪαϪ	κ(εράτια) γ	(τάλαντα) Βω
Ϩαλμίου	κ(εράτια) β	(τάλαντα) Αϡ
Ἱερημίας Πανε	κ(εράτια) β	(τάλαντα) Αϡ
Τατιαν(ὸς) Ἠλίας	κ(εράτια) ιε	(ταλάντων) (μυριὰς) [α Δρ]
Κυριακὸς Πατσοουϩε	κ(εράτια) β	(τάλαντα) Αϡ
Πατσαλαμαννα	κ(εράτια) ϛ	(τάλαντα) Εχ
Ἀβράμ(ις) τέκτων	κ(εράτια) ϛ	(τάλαντα) Εχ
Φῖβις Ταροοῦ	ν̣ο̣(μισμάτιον) α̣	(ταλάντων) (μυριὰς) α Ζ
Ἀπολλ(ῶς) ἐλαιουργ(ός)	κ(εράτια) ϛ	(τάλαντα) Εχ
. . . .	[κ(εράτια) ϛ]	[(τάλαντα) Εχ]
(in margin at line 28) (ταλάντων) (μυριάδες) ιθ ϛ[υ]		

10 παυλο^{υ} pap. 11 παχυμιο^{υ} pap. 15 ιερημS, ϊερημS pap. 16 κουϊ, Αϋ pap. 21 Κολλούθου 29 ϊερημιας pap. 30 ϊε pap. 37 ϊθ pap.

Folio 12 recto (= Page 24)

† Mecheir 4 likewise. Page 24.

As follows:

Lythis, laborer	2 ½ car.	2,300 tal.
Esaias, priest	6 ¼ car.	5,800 tal.
Panecheutes	4 car.	3,700 tal.
Senecio	12 car.	11,200 tal.
Petros son of Elias, likewise	3 car.	2,800 tal.
Heirs of Kah	1 ¼ car.	1,100 tal.
Monis, protokometes	1 sol.	17,000 tal.
Ioannes son of Paulos	12 car.	11,200 tal.
Konstantinos son of Pachymis	1 sol.	17,000 tal.
Ieremias son of Pane through Paulos the smith,	2 car.	1,900 tal
Loulous son of Ioannes, likewise	1 car.	900 tal.
Choor son of Anouphis, likewise	3 car.	2,800 tal.
Ieremias son of Elias through Ieremias, protokometes	1 sol.	17,000 tal.
Koui Snob	6 car.	5,600 tal.
Georgios son of Taurinos	6 car.	5,600 tal.
Apollos qes	2 car.	1,900 tal.
Plotion through Ieremias, protokometes	3 car.	2,800 tal.
Apa Nochis	17 ¾ car.	16,600 tal.
Enoch son of Kollouthos, likewise	1 car.	900 tal.
Minos son of Timoute	2 ¾ car.	2,500 tal.
Psas son of Komes	2 car.	1,900 tal.
Apollos, deacon	2 car.	1,900 tal.
Lota	3 car.	2,800 tal.
Mecheir 22. Account of Tatianos son of Herm( )		
Phibis (son of?) Pjaj	3 car.	2,800 tal.
Halmios	2 car.	1,900 tal.
Ieremias son of Pane	2 car.	1,900 tal.
Tatianos son of Elias	15 car.	[14,100] tal.
Kyriakos son of Patsoouhe	2 car.	1,900 tal.
Patsalamanna	6 car.	5,600 tal.
Abraamis, carpenter	6 car.	5,600 tal.
Phibis son of Taroous	1 sol.	17,000 tal.
Apollos, oil-worker	6 car.	5,600 tal.
. . . .	[6 car.]	[5,600 tal.]
(in margin)	196,[400] tal.	

Folio 12 verso (= Page 25)

(1 H.) † Μεχεὶρ δ ὁμο(ίως) κε σελ(ίς)

ΚαϪωϪ	κ(εράτια) β	(τάλαντα) Αϡ	
Μεχεὶρ κβ ἀπόδοσ(ις) νο(μισματίων) ιη εὐσ(τάθμων) ζυγ(ῷ)			
Πέτρ(ος) Ἠλίας	κ(εράτια) ϛ	(τάλαντα) Εχ	
υἱὸς Παρκατης	κ(εράτια) δ	(τάλαντα) Γψ	
Ἀπολλῶς Ἰωάν(νου)	κ(εράτια) ϛd	(τάλαντα) Εω	
Βάνος χαλκ(εύς)	κ(εράτια) β	(τάλαντα) Αϡ	
Ἀβρ(αάμις) Πεσοοῦ	κ(εράτια) δL	(τάλαντα) Δρ	
Θεόφιλ(ος)	κ(εράτια) θ	(τάλαντα) Ηφ	
Κουι Τικ	κ(εράτια) β	(τάλαντα) Αϡ	
υἱὸς φομ̅ν̅τ	κ(εράτια) β	(τάλαντα) Αϡ	
Πέτρ(ος) Ἠλίας ὁμο(ίως)	κ(εράτια) γ	(τάλαντα) Βω	
Ἀπολλῶτος Ἀτρῆτος	κ(εράτιον) α	(τάλαντα) ϡ	
Ἰωάννης Πναϩκας	κ(εράτια) β	(τάλαντα) Αϡ	[[ἀγρ( )]]
Ἐνῶχ Λουσία	κ(εράτιον) α	(τάλαντα) ϡ	
Ἀπολλῶτος ἐλαιουρ(γοῦ)	κ(εράτια) βLd	(τάλαντα) Βφ	
Ἄπε Ἀπαλο	κ(εράτια) β	(τάλαντα) Αϡ	
Βάνος χαλκ(εύς)	κ(εράτια) β	(τάλαντα) Αω	
Βίκτωρ Σαμηει	κ(εράτια) γ	(τάλαντα) Βω	
κληλ Καϩ	κ(εράτιον) α	(τάλαντα) ϡ	
Τατιαν(ὸς) Ἠλίας ὁμο(ίως)	κ(εράτια) γ	(τάλαντα) Βω	
Πλωτίων	κ(εράτιον) α	(τάλαντα) ϡ	
Ἰερημίας Πανε	κ(εράτια) αLd	(τάλαντα) Αχ	
Φῖβις Ταροοῦ	κ(εράτια) ϛ	(τάλαντα) Εχ	
κληρ(ονόμοι) διακόνου	κ(εράτια) ϛ	(τάλαντα) Εχ	
δ(ιὰ) τοῦ κυρίου Ἰωάν(νου) πραγμ(ατευτοῦ)			
Παπνοῦθ(ις) Κλύμ(αξ)	κ(εράτιον) α	(τάλαντα) ϡ	[[ἀγρ( )]]
Ἰωσῆφ(ις) Παύλου	κ(εράτια) ϛ	(τάλαντα) Εχ	[[ἀγρ( )]]
Σοίου καὶ Πιτεχου δ(ιὰ) Ἰωσηφ(ίου) Παύλ(ου)	κ(εράτια) δL	(τάλαντα) Δρ	[[ἀγ̣ρ̣( )]]
Κασίας Πινουτ(ίωνος)	κ(εράτιον) α	(τάλαντα) ϡ	
Κωρ ϪιϪ	κ(εράτιον) α	(τάλαντα) ϡ	
Φοι(βάμμων) ἀμπελουρ(γός)	κ(ερατίου) d	(τάλαντα) σ	ἀγρ( )
	(ταλάντων) (μυριάδες) η ω		

3 ϊη pap. 4 ϛ ex γ 5 υϊος pap. 6 ϊωανS pap. 10 κουϊ pap. 11 υϊος pap.? 18 Αω: α ex β, ω ex corr.? 20 κληλ = κληρ(ονόμοι) 23 ϊερημιας pap. 28 ϊωσηφ/ pap.

Folio 12 verso (= Page 25)

(1 H.) † Mecheir 4 likewise. Page 25.

Kajoj	2 car.	1,900 tal.	
Mecheir 22, payment of 18 full-weight solidi by (weight) standard.			
Petros son of Elias	6 car.	5,600 tal.	
Son of Parkates	4 car.	3,700 tal.	
Apollos son of Ioannes	6 ¼ car.	5,800 tal.	
Banos, smith	2 car.	1,900 tal.	
Abraamis son of Pesoous	4 ½ car.	4,100 tal.	
Theophilos	9 car.	8,500 tal.	
Koui Tik	2 car.	1,900 tal.	
Son of the smith	2 car.	1,900 tal.	
Petros son of Elias, likewise	3 car.	2,800 tal.	
Apollos son of Hatres	1 car.	900 tal.	
Ioannes son of Pnahkas	2 car.	1,900 tal.	~~unr.~~
Enoch son of Lousia	1 car.	900 tal.	
Apollos, oil-worker	2 ¾ car.	2,500 tal.	
Ape Apalo	2 car.	1,900 tal.	
Banos, smith	2 car.	1,800 tal.	
Victor son of Sameei	3 car.	2,800 tal.	
Heirs of Kah	1 car.	900 tal.	
Tatianos son of Elias, likewise	3 car.	2,800 tal.	
Plotion	1 car.	900 tal.	
Ieremias son of Pane	1 ¾ car.	1,600 tal.	
Phibis son of Taroous	6 car.	5,600 tal.	
Heirs of the deacon	6 car.	5,600 tal.	
through lord Ioannes, pragmateutes			
Papnouthis son of Klymax	1 car.	900 tal.	~~unr.~~
Iosephis son of Paulos	6 car.	5,600 tal.	~~unr.~~
Soios and Pitechou through Iosephis son of Paulos	4 ½ car.	4,100 tal.	~~unr.~~
Kasia daughter of Pinoution	1 car.	900 tal.	
Kor Jij	1 car.	900 tal.	
Phoibammon, wine producer	¼ car.	200 tal.	unr.
		80,800 tal.	

Folio 13 recto (= Page 26)

† Μεχεὶρ κβ ὁμο(ίως)	κς σελ(ίς)	
Μίνος Πις	κ(εράτιον) α	(τάλαντα) ϡ
Ἀπολλῶτος ἐλαιουρ(γοῦ)	κ(εράτια) βLd	(τάλαντα) Βφ
τῆς ἁγίας ἐκλησίας	νο(ισμάτια) ζ	(ταλάντων) (μυριάδες) ια Θ
Ἐνῶχ οἰκονόμ(ος)	νο(μισμάτια) α γ´	(ταλάντων) (μυριάδες) β Βχ
Λῦθις ἐργάτης	κ(εράτια) β	(τάλαντα) Αϡ
Ἰωσῆφ(ις) Ἀροοῦτ(ος)	κ(εράτια) β	(τάλαντα) Αϡ
Μακαρίου οἰκοδ(όμου)	κ(ερατίου) L	(τάλαντα) υ
Ἀτρῆτος Ὑπερεχ(ίου)	κ(εράτιον) α	(τάλαντα) ϡ
Γεώργ(ιος) Ταυρ(ίνου)	κ(εράτια) ε	(τάλαντα) Δψ
Εὖς Ἰωάννου	κ(εράτιον) α	(τάλαντα) ϡ
ΠανηϪνου	κ(εράτια) β	(τάλαντα) Αϡ
Βίκτωρ ματοι	κ(εράτια) ς	(τάλαντα) Εχ
Βίκτωρ Σαμηει	κ(ερατίου) Ld	(τάλαντα) ψ
κληρ(ονόμοι) Ἠλίας Πεσοοῦ	νο(μισμάτιον) α	(ταλάντων) (μυριὰς) α Ζ
Ἰωάννης Ζυνοδ(ώρου)	κ(εράτιον) α	(τάλαντα) ϡ
Τατιαν(ὸς) Ἠλίας δ(ιὰ) Πεσοοῦ	κ(εράτια) γ	(τάλαντα) Βω
Ἰωσῆφ(ις) Ὥρου	κ(εράτια) δ	(τάλαντα) Γψ
Μονίου Κόμες	κ(εράτια) γ	(τάλαντα) Βω
Σαραπίον Βαχη	κ(εράτια) γ	(τάλαντα) Βω
γυν(ὴ) Πενοβ	κ(ερατίου) d	(τάλαντα) σ
Ἐνῶχ Κυριακός	κ(εράτια) β	(τάλαντα) Αϡ
Βίκτωρ ϭες	κ(εράτια) β	(τάλαντα) Αϡ
Λαϩη	κ(εράτια) αL	(τάλαντα) Αυ
Μίνου Διοσκόρ(ου)	κ(εράτια) αd	(τάλαντα) Αρ
Ἰωσῆφ(ις) Ὥρου	κ(εράτια) γL	(τάλαντα) Γσ
Γεώρ(γιος) Ταυρ(ίνου)	κ(εράτια) γ	(τάλαντα) Βω
Ἰωνίου Ἰωσηφ(ίου)	κ(εράτια) γ	(τάλαντα) Βω
Ἰωάνν(ης) Λεῦτος	κ(εράτιον) α	(τάλαντα) ϡ
Φοιβάμ(μων) Ματρώνα	κ(εράτια) γ	(τάλαντα) Βω
Πευροτ Παχυμίου	κ(εράτια) β	(τάλαντα) Αϡ
Γεώρ(γιος) μάγυρ(ος)	κ(εράτια) γ	(τάλαντα) Βω
Μηνᾶ Ἐνῶχ	κ(εράτια) β	(τάλαντα) Αϡ
	(ταλάντων) (μυριάδες) κα Θυ	

4 ἐκκλησίας, ϊα pap. 7,18,26,28 ϊωσηφ/ pap. 8 ϋ pap. 11 ϊωαννου pap. 13 ματοϊ pap. 16 ϊωαννης pap., Ζηνοδ(ώρου) 20 Σαραπίων 21 γυνή 22 Κυριακοῦ 28 ϊωνιου pap. 29 ϊωαννS pap. 32 μάγειρος 34 Θϋ pap.

Folio 13 recto (= Page 26)

† Mecheir 22 likewise.	Page 26.	
Minos son of Pis	1 car.	900 tal.
Apollos, oil-worker	2 ¾ car.	2,500 tal.
The Holy Church	7 sol.	119,000 tal.
Enoch, oikonomos	1 1/3 sol.	22,600 tal.
Lythis, laborer	2 car.	1,900 tal.
Iosephis son of Haroous	2 car.	1,900 tal.
Makarios, mason	½ car.	400 tal.
Hatres son of Hyperechios	1 car.	900 tal.
Georgios son of Taurinos	5 car.	4,700 tal.
Eus daughter of Ioannes	1 car.	900 tal.
Panejnou	2 car.	1,900 tal.
Victor, soldier	6 car.	5,600 tal.
Victor son of Sameei	¾ car.	700 tal.
Heirs of Elias son of Pesoous	1 sol.	17,000 tal.
Ioannes son of Zenodoros	1 car.	900 tal.
Tatianos son of Elias through Pesoous	3 car.	2,800 tal.
Iosephis son of Horos	4 car.	3,700 tal.
Monis son of Komes	3 car.	2,800 tal.
Sarapion son of Bache	3 car.	2,800 tal.
Wife of Penob	¼ car.	200 tal.
Enoch son of Kyriakos	2 car.	1,900 tal.
Victor qes	2 car.	1,900 tal.
Lahe	1 ½ car.	1,400 tal.
Minos son of Dioskoros	1 ¼ car.	1,100 tal.
Iosephis son of Horos	3 ½ car.	3,200 tal.
Georgios son of Taurinos	3 car.	2,800 tal.
Ionios son of Iosephis	3 car.	2,800 tal.
Ioannes son of Leus	1 car.	900 tal.
Phoibammon son of Matrona	3 car.	2,800 tal.
Peurot son of Pachymis	2 car.	1,900 tal.
Georgios, meat-cook	3 car.	2,800 tal.
Menas son of Enoch	2 car.	1,900 tal.

219,400 tal.

Folio 13 verso (= Page 27)

† Μεχεὶρ κβ κζ σελ(ίς)

Μηνᾶ μάγυρ(ος)	κ(εράτια) γ	(τάλαντα) Βω
Ἰερημίας Πανε	κ(εράτια) γd	(τάλαντα) Γ
ϩελένα	κ(εράτια) θ	(τάλαντα) Ηφ
Κῦρος λαξόου	κ(εράτιον) α	(τάλαντα) ϡ
Ὧρος Βίκτωρ	κ(εράτιον) α	(τάλαντα) ϡ
Πατσαλαμανα	κ(εράτια) γd	(τάλαντα) Βω
ϩαμποι	κ(εράτια) γ	(τάλαντα) Βω
Πανηϫνου	κ(εράτια) δ	(τάλαντα) Γψ
Κύρα Ταυρ(ίνου)	κ(εράτιον) α	(τάλαντα) ϡ
Ἀτρῆτος Παρακοτε	κ(εράτιον) α	(τάλαντα) ϡ
Ἰωσῆφ(ις) Ὥρου	κ(εράτια) β	(τάλαντα) Αϡ
Μίνου Τιμουτη	κ(εράτια) β	(τάλαντα) Αω
Χωωρ Ἀνουφ(ίου)	κ(εράτια) εL	(τάλαντα) Ερ
Π̣ιτερ Ἀπολ(λῶτος)	κ(εράτια) β	(τάλαντα) Αϡ
Λωτα	κ(εράτια) β	(τάλαντα) Αϡ
Σαραπίον σιτομέτρ(ης)	κ(εράτια) β	(τάλαντα) Αϡ
Ἰερημίας Ἠλίας δ(ιὰ) Πεσοοῦ	κ(εράτια) ια	(ταλάντων) (μυριὰς) α σ
Ἰωάννης Παύλου δ(ιὰ) Πεσοοῦ	κ(εράτια) ϛ	(τάλαντα) Εχ
Φοι(βάμμων) Πινουτ(ίωνος) δ(ιὰ) Πεσοοῦ	κ(εράτιον) α	(τάλαντα) ϡ
Κασίας Πινουτ(ίωνος)	κ(εράτιον) α	(τάλαντα) ϡ
Παπνοῦθ(ις) Μίν(ου) Διοσκ(όρου)	κ(εράτια) β	(τάλαντα) Αϡ
Ἀνοῦφ(ις) Κωσταντ(ίνου)	κ(εράτια) β	(τάλαντα) Αϡ
Βίκτωρ Κερμιϫου	κ(εράτια) β	(τάλαντα) Αϡ
τῶν σκυδ(έων)	κ(εράτια) β	(τάλαντα) Αϡ
Μονίου Ἑρμαπόλ(λωνος)	κ(εράτιον) α	(τάλαντα) ϡ
γυν(ὴ) Ἀνουφ(ίου) Ἰακυβίου	κ(εράτια) δ	(τάλαντα) Γψ
Ἐνῶχ Κολλούθ(ου)	κ(εράτια) β	(τάλαντα) Αϡ
κληρ(ονόμοι) Κωσταντ(ίνου)	κ(εράτια) γ	(τάλαντα) Βω
Βίκτωρ καθαρ(ουργός)	κ(εράτια) β	(τάλαντα) Αϡ
Ἰακυβίου Κολ(λού)θ(ου)	κ(εράτια) γ	(τάλαντα) Βω
Ἀνοῦφ(ις) Μίνου	κ(εράτια) αL	(τάλαντα) Αυ

(ταλάντων) (μυριάδες) η Βψ

3 ϊερημιας pap. 4 Ηφ, Η ex corr. 6 Βίκτορος 7 Βω, Β ex ϡ 8 ϩαμποϊ pap. 9 ψ thickly overwritten (Col. 3) 12 ϊωσηφ/ pap. 17 Σαραπίων 18 ϊα pap. 19 ϊωαννης pap. 22 β ex α 25 σκυτ(έων) 27,31 ϊακυβιο^υ pap. 32 Αϋ

Folio 13 verso (= Page 27)

† Mecheir 22. Page 27.

Menas, meat-cook	3 car.	2,800 tal.
Ieremias son of Pane	3 ¼ car.	3,000 tal.
Helena	9 car.	8,500 tal.
Kyros, stonecutter	1 car.	900 tal.
Horos son of Victor	1 car.	900 tal.
Patsalamana	3 ¼ car.	2,800 tal.
Hampoi	3 car.	2,800 tal.
Panejnou	4 car.	3,700 tal.
Kyra daughter of Taurinos	1 car.	900 tal.
Hatres son of Parakote	1 car.	900 tal.
Iosephis son of Horos	2 car.	1,900 tal.
Minos son of Timoute	2 car.	1,800 tal.
Choor son of Anouphis	5 ½ car.	5,100 tal.
Piter son of Apollos	2 car.	1,900 tal.
Lota	2 car.	1,900 tal.
Sarapion, grain-measurer	2 car.	1,900 tal.
Ieremias son of Elias through Pesoous	11 car.	10,200 tal.
Ioannes son of Paulos through Pesoous	6 car.	5,600 tal.
Phoibammon son of Pinoution through Pesoous	1 car.	900 tal.
Kasia daughter of Pinoution	1 car.	900 tal.
Papnouthis son of Minos, grandson of Dioskoros	2 car.	1,900 tal.
Anouphis son of Konstantinos	2 car.	1,900 tal.
Victor son of Kermijou	2 car.	1,900 tal.
The cobblers	2 car.	1,900 tal.
Monis son of Hermapollon	1 car.	900 tal.
Wife of Anouphis son of Iakybis	4 car.	3,700 tal.
Enoch son of Kollouthos	2 car.	1,900 tal.
Heirs of Konstantinos	3 car.	2,800 tal.
Victor, baker	2 car.	1,900 tal.
Iakybis son of Kollouthos	3 car.	2,800 tal.
Anouphis son of Minos	1 ½ car.	1,400 tal.

82,700 tal.

Folio 14 recto (= Page 28)

† Μεχεὶρ κβ κη σελ(ίς)

Κύρου τέκτων(ος)	κ(εράτιον) α	(τάλαντα) ϡ
Πεσοοῦτος	κ(εράτια) ς	(τάλαντα) Εχ
Φῖβις Τοοσε	κ(εράτια) ς	(τάλαντα) Εχ
Ἀτρῆτος Ὑπερεχ(ίου)	κ(εράτιον) α	(τάλαντα) ϡ
Ἰωάννης Ἰακυβίου	κ(εράτια) γ	(τάλαντα) Βω
Μίνου Ἀνουφ(ίου)	κ(εράτιον) α	(τάλαντα) ϡ
Φῖβις ἀπὸ Ἁρμότν(εως)	κ(εράτια) γ	(τάλαντα) Βω
Ψᾶτος Κόμες	κ(εράτιον) α	(τάλαντα) ϡ

Φαμενὼθ α´ ἀπόδοσ(ις) νο(μισματίων) λ εὐσ(τάθμων)

Πατσαλαμανα	κ(εράτια) γ	(τάλαντα) Βω
Πιτεχου	κ(εράτιον) α	(τάλαντα) ϡ
κλ(ηρονόμοι) Πουηβ	κ(εράτια) β	(τάλαντα) Αϡ
κλ(ηρονόμοι) Καϩ	κ(εράτια) γ	(τάλαντα) Βω
γυναὶ Πειλιϣ	κ(εράτια) βL	(τάλαντα) Βφ
Μακαρίου Γερμαν(οῦ)	κ(εράτια) β	(τάλαντα) Αϡ
[γυ]ναὶ Πενοβ	κ(εράτια) δ	(τάλαντα) Γψ
Ἰωσῆφ(ις) Πινουτ(ίωνος)	κ(εράτια) γ	(τάλαντα) Βω
Ἐνῶχ γναφεύ(ς)	κ(εράτια) ς	(τάλαντα) Εχ
Ἰερημίας Πανε	κ(εράτια) δ	(τάλαντα) Γψ
Κελλη	κ(εράτια) γ	(τάλαντα) Βω
Ἀπολλῶτος Λασουκ	κ(εράτια) ε	(τάλαντα) Δψ
[Λ]αϩο	κ(εράτια) β	(τάλαντα) Αϡ
[Ἰ]ωάννης Λεῦτος	κ(εράτια) γ	(τάλαντα) Βω
Κουρ ΧιΧ	κ(εράτια) βL	(τάλαντα) Βτ̣
Ἀτρῆτο̣ς Σαμηει	κ(εράτια) γ	(τάλαντα) Βω
[Ὀ]νόφρ(ις) Πανουβε	κ(εράτια) β	(τάλαντα) Αϡ
ϩαμποι	κ(εράτια) ηLd	(τάλαντα) Ησ
Ἄβα Στεξ	κ(εράτιον) α	(τάλαντα) ϡ
Π̣κῦλις Παϣοτη	κ(εράτιον) α	(τάλαντα) ϡ
Ὥρου Σουριχη	κ(εράτια) γ	(τάλαντα) Βω
[Ψ]ᾶτος Ἰωάνν(ου)	κ(εράτια) β	(τάλαντα) Αϡ
[Μ]ηνᾶ Ἐνῶχ	κ(εράτια) ς	(τάλαντα) Εχ
[Σ]ο̣ίου Φιβίου	κ(εράτια) γ	(τάλαντα) Βω

2 τεκτωνS pap., read τέκτον(ος) 8 αρμοτνS pap. 15, 17 γυνή 28 ϩαμποϊ pap.

Folio 14 recto (= Page 28)

† Mecheir 22. Page 28.

	Kyros, carpenter	1 car.	900 tal.
	Pesoous	6 car.	5,600 tal.
4	Phibis son of Toose	6 car.	5,600 tal.
	Hatres son of Hyperechios	1 car.	900 tal.
	Ioannes son of Iakybis	3 car.	2,800 tal.
	Minos son of Anouphis	1 car.	900 tal.
8	Phibis from Harmotnis	3 car.	2,800 tal.
	Psas son of Komes	1 car.	900 tal.
	Phamenoth 1, payment of 30 full-weight solidi.		
	Patsalamana	3 sol.	2,800 tal.
12	Pitechou	1 car.	900 tal.
	Heirs of Poueb	2 car.	1,900 tal.
	Heirs of Kah	3 car.	2,800 tal.
	Wife of Peilish	2 ½ car.	2,500 tal.
16	Makarios son of Germanos	2 car.	1,900 tal.
	Wife of Penob	4 car.	3,700 tal.
	Iosephis son of Pinoution	3 car.	2,800 tal.
	Enoch, fuller	6 car.	5,600 tal.
20	Ieremias son of Pane	4 car.	3,700 tal.
	Kelle	3 car.	2,800 tal.
	Apollos son of Lasouk	5 car.	4,700 tal.
	Laho	2 car.	1,900 tal.
24	Ioannes son of Leus	3 car.	2,800 tal.
	Kour Jij	2 ½ car.	2,300 tal.
	Hatres son of Sameei	3 car.	2,800 tal.
	Onophris son of Panoube	2 car.	1,900 tal.
28	Hampoi	8 ¾ car.	8,200 tal.
	Aba Stex	1 car.	900 tal.
	Pkylis son of Pashote	1 car.	900 tal.
	Horos son of Souriche	3 car.	2,800 tal.
32	Psas son of Ioannes	2 car.	1,900 tal.
	Menas son of Enoch	6 car.	5,600 tal.
	Soios son of Phibis	3 car.	2,800 tal.

Folio 14 verso (= Page 29)

† Φαμενὼθ α	κθ σελ(ίς)	
Λακον	κ(εράτια) β	(τάλαντα) Αϡ
Ἀβρ(αάμις) τέκτων	κ(εράτια) ϛ	(τάλαντα) Εχ
Φοιβάμ(μων) Λωτα	κ(εράτια) γ	(τάλαντα) Βω
Ἀπορ δ(ιὰ) Βίκ(τορος) ἀπὸ Ἑρ(μουπόλεως)	κ(εράτια) ϛ	(τάλαντα) Εχ
Βίκτωρ ΓερμιϪου	κ(εράτια) ϛ	(τάλαντα) Εχ
Ἀπολλῶτος Ὠφελίου	κ(εράτια) β	(τάλαντα) Αϡ
Παπνοῦθ(ις) Μίνου Ἀνουφ(ίου)	κ(εράτια) βLd	(τάλαντα) Βφ
Ἀνοῦφ(ις) Μίνου Διοσκ(όρου)	κ(εράτια) δ	(τάλαντα) Γψ
Σ[ο]λομῶν Φιβίου	κ(εράτιον) α	(τάλαντα) ϡ
Ἀτρῆτος Πεβο	κ(εράτιον) α	(τάλαντα) ϡ
Φοιβάμμ(ων) Ματρώνα	κ(εράτια) ιβ	(ταλάντων) (μυριὰς) α Ασ
Λῦθις ἐργάτης	κ(εράτια) δ	(τάλαντα) Γψ
Πευροτ Παχυμίου	κ(εράτια) ζLd	(τάλαντα) Ζρ
Πκῦλις Κολ(λού)θου	κ(εράτια) β	(τάλαντα) Αϡ
Τατιανοῦ ϭες	κ(εράτια) θ	(τάλαντα) Ηφ
Βίκτωρ ϭες	κ(εράτια) β	(τάλαντα) Αϡ
Παῆσις Νωϩε	κ(εράτιον) α	(τάλαντα) ϡ
Μηνᾶ Θαβουνος	κ(εράτια) αL	(τάλαντα) Αυ
Πκῦλις Φύβης	κ(εράτια) γ	(τάλαντα) Βω
Ἀπολλῶς ϭες	κ(εράτια) β	(τάλαντα) Αϡ
Σαραπίον Ἰακυβίου	κ(εράτια) δ	(τάλαντα) Γψ
ϩελέννα	κ(εράτια) ιη	(ταλάντων) (μυριὰς) α Ζ
Ψᾶτος Κόμες	κ(εράτια) ϛ	(τάλαντα) Εχ
Ἰωνίου Ἰωσηφ(ίου)	κ(εράτια) ιη	(ταλάντων) (μυριὰς) α Ζ
Ἰωάννης Παύλ(ου)	νο(μισμάτια) β	(ταλάντων) (μυριάδες) γ Δ
Βίκτωρ καθαρ(ουργός)	κ(εράτια) δd	(τάλαντα) Γϡ
Κωσταντ(ίνου) ἰατροῦ	κ(εράτια) ιη	(ταλάντων) (μυριὰς) α Ζ
Ἰωάννης Ζυνοδ(ώρου)	κ(εράτια) β	(τάλαντα) Αϡ
Κῦρος λαξόου	κ(εράτια) γ	(τάλαντα) Βω
Ἀνοῦφ(ις) ἀπὸ Τβακε	κ(εράτια) β	(τάλαντα) Αϡ
Ἀνοῦφ(ιος) ϭες	κ(εράτια) θ	(τάλαντα) Ηφ
	(ταλάντων) (μυριάδες) ιη Ϛ	

7 Ὠφελίου, -λ̅ι̅ο̅ pap. 12 ϊβ pap. 16 θ ex γ 19 Αϋ pap. 20 Φοίβης 22 Σαραπίων; ϊακυβιου pap.
23 ϩελένα, ϊη pap. 25 ϊωνιου, ϊωσηφ/, ϊη pap. 26 ϊωαννης pap. 27 κ(ερ.) ex ν? 28 ϊη pap. 29 ϊωαννης pap.; read Ζηνοδ(ώρου)

Folio 14 verso (= Page 29)

† Phamenoth 1.	Page 29.	
Lakon	2 car.	1,900 tal.
Abraamis, carpenter	6 car.	5,600 tal.
Phoibammon son of Lota	3 car.	2,800 tal.
Apor through Victor from Hermopolis	6 car.	5,600 tal.
Victor son of Germijou	6 car.	5,600 tal.
Apollos son of Ophelios	2 car.	1,900 tal.
Papnouthis son of Minos, grandson of Anouphis	2 ¾ ca.	2,500 tal.
Anouphis son of Minos, grandson of Dioskoros	4 car.	3,700 tal.
Solomon son of Phibis	1 car.	900 tal.
Hatres son of Pebo	1 car.	900 tal.
Phoibammon son of Matrona	12 car.	11,200 tal.
Lythis, laborer	4 car.	3,700 tal.
Peurot son of Pachymis	7 ¾ car.	7,100 tal.
Pkylis son of Kollouthos	2 car.	1,900 tal.
Tatianos qes	9 car.	8,500 tal.
Victor qes	2 car.	1,900 tal.
Paesis son of Nohe	1 car.	900 tal.
Menas son of Thabounos	1 ½ car.	1,400 tal.
Pkylis son of Phoibe	3 car.	2,800 tal.
Apollos qes	2 car.	1,900 tal.
Sarapion son of Iakybis	4 car.	3,700 tal.
Helena	18 car.	17,000 tal.
Psas son of Komes	6 car.	5,600 tal.
Ionios son of Iosephis	18 car.	17,000 tal.
Ioannes son of Paulos	2 sol.	34,000 tal.
Victor, baker	4 ¼ car.	3,900 tal.
Konstantinos, doctor	18 car.	17,000 tal.
Ioannes son of Zenodoros	2 car.	1,900 tal.
Kyros, stonecutter	3 car.	2,800 tal.
Anouphis from Tbake	2 car.	1,900 tal.
Anouphis qes	9 car.	8,500 tal.
	186,000 tal.	

Folio 15 recto (= Page 30)

† Φαμενὼθ α	λ σελ(ίς)	
Μίνου Διοσκόρ(ου)	κ(εράτια) γL	(τάλαντα) Γσ
Ἰωάννης Ἰακυβίου	κ(εράτια) γ	(τάλαντα) Βω
Σαραπίον σιτομέτρ(ης)	κ(εράτια) θ	(τάλαντα) Ηφ
Γεώρ(γιος) μάγυρ(ος)	κ(εράτια) θ	(τάλαντα) Ηφ
Παρακοτε	κ(εράτια) ς	(τάλαντα) Εχ
Γεώρ(γιος) Ταυρ(ίνου)	κ(εράτια) δL	(τάλαντα) Δρ
Ἀτρῆτος Ὑπερεχ(ίου)	κ(εράτια) γ	(τάλαντα) Βω
Ἄπα Νοκις δ(ιὰ) Βίκ(τορος) ἀπὸ Ἑρμ(ουπόλεως)		
	κ(εράτια) ς	(τάλαντα) Εχ
Ἀνοῦφ(ις) Κωσταντ(ίνου)	κ(εράτια) θ	(τάλαντα) Ηφ
Χωωρ ῥάπτου	κ(εράτια) β	(τάλαντα) Α𐅷
Ἰωσῆφ(ις) Ὥρου	κ(εράτια) αL	(τάλαντα) Αυ
Ἰακυβίου χαλκ(έως)	κ(εράτια) β	(τάλαντα) Α𐅷
Κύρα Ταυρίνου	κ(εράτιον) α	(τάλαντα) 𐅷
τῆς ἁγίας ἐκλ(ησίας)	νο(μισμάτια) ς	(ταλάντων) (μυριάδες) ι´´ Β
τοῦ μαρτυρ(ίου)	νο(μισμάτια) β	(ταλάντων) (μυριάδες) γ Δ
Φῖβις Τοοσε	νο(μισμάτια) β	(ταλάντων) (μυριάδες) γ Δ
Φῖβις Ταροοῦ	νο(μισμάτιον) α	(ταλάντων) (μυριὰς) α Ζ
Ἰερημίας Ἠλίας	νο(μισμάτια) β	(ταλάντων) (μυριάδες) γ Δ
Ἀνοῦφ(ις) Πιουλ	κ(εράτια) γ	(τάλαντα) Βω
Λαϩη	κ(εράτια) αLd	(τάλαντα) Αφ
Τιτιανα Παρβας	κ(εράτια) γ	(τάλαντα) Βω
Βίκτωρ Ἰουλουμ(ένου)	κ(εράτια) αL	(τάλαντα) Αυ
Ἐνῶχ Κολ(λού)θ(ου)	κ(εράτια) γ	(τάλαντα) Βω
Ἀτρῆτος ῥάπτου	κ(εράτια) β	(τάλαντα) Α𐅷
Ἀπολλῶτος Ἀτρῆτ(ος)	κ(εράτια) β	(τάλαντα) Α𐅷
Ἀπολλῶτος Ἰωάν(νου)	κ(εράτια) ιη	(ταλάντων) (μυριὰς) α Ζ
κλ(ηρονόμοι) διακ(όνου)	κ(εράτια) ιη	(ταλάντων) (μυριὰς) α Ζ
Ἀπολλ(ῶς) ἐλαιουρ(γός)	κ(εράτια) ς	(τάλαντα) Εχ
κλ(ηρονόμοι) Θεοφίλ(ου)	κ(εράτια) ιη	(ταλάντων) (μυριὰς) α Ζ

(ταλάντων) (μυριάδες) λδ Ηφ

2 Διοσκόρ(ου), σ ex ο or remade 3 ϊωαννης, ϊακυβιο^υ pap. 4 Σαραπίων 5 μάγειρ(ος) 12 ϊωσηφ/, Αϋ pap. 13 ϊακυβιου pap. 15 ἐκκλ(ησίας) 19 ϊερημιας pap. 23 ϊουλουμS, Αϋ pap., υ ex φ 27 ϊωαν (no abbreviation mark), ϊη pap. 28, 30 ϊη pap.

Folio 15 recto (= Page 30)

	† Phamenoth 1.	Page 30.	
	Minos son of Dioskoros	3 ½ car.	3,200 tal.
	Ioannes son of Iakybis	3 car.	2,800 tal.
4	Sarapion, grain-measurer	9 car.	8,500 tal.
	Georgios, meat-cook	9 car.	8,500 tal.
	Parakote	6 car.	5,600 tal.
	Georgios son of Taurinos	4 ½ car.	4,100 tal.
8	Hatres son of Hyperechios	3 car.	2,800 tal.
	Apa Nokis through Victor from Hermopolis	6 car.	5,600 tal.
	Anouphis son of Konstantinos	9 car.	8,500 tal.
	Choor, tailor	2 car.	1,900 tal.
12	Iosephis son of Horos	1 ½ car.	1,400 tal.
	Iakybis, smith	2 car.	1,900 tal.
	Kyra daughter of Taurinos	1 car.	900 tal.
	The Holy Church	6 sol.	102,000 tal.
16	The Martyrion	2 sol.	34,000 tal.
	Phibis son of Toose	2 sol.	34,000 tal.
	Phibis son of Taroous	1 sol.	17,000 tal.
	Ieremias son of Elias	2 sol.	34,000 tal.
20	Anouphis son of Pioul	3 car.	2,800 tal.
	Lahe	1 ¾ car.	1,500 tal.
	Titiana son of Parbas	3 car.	2,800 tal.
	Victor son of Iouloumenos	1 ½ car.	1,400 tal.
24	Enoch son of Kollouthos	3 car.	2,800 tal.
	Hatres, tailor	2 car.	1,900 tal.
	Apollos son of Hatres	2 car.	1,900 tal.
	Apollos son of Ioannes	18 car.	17,000 tal.
28	Heirs of the deacon	18 car.	17,000 tal.
	Apollos, oilworker	6 car.	5,600 tal.
	Heirs of Theophilos	18 car.	17,000 tal.
		348,500 tal.	

Folio 15 verso (= Page 31)

† Φαμενὼθ α λα σελ(ίς)

Ϩαλμίου	κ(εράτια) δ	(τάλαντα) Γψ
Βάνος χαλκ(εύς)	κ(εράτια) β	(τάλαντα) Αϡ
Πέτρ(ος) Ἠλίας	κ(εράτια) ιη	(ταλάντων) (μυριὰς) α Ζ
Τατιαν(ὸς) Ἠλίας	κ(εράτια) ιη	(ταλάντων) (μυριὰς) α Ζ
Μίνος Πις	κ(εράτια) γ	(τάλαντα) Βω
Μίνος ἀναγνώστ(ης)	κ(εράτια) β	(τάλαντα) Αϡ
[[Σαραπίον Βαχ(η)	κ(εράτια) ι̣γ	(τάλαντα) *vacat*]]
Βίκτωρ Σαμηει	κ(εράτια) ιβ	(ταλάντων) (μυριὰς) α Ασ
Κουι Τικ	κ(εράτια) ς	(τάλαντα) Εχ
Κωσταντ(ῖνος) Παχυμ(ίου)	κ(εράτια) ιε	(ταλάντων) (μυριὰς) α Δ
Ἄπα Ἠσαίας πρεσβύτερ(ος)	κ(εράτια) ς	(τάλαντα) Εχ
[Ε]ὖ̣ς Ἰωάννου	κ(εράτια) ς	(τάλαντα) Εχ
Κ̣ουι Σνοβ	κ(εράτια) ιβ	(ταλάντων) (μυριὰς) α Ασ
υἱὸς φομντ	κ(εράτια) ιβ	(ταλάντων) (μυριὰς) α Ασ
[Ἰ]σακίου κλ(ηρονόμου) Ἠλίας	κ(εράτια) ιζ	(ταλάντων) *vacat*
Ψ̣ανκελελε ἐν χρ(υσῷ)	κ(εράτια) ιζd	(ταλάντων) (μυριὰς) α Ϛτ ἀγρ( )
Φαμενὼθ ιζ ἀπόδοσ(ις) νο(μισματίων) ιη εὐσ(τάθμων)		
Λουλοῦτος Ἰωάννου	κ(εράτιον) α	(τάλαντα) ϡ
Πευροτ Παχυμίου	κ(εράτια) ς	(τάλαντα) Εχ
Μίνου Ἀνουφ(ίου)	κ(εράτια) γ	(τάλαντα) Βω
[Φ]οιβάμμ(ων) Πινουτ(ίωνος)	κ(εράτια) ε	(τάλαντα) Δχ
[Σα]ραπίον Πασωθ(ίου)	κ(εράτια) γ	(τάλαντα) Βω
[τ]ῶν σκυτέων	κ(εράτια) γ	(τάλαντα) Βω
[Πα]πνοῦθ(ις) Μίνου Ἀνου̣φ(ίου)	κ(εράτια) δLd	(τάλαντα) Δτ
[Μο]νίου Κό̣μες	κ(εράτια) β	(τάλαντα) Αϡ
[Τε]ϣνεενε	κ(εράτιον) α	(τάλαντα) ϡ
[Βίκ]τωρ καθαρ(ουργός)	κ(εράτια) αLd	(τάλαντα) Αχ
[Ἀνο]ῦφ(ις) Μίν(ου) Διοσκ(όρου)	κ(εράτια) δ	(τάλαντα) Γψ
[. .]. ὡ̣μ(ιος) Ἀπολ(λῶτος)	κ(εράτια) δL	(τάλαντα) Δσ
[Βίκ]τωρ Ἰλουμ(ένου)	κ(εράτια) αL	(τάλαντα) Αυ
[Πι]τ̣ερ Ἀπολ(λῶτος)	κ(εράτιον) α	(τάλαντα) ϡ
Μόνιος Κ[ό]μ̣ες̣	[κ(εράτια)]	(τάλαντα) [ ]
(in line 27, between Cols. 1 and 2)	(ταλάντων) (μυριάδες) ις Γϡ	

4-5 ϊη pap. 9 ϊβ pap. 10,14 κουϊ pap. 11 ϊε pap. 12 ησαϊας pap. 14 κουϊ, ϊβ pap. 15 ϊβ pap. 16 ϊζ pap. 17 ϊζd pap. 18 ϊη pap. 23 Σαραπίων 31 ϊλουμS pap., read Ἰουλουμ(ένου)

Folio 15 verso (= Page 31)

† Phamenoth 1.	Page 31.		
Halmios	4 car.	3,700 tal.	
Banos, smith	2 car.	1,900 tal.	
Petros son of Elias	18 car.	17,000 tal.	
Tatianos son of Elias	18 car.	17,000 tal.	
Minos son of Pis	3 car.	2,800 tal.	
Minos, reader	2 car.	1,900 tal.	
[[Sarapion son of Bache	13 car.	*vacat* tal.]]	
Victor son of Sameei	12 car.	11,200 tal.	
Koui Tik	6 car.	5,600 tal.	
Konstantinos son of Pachymis	15 car.	14,000 tal.	
Apa Esaias, priest	6 car.	5,600 tal.	
Eus daughter of Ioannes	6 car.	5,600 tal.	
Koui Snob	12 car.	11,200 tal.	
Son of the smith	12 car.	11,200 tal.	
Isakis heir of Elias	17 car.	*vacat* tal.	
Psankelele in gold	17 ¼ car.	16,300 tal.	unr.
Phamenoth 17, payment of 18 full-weight solidi.			
Loulous son of Ioannes	1 car.	900 tal.	
Peurot son of Pachymis	6 car.	5,600 tal.	
Minos son of Anouphis	3 car.	2,800 tal.	
Phoibammon son of Pinoution	5 car.	4,600 tal.	
Sarapion son of Pasothios	3 car.	2,800 tal.	
The cobblers	3 car.	2,800 tal.	
Papnouthis son of Minos, grandson of Anouphis	4 ¾ car.	4,300 tal.	
Monis son of Komes	2 car.	1,900 tal.	
[Te]shneene	1 car.	900 tal.	
Victor, baker	1 ¾ car.	1,600 tal.	
Anouphis son of Minos, grandson of Dioskoros	4 car.	3,700 tal.	
[..].omis son of Apollos	4 ½ car.	4,200 tal.	
Victor son of Iouloumenos	1 ½ car.	1,400 tal.	
Piter son of Apollos	1 car.	900 tal.	
Monis son of Komes	[car.]	[ ] tal.	
	163,900 tal.		

Folio 16 recto (= Page 32)

† Φαμενὼθ ιζ λβ σελ(ίς)

Μονίου Ἑρμαπόλ(λωνος)	κ(εράτια) αLd	(τάλαντα) Αχ
Λαϩη Πανουβε	κ(εράτιον) α	(τάλαντα) ϡ
Ἀβράμμ(ις) ϭες	κ(εράτια) βL	(τάλαντα) Βτ
Ἄβα Στεξ	κ(εράτιον) α	(τάλαντα) ϡ
[[Ἰωσῆφ(ις) Ὥρου	κ(εράτια) ιϛ	(ταλάντων) (μυριὰς) α Ε]]
Μακάρ(ιος) οἰκοδόμ(ος)	κ(εράτια) γ	(τάλαντα) Βω
Πεσοοῦ	κ(εράτια) κα	(ταλάντων) (μυριὰς) α Θω
Κωμήτα Σαραπ(ίωνος) Θεονίλ(λης) κ(εράτια) β		(τάλαντα) Αϡ
Ἰωάνν(ης) ἀδελ(φός)	κ(εράτιον) α	(τάλαντα) ϡ
Σαραπί(ων) Θεονίλ(λης) ὁμοί(ως) κ(εράτιον) α		(τάλαντα) ϡ
Ἀπολλῶτ(ος) ἐλαιουρ(γοῦ)	κ(εράτια) ζ	(τάλαντα) Ϛφ
Ἀβράμ(ις) Πεσοοῦ	κ(εράτια) γ	(τάλαντα) Βω
κλ(ηρονόμοι) διακόν(ου)	κ(εράτια) θ	(τάλαντα) Ηφ
Πέτρ(ος) Ἠλίας	κ(εράτια) θ	(τάλαντα) Ηφ
Τατιανὸς Ἠλίας	κ(εράτια) θ	(τάλαντα) Ηφ
Ψᾶτος Κόμες	κ(εράτια) βLd	(τάλαντα) Βφ
κλ(ηρονόμοι) Σενικίον	νο(μισμάτιον) α	(ταλάντων) (μυριὰς) α Ζ
Φῖβις ἀπὸ Ἀρμ(ότνεως)	κ(εράτια) γ	(τάλαντα) Βω
Πίστος	κ(εράτια) γ	(τάλαντα) Βω
ϩαμποι	κ(εράτιον) . .	(τάλαντα) . .
γυν(ή) Ἀνουφ(ίου) Ἰακ(υβίου)	κ(εράτια) ϛ	(τάλαντα) Εχ
Γεώρ(γιος) Ταυρ(ίνου)	κ(εράτια) ζ	(τάλαντα) Ϛφ
Πκῦλ(ις) Φύβης	κ(εράτιον) α	(τάλαντα) ϡ
Παῦλ(ος) Καλατους	κ(εράτια) γ	(τάλαντα) Βω
Ἰακυβίου χαλκ(εύς)	κ(εράτιον) α	(τάλαντα) ϡ
Κυριακὸς Πατσοουϩε	κ(εράτια) β	(τάλαντα) Αϡ
Τϫεερ	κ(εράτιον) α	(τάλαντα) ϡ
Λῦθις ἐργάτης	κ(εράτιον) α	(τάλαντα) ϡ
traces		

4 αβραμμS pap. 6 ϊωσηφ/, ϊς pap. 9 Κωμήτας 10 ϊωαννS pap. 16 θ ex γ (?) 21 ϩαμποϊ pap. 24 Φοίβης 26 ϊακυβιου pap.

Folio 16 recto (= Page 32)

† Phamenoth 17. Page 32.

Monis son of Hermapollon	1 ¾ car.	1,600 tal.
Lahe son of Panoube	1 car.	900 tal.
Abraamis qes	2 ½ car.	2,300 tal.
Aba Stex	1 car.	900 tal.
[[Iosephis son of Horos	16 car.	15,000 tal.]]
Makarios, mason	3 car.	2,800 tal.
Pesoous	21 car.	19,800 tal.
Kometas son of Sarapion, grandson of Theonilla,	2 car.	1,900 tal.
Ioannes his brother	1 car.	900 tal.
Sarapion son of Theonilla, likewise	1 car.	900 tal.
Apollos, oilworker	7 car.	6,500 tal.
Abraamis son of Pesoous	3 car.	2,800 tal.
Heirs of the deacon	9 ar.	8,500 tal.
Petros son of Elias	9 car.	8,500 tal.
Tatianos son of Elias	9 car.	8,500 tal.
Psas son of Komes	2 ¾ car.	2,500 tal.
Heirs of Senecio	1 sol.	17,000 tal.
Phibis from Harmotnis	3 car.	2,800 tal.
Pistos	3 car.	2,800 tal.
Hampoi	- car.	- tal.
Wife of Anouphis son of Iakybis	6 car.	5,600 tal.
Georgios son of Taurinos	7 car.	6,500 tal.
Pkylis son of Phoibe	1 car.	900 tal.
Paulos son of Kalatous	3 car.	2,800 tal.
Iakybis, smith	1 car.	900 tal.
Kyriakos son of Patsoouhe	2 car.	1,900 tal.
Tjeer	1 car.	900 tal.
Lythis, laborer	1 car.	900 tal.
traces		

Folio 16 verso (= Page 33)

† Φαμενὼθ ιζ λγ σελ(ίς)

υἱὸς Παρκατης	κ(εράτια) β	(τάλαντα) Αϡ
Κωρ ΧιΧ	κ(εράτια) β	(τάλαντα) Αϡ
Μαθητής	κ(εράτιον) α	(τάλαντα) ϡ
Ἀπολ(λῶς) Ἰωάνν(ου)	κ(εράτια) β	(τάλαντα) Αϡ
Ἰωάννης Ἀκωρίου	κ(εράτια) γ	(τάλαντα) Βω
Τατιαν(ὸς) Βάν(ου) χαλ(κέως)	κ(εράτιον) α	(τάλαντα) ϡ
Ἐνῶχ Λουσία	κ(εράτια) β	(τάλαντα) Αϡ
Βίκτωρ ϭεc	κ(εράτιον) α	(τάλαντα) ϡ
Μηνᾶ Ἐνῶχ	κ(εράτιον) α	(τάλαντα) ϡ
γυν(ὴ) Πειλιϣ	κ(εράτιον) α	(τάλαντα) ϡ
Ὥρου Σουριχ(η)	κ(εράτιον) α	(τάλαντα) ϡ
Ἰακ(ῦβις) Κολ(λούθου)	κ(εράτιον) α	(τάλαντα) ϡ
Ἀβρ(αάμις) τέκτ(ων)	κ(εράτιον) α	(τάλαντα) ϡ
Ἐνῶχ γναφ(εύς)	κ(εράτιον) α	(τάλαντα) ϡ
Ἀτρῆτος Παρακ(οτε)	κ(εράτιον) α	(τάλαντα) ϡ
Ἀνοῦφ(ις) Κωσταν(τίνου)	κ(εράτια) β	(τάλαντα) Αϡ
Φοιβάμ(μων) Ματρών(ας)	κ(εράτια) β	(τάλαντα) Αϡ
ϩαλμίου	κ(εράτιον) α	(τάλαντα) ϡ
Ἄπα Ἡσαίας	κ(εράτιον) α	(τάλαντα) ϡ
Ἰωάνν(ης) Ζυνοδ(ώρου)	κ(εράτιον) α	(τάλαντα) ϡ
Μηνᾶ Θαβουν(ος)	κ(ερατίου) L	(τάλαντα) υ
κλ(ηρονόμοι) Θεοφίλ(ου)	κ(εράτια) θ	(τάλαντα) Ηφ
κλ(ηρονόμοι) Καϩ	κ(εράτιον) α	(τάλαντα) ϡ
Φῖβις Ἰωσηφ(ίου)	κ(εράτιον) α	(τάλαντα) ϡ
Θεόφιλ(ος)	κ(εράτια) γ	(τάλαντα) Βω
[[Βίκτωρ Σαμηει	κ(εράτια) γ	(τάλαντα) Βω]]
υἱὸς φομντ	κ(εράτια) γ	(τάλαντα) Βω
Σαραπίον Ἰακ(υβίου)	κ(εράτια) ς	(τάλαντα) Εχ
Ὀνοβηρ Πανουβε	κ(εράτιον) α	(τάλαντα) ϡ

(ταλάντων) (μυριάδες) δ Η̣χ

2 υϊος pap. 5 ϊωαννS pap. 6 ϊωαννης pap. 13 ϊακ/ pap. 20 ησαϊας pap. 21 ϊωαννS; read Ζηνοδ(ώρου) 22 ϋ pap. 25 ϊωσηφ/ pap. 28 υϊος pap. 29 Σαραπίων; ϊακ/ pap.

Folio 16 verso (= Page 33)

† Phamenoth 17.	Page 33.	
Son of Parkates	2 car.	1,900 tal.
Kor son of Jij	2 car.	1,900 tal.
Mathetes	1 car.	900 tal.
Apollos son of Ioannes	2 car.	1,900 tal.
Ioannes son of Akoris	3 car.	2,800 tal.
Tatianos son of Banos, smith	1 car.	900 tal.
Enoch son of Lousia	2 car.	1,900 tal.
Victor qes	1 car.	900 tal.
Menas son of Enoch	1 car.	900 tal.
Wife of Peilish	1 car.	900 tal.
Horos son of Souriche	1 car.	900 tal.
Iakybis son of Kollouthos	1 car.	900 tal.
Abraamis, carpenter	1 car.	900 tal.
Enoch, fuller	1 car.	900 tal.
Hatres son of Parakote	1 car.	900 tal.
Anouphis son of Konstantinos	2 car.	1,900 tal.
Phoibammon son of Matrona	2 car.	1,900 tal.
Halmios	1 car.	900 tal.
Apa Esaias	1 car.	900 tal.
Ioannes son of Zenodoros	1 car.	900 tal.
Menas son of Thabounos	½ car.	400 tal.
Heirs of Theophilos	9 car.	8,500 tal.
Heirs of Kah	1 car.	900 tal.
Phibis son of Iosephis	1 car.	900 tal.
Theophilos	3 car.	2,800 tal.
[[Victor son of Sameei	3 car.	2,800 tal.]]
son of the smith	3 car.	2,800 tal.
Sarapion son of Iakybis	6 car.	5,600 tal.
Onober son of Panoube	1 car.	900 tal.
	48,600 tal.	

Folio 17 recto (= Page 34)

† Φαμενὼθ ιζ λδ σελ(ίς)

Τατιαν(ὸς) Παρβας	κ(εράτιον) α	(τάλαντα) ϡ
Πεκῦσις τέκ(των)	κ(εράτια) β	(τάλαντα) Αϡ
Ἰωσῆφ(ις) γραμμ(ατ--)	κ(εράτια) γd	(τάλαντα) Γ
Σοίου καὶ Πιηοῦτ(ος)	κ(εράτια) β	(τάλαντα) Αϡ
Πιτεχου	κ(εράτιον) α	(τάλαντα) ϡ
γυν(ὴ) Πενοβ	κ(εράτιον) α	(τάλαντα) ϡ
κλ(ηρονόμοι) Ἠλίας	κ(εράτια) δLd	(τάλαντα) Δυ
Ἐνῶχ Κυριακ(οῦ)	κ(εράτιον) α	(τάλαντα) ϡ
Λωτα	κ(εράτιον) α	(τάλαντα) ϡ
Λαϩο	κ(εράτιον) α	(τάλαντα) ϡ
Ἰερημίας πρωτ(οκωμήτης)	κ(εράτια) β	(τάλαντα) Αϡ
Ἀπολ(λῶς) ϭες	κ(εράτιον) α	(τάλαντα) ϡ
Μακάρ(ιος) Γερμ(ανοῦ)	κ(εράτιον) α	(τάλαντα) ϡ
Σαραπίον σιτ(ομέτρης)	κ(εράτιον) α	(τάλαντα) ϡ
Πατϫιτς	κ(εράτιον) α	(τάλαντα) ϡ
Ἰερημίας Πανε	κ(εράτια) δ	(τάλαντα) Γψ
Ἰωάνν(ης) Λεῦτος	κ(εράτιον) α	(τάλαντα) ϡ
Κῦρος λαξόου	κ(εράτιον) α	(τάλαντα) ϡ
Κουι Τικ	κ(εράτιον) α	(τάλαντα) ϡ
ϩελένα	κ(εράτια) ς	(τάλαντα) Εχ
Μηνᾶ μάγυρ(ος)	κ(εράτια) γ	(τάλαντα) Βω
Πανηϫνου	κ(εράτιον) α	(τάλαντα) ϡ
Ἀτρῆτος Πεβῶ	κ(εράτιον) α	(τάλαντα) ϡ
Ἀπορ	κ(εράτια) γ	(τάλαντα) Βω
Ἐνῶχ οἰκον(όμος)	κ(εράτια) κδ	(ταλάντων) (μυριάδες) β Βχ
Παπνοῦθ(ις) Κλεμ( )	κ(εράτια) θ	(τάλαντα) Ηφ
Ἰωάννης Ἰακ(υβίου)	κ(εράτιον) α	(τάλαντα) ϡ
Ἀτρῆτος ῥάπτου	κ(εράτιον) α	(τάλαντα) ϡ

(ταλάντων) (μυριάδες) ζ Δυ

4 ϊωσηφ/ pap. 5 σοϊου, πιηουτS pap. 8 Δϋ pap. 12, 17 ϊερημιας pap. 15 Σαραπίων; σιτS pap. 18 ϊωαννS pap. 20 κουϊ pap. 22 μάγειρος 28 ϊακ pap.

Page 17 recto (= Page 34)

† Phamenoth 17. Page 34.

Tatianos son of Parbas	1 car.	900 tal.
Pekysis, carpenter	2 car.	1,900 tal.
Iosephis, gramm( )	3 ¼ car.	3,000 tal.
Soios and Pieous	2 car.	1,900 tal.
Pitechou	1 car.	900 tal.
Wife of Penob	1 car.	900 tal.
Heirs of Elias	4 ¾ car.	4,400 tal.
Enoch son of Kyriakos	1 car.	900 tal.
Lota	1 car.	900 tal.
Laho	1 car.	900 tal.
Ieremias, protokometes	2 car.	1,900 tal.
Apollos qes	1 car.	900 tal.
Makarios son of Germanos	1 car.	900 tal.
Sarapion, grain-measurer	1 car.	900 tal
Patjits	1 car.	900 tal.
Ieremias son of Pane	4 car.	3,700 tal.
Ioannes son of Leus	1 car.	900 tal.
Kyros, stonecutter	1 car.	900 tal.
Koui Tik	1 car.	900 tal.
Helena	6 car.	5,600 tal.
Menas, meat-cook	3 car.	2,800 tal.
Panejnou	1 car.	900 tal.
Hatres son of Pebos	1 car.	900 tal.
Apor	3 car.	2,800 tal.
Enoch, oikonomos	24 car.	22,600 tal.
Papnouthis son of Klem( )	9 car.	8,500 tal.
Ioannes son of Iakybis	1 car.	900 tal.
Hatres, tailor	1 car.	900 tal.

74,400 tal.

Folio 17 verso (= Page 35)

† Φαμενὼθ ιζ   λε σελ(ίς)

Ἄπα Νοκις	κ(εράτια) ϛ	(τάλαντα) Εχ
Φίβις Τοοσε	κ(εράτια) κδ	(ταλάντων) (μυριάδες) β Βχ
Βίκτωρ Ἀπολ(λῶτος)	κ(εράτια) β	(τάλαντα) Αϡ
τῆς ἁγίας ἐκλ(ησίας)	νο(μισμάτια) β	(ταλάντων) (μυριάδες) γ Δ//
Νόννα Στεφ(άνου)	κ(εράτια) γ	(τάλαντα) Βω
Σαραπίον Βαχ(η)	κ(εράτιον) α	(τάλαντα) ϡ
Ἄπε Ἀπαλο	κ(εράτια) γ	(τάλαντα) Βω
Π[[.]]τουλ	κ(ερατίου) Ld	(τάλαντα) ψ
Φῖβις Ταροοῦ	κ(εράτια) θ	(τάλαντα) Ηφ
Παῆσις Νωϩε	κ(εράτια) β	(τάλαντα) Αϡ
[[Ἰσάκ(ις) κλ(ηρονόμος) Ἡλίας	κ(εράτια) ιζ	(ταλάντων) (μυριὰς) α ϛ]]
Σαραπίον Βαχ(η)	κ(εράτια) γ	(τάλαντα) Βω

. . . Φαρμ(οῦθι) η

Σοίου Φιβίου	κ(εράτια) δ	(τάλαντα) Γψ
Ἀτρῆτος Πεβο	κ(εράτια) β	(τάλαντα) Αϡ
ϩαμποι	κ(εράτια) εd	(τάλαντα) Δϡ
Κουι Ϣα	κ(εράτια) ϛ	(τάλαντα) Εχ
Πιουλ	κ(εράτια) β	(τάλαντα) Αϡ
Ἰωνίου Ἰωσηφ(ίου)	κ(εράτια) ε	(τάλαντα) Δχ
Ὥρου Σουριχη	κ(εράτια) ε	(τάλαντα) Δχ
Ἐνῶχ Κολλούθ(ου)	κ(εράτια) δ	(τάλαντα) Γψ
Ἐνῶχ γναφ(εύς)	κ(εράτια) ε	(τάλαντα) Δχ
Κελλη	κ(εράτια) βL	(τάλαντα) Βτ
ΛοοϪε	κ(εράτια) γd	(τάλαντα) Γ
Παρακοτε	κ(εράτια) γ	(τάλαντα) Βω
Ἰωάννης Πανουβε	κ(εράτια) β	(τάλαντα) Αϡ
Ἰωάννης Λεῦτος	κ(εράτια) β	(τάλαντα) Αϡ

(ταλάντων) (μυριάδες) ιγ Αϡ

5 ἐκκλ(ησίας); numerals ex corr. in both columns   7,13 Σαραπίων   12 ϊσακ/ pap.   14 φαρμS pap.   17 ϩαμποϊ pap.   18 κουϊ pap.   20 ϊωνιου, ϊωσηφ/ pap.   29 ϊγ pap.

Folio 17 verso (= Page 35)

† Phamenoth 17.	Page 35.	
Apa Nokis	6 car.	5,600 tal.
Phibis son of Toose	24 car.	22,600 tal.
Victor son of Apollos	2 car.	1,900 tal.
The Holy Church	2 sol.	34,000 tal.
Nonna daughter of Stephanos	3 car.	2,800 tal.
Sarapion son of Bache	1 car.	900 tal.
Ape Apalo	3 car.	2,800 tal.
Ptoul	¾ car.	700 tal.
Phibis son of Taroous	9 car.	8,500 tal.
Paesis son of Nohe	2 car.	1,900 tal.
[[Isakis heir of Elias	17 car.	16,000 tal.]]
Sarapion son of Bache	3 car.	2,800 tal.
. . . of Pharmouthi 8		
Soiou son of Phibis	4 car.	3,700 tal.
Hatres son of Pebo	2 car.	1,900 tal.
Hampoi	5 ¼ car.	4,900 tal.
Koui Sha	6 car.	5,600 tal.
Pioul	2 car.	1,900 tal.
Ionios son of Iosephis	5 car.	4,600 tal.
Horos son of Souriche	5 car.	4,600 tal.
Enoch son of Kollouthos	4 car.	3,700 tal.
Enoch, fuller	5 car.	4,600 tal.
Kelle	2 ½ car.	2,300 tal.
Looje	3 ¼ car.	3,000 tal.
Parakote	3 car.	2,800 tal.
Ioannes son of Panoube	2 car.	1,900 tal.
Ioannes son of Leus	2 car.	1,900 tal.
	131,900 tal.	

Folio 18 recto (= Page 36)

† Φαρμοῦθι η ἀπ`ό´δοσ(ις) νο(μισματίων) κδ εὐσ(τάθμων)

—————— λς σελ(ίς)

Μονίου Κόμες	κ(εράτιον) α	(τάλαντα) ϡ
Ἀβράμμ(ις) Πεσοοῦ	κ(εράτια) ιη	(ταλάντων) (μυριὰς) α Ζ//
Κωρ ϫιϫ	κ(εράτια) δ	(τάλαντα) Γψ
Ἰερημί`α´ς ϭεc	κ(εράτια) ιθd	(ταλάντων) (μυριὰς) α Ηρ
Ἀβρ(αάμις) ϭεc	κ(εράτια) β	(τάλαντα) Αϡ
Τ[[α]]ιτιανε Παρβας	κ(εράτια) β	(τάλαντα) Αϡ
Κυριακὸς Πατσοουϩε	κ(εράτια) ε	(τάλαντα) Δχ
Ἀκουι γναφ(εύς)	κ(εράτιον) α	(τάλαντα) ϡ
Ἰακυβίου Κολλ(ούθου)	κ(εράτια) αL	(τάλαντα) Αυ
Μηνᾶ Ἐνῶχ	κ(εράτια) ς	(τάλαντα) Εχ
Πιτεχου	κ(ερατίου) Ld	(τάλαντα) ψ
κληλ Καϩ	κ(εράτια) γ	(τάλαντα) Βω
γυν(ὴ) Πενοβ	κ(εράτια) γ	(τάλαντα) Βω
Λοοϫε	κ(εράτια) β	(τάλαντα) Αϡ
Παῆσις Νωϩε	κ(εράτια) αL	(τάλαντα) Αυ
Ὥρου Σουριχη	κ(εράτια) γ	(τάλαντα) Βω
Ἀτρῆτος ῥά{τ}πτου	κ(εράτια) γ	(τάλαντα) Βω
Ἰωάννης Πατσαλ(αμανα)	κ(εράτια) γ	(τάλαντα) Βω
Ἰωάννης κλ(ηρονόμος) Παύλ(ου)	κ(εράτια) κε	(ταλάντων) (μυριάδες) β Γφ
Ἄμα Τασοῦ	κ(εράτια) ιη	(ταλάντων) (μυριὰς) α Ζ
Μακαρίου Γερμ(ανοῦ)	κ(εράτια) ς	(τάλαντα) Εχ
Λῦθις ἐργάτης	κ(εράτια) β	(τάλαντα) Αϡ
Καπαι ἀμπελ(ουργός)	κ(εράτια) αL	(τάλαντα) Αυ
Κωσταν(τῖνος) Παχυμ(ίου)	κ(εράτια) ς	(τάλαντα) Εχ
Τατιαν(ὸς) χαλκ(εύς)	κ(εράτια) δL	(τάλαντα) Δρ
Πανηϫνου	κ(εράτια) β	(τάλαντα) Αϡ
Πκῦλ(ις) Πασωθ(ίου)	κ(εράτιον) α	(τάλαντα) ϡ
Βίκ(τωρ) καθαρ(ουργός)	κ(εράτια) ς	(τάλαντα) Εχ
Κύρα Ταυρ(ίνου)	κ(ερατίου) L	(τάλαντα) υ
Φοιβάμμ(ων) Ματρῶν(ας)	κ(εράτια) θ	(τάλαντα) Ηφ

(ταλάντων) (μυριάδες) ιε´´ υ

1 φαρμουθι// pap. 3 αβραμμS, ϊη pap. 5 ϊερημι`α´ς, ϊθ pap. 7 Τιτ- ex Τατ- 9 ακουϊ pap. 10 ϊακυβιο^{υ}, Αϋ pap. 13 κληλ = κληρ(ονόμοι) 14 γυνή 16 Παῆσις, second ς perhaps corr.; Αϋ pap. 19, 20 ϊωαννης pap. 22 γερμS pap. 24 καπαϊ pap. 30 ϋ pap. 32 ϋ pap.

Folio 18 recto (= Page 36)

† Pharmouthi 8. Payment of 24 full-weight solidi.

Page 36.

	Monis son of Komes	1 car.	900 tal.
	Abrammis son of Pesoous	18 car.	17,000 tal.
4	Kor (son of?) Jij	4 car.	3,700 tal.
	Ieremias qes	19 ¼ car.	18,100 tal.
	Abraamis qes	2 car.	1,900 tal.
	Titiane son of Parbas	2 car.	1,900 tal.
8	Kyriakos son of Patsoouhe	5 car.	4,600 tal.
	Akoui, fuller	1 car.	900 tal.
	Iakybis son of Kollouthos	1 ½ car.	1,400 tal.
	Menas son of Enoch	6 car.	5,600 tal.
12	Pitechou	¾ car.	700 tal.
	Heirs of Kah	3 car.	2,800 tal.
	Wife of Penob	3 car.	2,800 tal.
	Looje	2 car.	1,900 tal.
16	Paesis son of Nohe	1 ½ car.	1,400 tal.
	Horos son of Souriche	3 car.	2,800 tal.
	Hatres, tailor	3 car.	2,800 tal.
	Ioannes son of Patsalamana	3 car.	2,800 tal.
20	Ioannes heir of Paulos	25 car.	23,500 tal.
	Ama Tasous	18 car.	17,000 tal.
	Makarios son of Germanos	6 car.	5,600 tal.
	Lythis, laborer	2 car.	1,900 tal.
24	Kapai, wine producer	1 ½ car.	1,400 tal.
	Konstantinos son of Pachymis	6 car.	5,600 tal.
	Tatianos, smith	4 ½ car.	4,100 tal.
	Panejnou	2 car.	1,900 tal.
28	Pkylis son of Pasothis	1 car.	900 tal.
	Victor, baker	6 car.	5,600 tal.
	Kyra daughter of Taurinos	½ car.	400 tal.
	Phoibammon son of Matrona	9 car.	8,500 tal.

150,400 tal.

Folio 18 verso (= Page 37)

† Φαρμ(οῦθι) η ἀπόδοσι(ς) ὁμοί(ως) λζ σελ(ίς)

Ἀπολ(λῶς) Ὠφελ(ίου)	κ(εράτιον) α	(τάλαντα) ϡ
Ἠλίας Πατσαλαμ(ανα)	κ(εράτια) γ	(τάλαντα) Βω
Ἰωάννης Ἰακυβίου	κ(εράτια) ε	(τάλαντα) Δχ
Ἰωάνν(ης) Ζυνοδ(ώρου)	κ(εράτια) αL	(τάλαντα) Αυ
Ἀπολ(λῶς) Ἰωάννου	κ(εράτια) θ	(τάλαντα) Ηφ
κλ(ηρονόμοι) διακόνου	κ(εράτια) ιη	(ταλάντων) (μυριὰς) α Ζ´´
Βίκτωρ Ἰουλουμ(ένου)	κ(εράτια) αL	(τάλαντα) Αυ
Λῦθις ἐργάτης	κ(εράτια) γ	(τάλαντα) Βω
Ἰωνίου Ἰωσηφ(ίου)	κ(εράτια) γ	(τάλαντα) Βω
κλ(ηρονόμοι) Πουηηβ	κ(εράτιον) α	(τάλαντα) ϡ
Ἰωάννης Λεῦτος	κ(εράτια) ϛ	(τάλαντα) Εχ
Ἰωάννης Πατσαλ(αμανα)	κ(εράτια) βL	(τάλαντα) Βτ
Ἀπολ(λῶς) Λασουκ	κ(εράτια) αL	(τάλαντα) Αυ
Κωσταντ(ῖνος) Παχυμίου	κ(εράτια) ϛ	(τάλαντα) Εχ
Ἐνῶχ Κολλούθ(ου)	κ(εράτια) αd	(τάλαντα) Αρ
Ἐνῶχ Λουσία	κ(εράτια) β	(τάλαντα) Αϡ
Σαραπίον Βαχη	κ(εράτιον) α	(τάλαντα) ϡ
Ἀπολ(λῶς) Ἀτρῆτος	κ(εράτια) ϛ	(τάλαντα) Εχ
Φοι(βάμμων) Πινουτ(ίωνος)	κ(εράτια) γ	(τάλαντα) Βω
Κουι Νου	κ(εράτια) αL	(τάλαντα) Αυ
υἱὸς Καλατους	κ(εράτια) γ	(τάλαντα) Βω
γυν(ὴ) Πενοβ	κ(εράτιον) α	(τάλαντα) ϡ
Βίκτωρ Ἑλλῶτος	κ(εράτια) ε	(τάλαντα) Δχ
Ἰερημίας Πανε	κ(εράτια) ϛ	(τάλαντα) Εχ
Παπνοῦθ(ις) Κλεμ( )	κ(εράτια) θ	(τάλαντα) Ηφ
τῆς ἁγίας ἐκλ(ησίας)	νο(μισμάτια) ι//	(ταλάντων) (μυριάδες) ιζ ´´
Πέτρ(ος) Ἠλίας	νο(μισμάτιον) α	(ταλάντων) (μυριὰς) α Ζ´´
Φῖβις Τοοσε	νο(μισμάτιον) α	(ταλάντων) (μυριὰς) α Ζ´´
τοῦ ἁγίου μαρτυρ(ίου)	νο(μισμάτια) β	(ταλάντων) (μυριάδες) γ Δ
Παρακοτε	κ(εράτια) εL	(τάλαντα) Ερ
Τατιαν(ὸς) Ἠλία	νο(μισμάτιον) α	(ταλάντων) (μυριὰς) α Ζ´´

(ταλάντων) (μυριάδες) λε Δσ

1 φαρμS pap. 4 ϊωαννης, ϊακυβιο^υ pap. 5 Ζηνοδ(ώρου); Αϋ pap. 6 ϊωαννου pap. 7 ϊη pap. 8 ϊουλουμS, Αϋ pap. 10 ϊωνιου, ϊωσηφ/ pap. 12, 13 ϊωαννης pap. 14 λασουκ/, Αϋ pap. 18 Σαραπίων 21 Αϋ pap. 22 υϊος pap. 25 ϊερημιας pap. 27 ἐκκλ(ησίας); ϊ, ϊζ pap.

Folio 18 verso (= Page 37)

† Pharmouthi 8, payment likewise.		Page 37.
Apollos son of Ophelios	1 car.	900 tal.
Elias son of Patsalamana	3 car.	2,800 tal.
Ioannes son of Iakybis	5 car.	4,600 tal.
Ioannes son of Zenodoros	1 ½ car.	1,400 tal.
Apollos son of Ioannes	9 car.	8,500 tal.
Heirs of the deacon	18 car.	17,000 tal.
Victor son of Iouloumenos	1 ½ car.	1,400 tal.
Lythis, laborer	3 car.	2,800 tal.
Ionios son of Iosephis	3 car.	2,800 tal.
Heirs of Poueeb	1 car.	900 tal.
Ioannes son of Leus	6 car.	5,600 tal.
Ioannes son of Patsalamana	2 ½ car.	2,300 tal.
Apollos son of Lasouk	1 ½ car.	1,400 tal.
Konstantinos son of Pachymis	6 car.	5,600 tal.
Enoch son of Kollouthos	1 ¼ car.	1,100 tal.
Enoch son of Lousia	2 car.	1,900 tal.
Sarapion son of Bache	1 car.	900 tal.
Apollos son of Hatres	6 car.	5,600 tal.
Phoibammon son of Pinoution	3 car.	2,800 tal.
Koui Nou	1 ½ car.	1,400 tal.
Son of Kalatous	3 car.	2,800 tal.
Wife of Penob	1 car.	900 tal.
Victor son of Hellos	5 car.	4,600 tal.
Ieremias son of Pane	6 car.	5,600 tal.
Papnouthis son of Klem( )	9 car.	8,500 tal.
The Holy Church	10 sol.	170,000 tal.
Petros son of Elias	1 sol.	17,000 tal.
Phibis son of Toose	1 sol.	17,000 tal.
The Holy Martyrion	2 sol.	34,000 tal.
Parakote	5 ½ sol.	5,100 tal.
Tatianos son of Elias	1 sol.	17,000 tal.

354,200 tal.

Folio 19 recto (= Page 38)

† Φαρμοῦθ(ι) η ἀπόδοσι(ς) ὁμοί(ως)		λη σελ(ίς)
Φῖβις Ἰωσηφ(ίου)	νο(μισμάτιον) α	(ταλάντων) (μυριὰς) α Ζ´´
Χωωρ Ἀνουφ(ίου)	κ(εράτια) ις	(ταλάντων) (μυριὰς) α Ε
Ἰωνίου Ἰωσηφ(ίου)	κ(εράτια) ϛ	(τάλαντα) Εχ
Κουι Ϣα καὶ Λαϩο	κ(εράτια) ιLd	(ταλάντων) (μυριὰς) α// ρ
Φοιβάμ(μων) χαλκ(εύς)	κ(εράτια) β	(τάλαντα) Αϡ
Μηνᾶ Ἐνῶχ	κ(εράτια) η	(τάλαντα) Ζφ
Ἀπολ(λῶς) Ἀνουφ(ίου) δ(ιὰ) Λαϩο κ(ερατίου) L		(τάλαντα) υ
Ψᾶτος Κόμες	κ(εράτια) ϛ	(τάλαντα) Εχ
Ἀπολ(λῶς) διάκ(ονος)	κ(εράτιον) α	(τάλαντα) ϡ
Ἀπολ(λῶς) ἐλαιουρ(γός)	κ(εράτιον) α	(τάλαντα) ϡ
Παῆσις Νωϩε	κ(εράτια) γ	(τάλαντα) Βω
Τατιαν(ὸς) φομντ δ(ιὰ) Τατιαν(οῦ) Ἑρμ( ) ἐν χρ(υσῷ)		
	νο(μισμάτιον) α	(ταλάντων) (μυριὰς) α Ζ
Σερῆνος Κωσταντ(ίνου)	κ(εράτια) αL	(τάλαντα) Αυ
Ἐνῶχ οἰκονόμ(ος) ἐν χρ(υσῷ)	νο(μισμάτιον) α π(αρὰ) ϛLd	(ταλάντων) (μυριὰς) α Ϛρ
Ἰερημίας Ἠλίας ἐν χρ(υσῷ)	νο(μισμάτιον) α π(αρὰ) η	(ταλάντων) (μυριὰς) α Ε
Σαραπίον σιτομέτρ(ης)	νο(μισμάτια) β γ°	(ταλάντων) (μυριάδες) ε Αϡ
Ἄμα Τασου μονάζ(ουσα)	νο(μισματίου) γ´	(τάλαντα) Ϛψ
Ἄπα Ἰωνίου Φαρμ(οῦθι) ια	κ(εράτια) ιθ	(ταλάντων) (μυριὰς) α Ζϡ
τοῦ ἁγίου μαρτυρ(ίου) Φαρμ(οῦθι) ια	κ(εράτια) ιηL	(ταλάντων) (μυριὰς) α Ζφ
Φαρμ(οῦθι) κδ		
Ἰσίδωρ(ος) Κα̣λη	κ(εράτια) δ	(τάλαντα) Γψ
γυν(ὴ) Πενοβ	κ(εράτια) βL	(τάλαντα) Βτ
Ἀτρῆτος ῥάπτο(υ)	κ(εράτια) β	(τάλαντα) Αϡ
Σαραπίον Θεονίλ(λης)	κ(εράτια) βd	(τάλαντα) Βρ
Κωρ ϪιϪ	κ(εράτια) εd	(τάλαντα) Δϡ κς ωυ
Μίνος Πις	κ(εράτια) εL	(τάλαντα) Ερ
κληλ Καϩ	κ(εράτια) γ	(τάλαντα) Βω
Εὖς Ἰωάνν(ου)	κ(εράτια) γ	(τάλαντα) Βω
Ἠσαίας πρεσβύτερ(ος)	κ(εράτια) ιε	(ταλάντων) (μυριὰς) α Δρ
Μίν(ος) ἀναγνώστ(ης)	κ(εράτια) ηL	(τάλαντα) Ζϡ
Διόσκορ(ος) Ὥρου	κ(εράτιον) α	(τάλαντα) ϡ
Ἀ̣νοῦφ(ις) Κωσταν(τίνου)	κ(εράτια) αL	(τάλαντα) Αυ
	(ταλάντων) (μυριάδες) κς Αυ	

2 ϊωσηφ/ pap. 3 ϊς pap.; ϛ ex L, Col. 3 corr. 4 ϊωνιου, ϊωσηφ/ pap. 5 κουϊ, ϊLd pap. 7 Ζφ ex Η 8 ϋ pap. 14 Αϋ pap. 16 ϊερημιας pap. 17,25 Σαραπίων 19,20 κ(εράτια) ex νο(μ.) 19 ϊωνιου, ϊα, ϊθ pap. 20 ϊα, ϊηL pap. 22 ϊσιδωρ/ pap. 28 κληλ = κληρ(ονόμοι) 30 ϊε pap.

Folio 19 recto (= Page 38)

† Pharmouthi 8, payment likewise. Page 38.

Phibis son of Iosephis	1 sol.	17,000 tal.
Choor son of Anouphis	16 car.	15,000 tal.
Ionios son of Iosephis	6 car.	5,600 tal.
Koui Sha and Laho	10 ¾ car.	10,100 tal.
Phoibammon, smith	2 car.	1,900 tal.
Menas son of Enoch	8 car.	7,500 tal.
Apollos son of Anouphis through Laho	½ car.	400 tal.
Psas son of Komes	6 car.	5,600 tal.
Apollos, deacon	1 car.	900 tal.
Apollos, oilworker	1 car.	900 tal.
Paesis son of Nohe	3 car.	2,800 tal.
Tatianos son of the smith through Tatianos son of Herm( ), in gold	1 sol.	17,000 tal.
Serenos son of Konstantinos	1 ½ car.	1,400 tal.
Enoch, oikonomos, in gold	1 sol. minus 6 ¾ (car.)	16,100 tal.
Ieremias son of Elias, in gold	1 sol. minus 8 (car.)	15,000 tal.
Sarapion, grain-measurer	2 1/3 sol.	51,900 tal.
Ama Tasous, nun	1/3 sol.	6,700 tal.
Apa Ionios, Pharmouthi 11	19 car.	17,900 tal.
The Holy Martyrion, Pharmouthi 11,	18 ½ car.	17,500 tal.

<u>Pharmouthi 24</u>

Isidoros son of Kale	4 car.	3,700 tal.
Wife of Penob	2 ½ car.	2,300 tal.
Hatres, tailor	2 car.	1,900 tal.
Sarapion son of Theonilla	2 ¼ car.	2,100 tal.
Kor (son of ?) Jij	5 ¼ car.	4,900 tal.
Minos son of Pis	5 ½ car.	5,100 tal.
Heirs of Kah	3 car.	2,800 tal.
Eus daughter of Ioannes	3 car.	2,800 tal.
Esaias, priest	15 car.	14,100 tal.
Minos, reader	8 ½ car.	7,900 tal.
Dioskoros son of Horos	1 car.	900 tal.
Anouphis son of Konstantinos	1 ½ car.	1,400 tal.

2[6]1,400 tal.

Folio 19 verso (= Page 39)

† Φαρμ(οῦθι) κδ	λθ σελ(ίς)	
Λουλ(οῦς) Ἰωάνν(ου)	κ(εράτια) αL	(τάλαντα) Αυ
Ἀπορ	κ(εράτια) εL	(τάλαντα) Ερ
[[Σοίου Φιβίου	κ(εράτια) αd	(τάλαντα) Ασ]]
Σαραπίον Βαχη	κ(εράτια) β	(τάλαντα) Α⅄
Ἐνῶχ Λουσία	κ(εράτια) ς	(τάλαντα) Εχ
Βίκτωρ Ἰουλουμ(ένου)	κ(εράτια) γ	(τάλαντα) Βω
Βίκτωρ Σαμηει	νο(μισμάτιον) α	(ταλάντων) (μυριὰς) α Ζ
ὁμοί(ως)	κ(εράτια) ιε	(ταλάντων) (μυριὰς) α Δρ
Ἀπολ(λῶς) Λασουκ	κ(εράτια) δ	(τάλαντα) Γψ
Ψᾶ̣τος Κόμες	κ(εράτια) ηLd	(τάλαντα) Ησ
Φοι(βάμμων) Πινουτίων	κ(εράτια) ς	(τάλαντα) Εχ
Ἀπολλ(ῶς) Ἀτρῆτος	κ(εράτια) δd	(τάλαντα) Γ⅄
Μακάρ(ιος) οἰκοδόμ(ος)	κ(εράτια) γL	(τάλαντα) Γτ
Βίκτωρ ϭεc	κ(εράτια) θ	(τάλαντα) Ηφ
υἱὸς Σαρ(απίωνος) Λασυγ̣	κ(εράτια) ι̣η	(ταλάντων) [[Α ⅄]] (μυριὰς) α Ζ
Χωωρ Ἀνουφ(ίου)	κ(εράτια) ς	(τάλαντα) Εχ
Πέτρ(ος) Ἠλίας	κ(εράτια) ιη	(ταλάντων) (μυριὰς) α Ζ
Ἀνοῦφ(ις) Μίνου	κ(εράτιον) α	(τάλαντα) ⅄
Ἀτρῆτος Ὑπερεχ(ίου)	κ(εράτια) ςLd	(τάλαντα) Ϛτ
Ἐνῶχ γναφ(εύς)	κ(εράτια) β	(τάλαντα) Α⅄
Παπνοῦθ(ις) Μίνου	κ(εράτια) δd	(τάλαντα) Γ⅄
Ἄπα Νοκις	κ(εράτια) ς	(τάλαντα) Εχ
Ἰακυβίου χαλ(κέως)	κ(εράτια) β	(τάλαντα) Α⅄
ϩελένα	νο(μισμάτιον) α	(ταλάντων) (μυριὰς) α Ζ
Κωσταντ(ῖνος) Παχυμ(ίου)	νο(μισμάτιον) α	(ταλάντων) (μυριὰς) α Ζ
Κουι Τικ	κ(εράτια) ιγd	(ταλάντων) (μυριὰς) α Βυ
Βίκτωρ Γερμ(ιχου)	κ(εράτια) δ	(τάλαντα) Γψ
Κελλη	κ(εράτια) γ	(τάλαντα) Βω
Τατιανὸς Ἠλίας	νο(μισμάτιον) α	(ταλάντων) (μυριὰς) α Ζ
Τατιαν(οῦ) ῥάπτου	κ(εράτιον) α	(τάλαντα) ⅄
υἱὸς Καλατους	κ(εράτια) β	(τάλαντα) Α⅄

(ταλάντων) (μυριάδες) κα Γ⅄

2 λουλ/, ϊωαννS, Αϋ pap. 5 Σαραπίων 7 ϊουλουμS pap. 9 ϊε pap. 12 Πινουτίωνος 16 υϊος pap. 18 ϊε pap. 24 ϊακυβιου pap. 27 κουϊ, ϊγ, Βϋ pap. 32 υϊος pap.

Folio 19 verso (= Page 39)

† Pharmouthi 24.	Page 39.	
Loulous son of Ioannes	1 ½ car.	1,400 tal.
Apor	5 ½ car.	5,100 tal.
[[Soios son of Phibis	1 ¼ car.	1,200 tal.]]
Sarapion son of Bache	2 car.	1,900 tal.
Enoch son of Lousia	6 car.	5,600 tal.
Victor son of Iouloumenos	3 car.	2,800 tal.
Victor son of Sameei	1 sol.	17,000 tal.
Likewise	15 car.	14,100 tal.
Apollos son of Lasouk	4 car.	3,700 tal.
Psas son of Komes	8 ¾ car.	8,200 tal.
Phoibammon son of Pinoution	6 car.	5,600 tal.
Apollos son of Hatres	4 ¼ car.	3,900 tal.
Makarios, mason	3 ½ car.	3,300 tal.
Victor qes	9 car.	8,500 tal.
Son of Sarapion son of Lasug	18 car.	[[1,900]] 17,000 tal.
Choor son of Anouphis	6 car.	5,600 tal.
Petros son of Elias	18 car.	17,000 tal.
Anouphis son of Minos	1 car.	900 tal.
Hatres son of Hyperechios	6 ¾ car.	6,300 tal.
Enoch, fuller	2 car.	1,900 tal.
Papnouthis son of Minos	4 ¼ car.	3,900 tal.
Apa Nokis	6 car.	5,600 tal.
Iakybis, smith	2 car.	1,900 tal.
Helena	1 sol.	17,000 tal.
Konstantinos son of Pachymis	1 sol.	17,000 tal.
Koui Tik	13 ¼ car.	12,400 tal.
Victor son of Germijou	4 car.	3,700 tal.
Kelle	3 car.	2,800 tal.
Tatianos son of Elias	1 sol.	17,000 tal.
Tatianos, tailor	1 car.	900 tal.
Son of Kalatous	2 car.	1,900 tal.

213,900 tal.

Folio 20 recto (= Page 40)

† Φαρμ(οῦθι) κδ	μ σελ(ίς)	
Ἄπε Ἀπαλο	κ(εράτια) γd	(τάλαντα) Γ
Ἠλίας Κολ(λούθου)	κ(εράτια) αL	(τάλαντα) Αυ
γυν(ή) Ἀνουφ(ίου) Ἰακ(υβίου)	κ(εράτια) ϛ	(τάλαντα) Εχ
Κουι Σνοβ	κ(εράτια) ϛ	(τάλαντα) Εχ
Ἰερημίας δες	κ(εράτια) θ	(τάλαντα) Ηφ
κλ(ηρονόμοι) Θεοφίλ(ου)	νο(μισμάτιον) α	(ταλάντων) (μυριὰς) α Ζ
Ἀνοῦφ(ις) Μίνου	κ(εράτια) αL	(τάλαντα) Αυ
τῆς ἁγίας ἐκλ(ησίας)	νο(μισμάτιον) α	(ταλάντων) (μυριὰς) α Ζ
ὁμοί(ως)	νο(μισμάτια) ι´´	(ταλάντων) (μυριάδες) ιζ
Γεώρ(γιος) Ταυρ(ίνου)	κ(εράτια) ιβ	(ταλάντων) (μυριάδες) α Ασ
Παρακοτε	κ(εράτια) ζd	(τάλαντα) Ϛω
Πατσαλαμ(ανα)	κ(εράτια) ϛL	(τάλαντα) Ϛρ
Κουι Νου	κ(εράτια) β	(τάλαντα) Αϡ
θυγάτηρ Φανουβ	κ(εράτια) αL	(τάλαντα) Αυ
Φῖβις Ἰωσηφ(ίου)	κ(εράτια) θ	(τάλαντα) Ηφ
κλ(ηρονόμοι) διακόνου̣	κ(εράτια) δ	(τάλαντα) Γψ
Μαρία Βίκτωρ	κ(εράτια) ε	(τάλαντα) Δχ
Ἰερημίας κλ(ηρονόμος) Ἠλίας	νο(μισμάτια) γ	(ταλάντων) (μυριάδες) ε Α
ΠανηϪνου	κ(ερατίου) L	(τάλαντα) υ
Σαραπίον Ἰακ(υβίου)	κ(εράτια) ϛ	(τάλαντα) Εχ
Φοι(βάμμων) Πινουτίων	κ(εράτιον) α	(τάλαντα) ϡ
Φῖβις Τοοσε	κ(εράτια) ϛ	(τάλαντα) Εχ
κλ(ηρονόμοι) Ἠλίας	κ(εράτια) κγL/	(ταλάντων) (μυριάδες) β Βρ
Ἀνοῦφ(ις) Μίνου	κ(εράτια) β	(τάλαντα) Αϡ

(ταλάντων) (μυριάδες) λϛ Ασ

3 Αϋ pap. 4 ϊακ/ pap. 5, 14 κουϊ pap. 6 ϊερημιας pap. 8 Αϋ pap. 9 ἐκκλ(ησίας) 9 νο(μ.) α, α ex corr. (ι?) 10 ϊ, ϊζ pap. 11 ϊβ pap. 18 Βίκτορος 19 ϊερημιας pap. 20 ϋ pap. 21 Σαραπίων 22 Πινουτίωνος

Folio 20 recto (= Page 40)

† Pharmouthi 24. Page 40.

Ape Apalo	3 ¼ car.	3,000 tal.
Elias son of Kollouthos	1 ½ car.	1,400 tal.
Wife of Anouphis son of Iakybis	6 car.	5,600 tal.
Koui Snob	6 car.	5,600 tal.
Ieremias qes	9 car.	8,500 tal.
Heirs of Theophilos	1 sol.	17,000 tal.
Anouphis son of Minos	1 ½ car.	1,400 tal.
The Holy Church	1 sol.	17,000 tal.
Likewise	10 sol.	170,000 tal.
Georgios son of Taurinos	12 car.	11,200 tal.
Parakote	7 ¼ car.	6,800 tal.
Patsalamana	6 ½ car.	6,100 tal.
Koui Nou	2 car.	1,900 tal.
Daughter of Phanoub	1 ½ car.	1,400 tal.
Phibis son of Iosephis	9 car.	8,500 tal.
Heirs of the deacon	4 car.	3,700 tal.
Maria daughter of Victor	5 car.	4,600 tal.
Ieremias heir of Elias	3 sol.	51,000 tal.
Panejnou	½ car.	400 tal.
Sarapion son of Iakybis	6 car.	5,600 tal.
Phoibammon son of Pinoution	1 car.	900 tal.
Phibis son of Toose	6 car.	5,600 tal.
Heirs of Elias	23 ½ car.	22,100 tal.
Anouphis son of Minos	2 car.	1,900 tal.

361,200 tal.

Folio 20 verso

† β` εἴσπραξ(ις) (ὑπὲρ) μερ(ισμοῦ) δεκ(άτης) ἰνδ(ικτίωνος) Παχ(ὼν) κ
ο(ὕτως)

Πε . ε ἀρτοκ(όπος)	κ(εράτια) αd	(τάλαντα) Ασ
Μαρίας Παλικοῦ	κ(εράτια) αLd	(τάλαντα) Αχ
Βίκτωρ τέκ(των)	κ(εράτια) βL	(τάλαντα) Βτ
Σάννα Παμίδου	κ(εράτια) γ	(τάλαντα) Βω
Γεώρ(γιος) Μαθείας	κ(εράτια) γ	(τάλαντα) Βω
Καπαι	κ(εράτιον) α	(τάλαντα) ϡ
Παπνοῦθ(ις) Κλεμ( )	κ(ερατίου) L	(τάλαντα) υ
Ἰ̣σ̣ὰκ χωλός	κ(εράτια) β	(τάλαντα) Αϡ
Ἀτρῆτος Ὑπερεχ(ίου)	κ(εράτια) εL	(τάλαντα) Ερ
Φῖβις Λουσία	κ(εράτια) αL	(τάλαντα) Αυ
Εὖς Ἰωάννου	κ(ερατίου) Ld	(τάλαντα) ψ
Τατιανὸς Ἠλίας	κ(εράτια) λϛ	(ταλάντων) (μυριάδες) γ Δ
Ἀπορ	κ(εράτια) β	(τάλαντα) Αϡ
Πκῦλ(ις) Πέτρ(ου)	κ(εράτια) ια	(ταλάντων) (μυριὰς) α΄΄ σ
Μονίου Πακοῦ	κ(εράτια) ιη	(ταλάντων) (μυριὰς) α Ζ
Ἰερημίας Ἠλ{ηλ}ίου	κ(εράτια) ιη	(ταλάντων) (μυριὰς) α Ζ
Ἠ̣λ̣ίας̣ Κελελε̣	κ(εράτια) ιϛ	(ταλάντων) (μυριὰς) α Ε
Ἰωάννης Λ̣εῦ̣τ̣[ος]	κ(εράτια) βd	(τάλαντα) Βρ
Ἀνοῦφ(ις) Παμ̣ί̣[δο]υ̣	[κ(εράτια) ϛd]	(τάλαντα) Εω
Ἰσάκ(ις) κλ(ηρονόμος) Ἠλίου	[κ(εράτια) αd]	(τάλαντα) Ασ
Φοι(βάμμων) Πινουτ(ίωνος)	[κ(εράτια) εL]	(τάλαντα) Ερ
Ἰσάκ(ις) κλ(ηρονόμος) Ἠλίου	[κ(εράτια) ιαL?]	(ταλάντων) (μυριὰς) α ϡ
Βίκτωρ Γερμ(ι⌧ου)	κ(εράτια) [εLd]	(τάλαντα) Ευ
Σερῆν(ος) καὶ Σενικ(ίον)	κ(εράτια) λϛ	(ταλάντων) (μυριάδες) γ Δ
Ἰακ(ῦβις) χαλ(κεύς)	κ(εράτια) δ̣	(τάλαντα) Γψ
Φῖβις Π⌧α⌧	κ(εράτια) δ	(τάλαντα) Γψ
Πέτρ(ος) Ἠλίας	κ(εράτια) ιζ	(ταλάντων) (μυριὰς) [α Εϡ]
τῆς ἁγίας ἐκλ(ησίας)	{κ(εράτια)} νο(μισμάτια) γ	(ταλάντων) (μυριάδες) ε Α
Κουι Συοβ	κ(εράτια) θ	(τάλαντα) [Η]φ
γυν(ὴ) Ἀνουφ(ίου) Ἰακ(υβίου)	κ(εράτια) ϛ	(τάλαντα) Ε̣χ

(ταλάντων) (μυριάδες) κ̣[ϛ Θρ]

7 καπαϊ pap. 8 ϋ pap. 11 Αϋ pap. 15 ϊα pap. 16, 17 ϊη pap. 18 ϊϛ pap. 23 ϊσακ/ pap. 24 Εϋ pap. 26, 31 ϊακ/ pap. 28 Ἠλίου 29 ἐκκλ(ησίας)

Folio 20 verso

† 2nd collection for merismos of the 10th indiction, Pachon 20.
As follows:

Pe . e, baker	1 ¼ car.	1,200 tal.
Maria daughter of Palikous	1 ¾ car.	1,600 tal.
Victor, carpenter	2 ½ car.	2,300 tal.
Sanna daughter of Pamides	3 car.	2,800 tal.
Georgios son of Mathias	3 car.	2,800 tal.
Kapai	1 car.	900 tal.
Papnouthis son of Klem( )	½ car.	400 tal.
Isak the lame	2 car.	1,900 tal.
Hatres son of Hyperechios	5 ½ car.	5,100 tal.
Phibis son of Lousia	1 ½ car.	1,400 tal.
Eus daughter of Ioannes	¾ car.	700 tal.
Tatianos son of Elias	36 car.	34,000 tal.
Apor	2 car.	1,900 tal.
Pkylis son of Petros	11 car.	10,200 tal.
Monis son of Pakous	18 car.	17,000 tal.
Ieremias son of Elias	18 car.	17,000 tal.
Elias son of Kelele	16 car.	15,000 tal.
Ioannes son of Leus	2 ¼ car.	2,100 tal.
Anouphis son of Pamides	[6 ¼ car.]	5,800 tal.
Isakis heir of Elias	[1 ¼ car.]	1,200 tal.
Phoibammon son of Pinoution	[5 ½ car.]	5,100 tal.
Isakis heir of Elias	[11 ½ car.?]	10,900 tal.
Victor son of Germijou	[5 ¾] car.	5,400 tal.
Serenos and Senecio	36 car.	34,000 tal.
Iakybis, smith	4 car.	3,700 tal.
Phibis son of Pjaj	4 car.	3,700 tal.
Petros son of Elias	17 car.	1[5,900] tal.
The Holy Church	3 {car.} sol.	51,000 tal.
Koui Snob	9 car.	[8],500 tal.
Wife of Anouphis son of Iakybis	6 car.	5,600 tal.
	2[69,100 tal.]	

Folio 21 recto

Plate 3

† λόγ(ος) κώμ(ης) Τεμσευ Σκώρ(δων)
δεκάτης ἰνδ(ικτίωνος)
οὕ(τως)
(ὑπὲρ) τοῦ πάκτου
νο(μισμάτια) τνδ εὔσ(ταθμα) ἀπὸ (ταλάντων) (μυριάδων) β Ε
ὁμοί(ως) (ὑπὲρ) ταπάν(ης) τοῦ βοηθ(οῦ)
(ταλάντων) (μυριάδες) ιη//
γί(νονται) (ταλάντων) (μυριάδες) ϡγ
ἀφ᾽ (ὧν) δ(ιὰ) πρώτ(ης) εἰσπράξ(εως)
(ταλάντων) (μυριάδας) ψπϛ Βσ

2 ϊνδ/ pap. 4 π of πάκτου ex corr. 6 δαπάν(ης); βοηθοῦ, η ex υ 7 ϊη// pap. 8 γί(νονται): γ//ι/ pap.

Folio 21 verso

† Θὼθ ἀπόδοσι(ς) ἰνδ(ικτίωνος) ι
Ἰωάνν(ου) πραγμ(ατευτοῦ)

δ(ιὰ) κοιν(οῦ) τῆς κώμ(ης) νο(μισμάτια) οβ Ἀλεξ(ανδρείας)
[[ὁμοί(ως) (ὑπὲρ) παραλ(ληλισμοῦ)]]
Φῖβις Τοοσε (ὑπὲρ) παραλ(ληλισμοῦ) νο(μισμάτια) γ
Μηνᾶ μάγυρ(ος) (ὑπὲρ) τοῦ αὐτοῦ νο(μισμάτιον) α

1 ϊνδ/ pap. 6 μάγειρ(ος), (ὑπὲρ) ex corr. (τοῦ?)

[Folio 22 recto is blank]

Folio 21 recto

† Account of the village of Temseu Skordon,
of the tenth indiction,
as follows:
For the *pakton*
354 sol. of full weight, at a rate of 25,000 tal.
Likewise for the expense of the assistant
180,000 tal.
Total, 9,030,000 tal.
From which through the first collection
7,862,200 tal.

Folio 21 verso

† Thoth, payment for indiction 10
of Ioannes the pragmateutes.

Through the corporation of the village, 72 Alexandrian solidi
[[likewise for *parallelismos*]]
Phibis son of Toose, for *parallelismos*, 3 sol.
Menas, meat-cook, for the same, 1 sol.

[Folio 22 recto is blank]

Folio 22 verso

† κατὰ σελ(ίδα) τόπ(ου) Δημέου μερ(ισμοῦ) δεκάτης ἰνδ(ικτίωνος)
(2 hand) ———————
α σελ(ὶς) (ταλάντων) (μυριάδες) ιγ Βψ
β σελ(ὶς) (ταλάντων) (μυριάδες) ι// Θχ
γ σελ(ὶς) (ταλάντων) (μυριάδες) η Ζυ
δ σελ(ὶς) (ταλάντων) (μυριάδες) ε Ζφ
ε σελ(ὶς) (ταλάντων) (μυριάδες) θ Ασ
ϛ σελ(ὶς) (ταλάντων) (μυριάδες) γ Ηφ

(ταλάντων) (μυριάδες) να ϛⲗ

(3.5 cm blank)

πλ(έον) κ(εράτια) λϛ
[νο(μισμάτια)?] τιδ κ(εράτια) ιαL
νο(μισμάτια) ια κ(εράτια) καL
. . .ς τκϛ κ(εράτια) [[. .]]
traces
traces λο
traces τκϛ
[[λόγ(ος) . . . . ἀφ' (ὧν)
ἀπόδοσ(ις) κερ(ατισμοῦ) νο(μισμάτια) λϛ κ(εράτια) ιβ ζυ(γῷ) τῆς κώμης
ὁμο(ίως) ἐν χρ(υσῷ) νο(μισμάτιον) α . . . .
λόγ(ος) τῶν κτητόρ(ων) ἐν χρυσ(ῷ)
Σερῆνος Κωσταντ(ίνου) κ(εράτια) αL ἀκρ( )
Ἰσάκ(ις) κλ(ηρονόμος) Ἠλίας [
Ἐνῶχ οἰκονόμ(ος) νο(μισμάτιον) α κ(εράτια) ϛ ἀγρ( )
Τατιανὸς Ἠλίας νο(μισμάτιον) α ἀγρ( )]]

(faint traces of 5 more lines)

1 δημεō pap. 3 ϊ pap. 4 Ζϋ pap. 10 ϊαL pap. 17 ϊβ pap. 20 ἀγρ( ) ?

Folio 22 verso

† Page-by-page (totals) for Topos Demeou for the merismos of the tenth indiction

Page 1, 132,700 tal.
Page 2, 109,600 tal.
Page 3, 87,400 tal.
Page 4, 57,500 tal.
Page 5, 91,200 tal.
Page 6, 38,500 tal.

516,900 tal.

(3.5 cm blank)

balance, 36 car.
314 sol., 11 ½ car.
11 sol. 21 ½ car.
. . . 326 (car.) [[. .]
traces
traces
traces
[[Account . . . from which
Payment of keratismos, 36 sol. 12 car. by the village (weight) standard
Likewise in gold, 1 sol. . . .
Account of the landowners, in gold
Serenos son of Konstantinos, 1 ½ car. unr. (?)
Isakis, heir of Elias [
Enoch, oikonomos, 1 sol. 6 car. unr.
Tatianos son of Elias, 1 sol. . . . unr.]]

(faint traces of 5 more lines)

Folio 23 recto Plate 4

Column i

† λόγ(ος) κατὰ σελ(ίδα) μερ(ισμοῦ) δεκάτης ἰνδ(ικτίωνος)

α σελ(ὶς)	(ταλάντων) (μυριάδες) λθ Ζσ
β σελ(ὶς)	(ταλάντων) (μυριάδες) ιζ Θϡ
γ σελ(ὶς)	(ταλάντων) (μυριάδες) η Εσ
δ σελ(ὶς)	(ταλάντων) (μυριάδες) ιγ Ϛσ
ε σελ(ὶς)	(ταλάντων) (μυριάδες) λε Δϡ
ς σελ(ὶς)	(ταλάντων) (μυριάδες) ς Βω
ζ σελ(ὶς)	(ταλάντων) (μυριάδες) κα Ϛφ
η σελ(ὶς)	(ταλάντων) (μυριάδες) ιγ Α
θ σελ(ὶς)	(ταλάντων) (μυριάδες) η// [[ω]] ϡ
ι σελ(ὶς)	(ταλάντων) (μυριάδες) ις Ασ
ια σελ(ὶς)	(ταλάντων) (μυριάδες) λβ Θυ
ιβ σελ(ὶς)	(ταλάντων) (μυριάδες) ιε Ηψ
ιγ σελ(ὶς)	(ταλάντων) (μυριάδες) ιθ Β
ιδ σελ(ὶς)	(ταλάντων) (μυριάδες) κε Βχ
ιε σελ(ὶς)	(ταλάντων) (μυριάδες) ιβ Γυ
ις σελ(ὶς)	(ταλάντων) (μυριάδες) κζ Ερ
ιζ σελ(ὶς)	(ταλάντων) (μυριάδες) ια Εχ
ιη σελ(ὶς)	(ταλάντων) (μυριάδες) ιβ Θσ
ιθ σελ(ὶς)	(ταλάντων) (μυριάδες) κη Θρ
κ σελ(ὶς)	(ταλάντων) (μυριάδες) ι // Γσ
κα σελ(ὶς)	(ταλάντων) (μυριάδες) ζ Ζυ
κβ σελ(ὶς)	(ταλάντων) (μυριάδες) κζ Γχ
κγ σελ(ὶς)	(ταλάντων) (μυριάδες) ιδ τ
κδ σελ(ὶς)	(ταλάντων) (μυριάδες) ιθ Ϛυ
κε σελ(ὶς)	(ταλάντων) (μυριάδες) η// ω
κς σελ(ὶς)	(ταλάντων) (μυριάδες) κα Θυ
κζ σελ(ὶς)	(ταλάντων) (μυριάδες) η Β[ψ]
κη σελ(ὶς)	(ταλάντων) (μυριάδες) θ Ατ
κθ σελ(ὶς)	(ταλάντων) (μυριάδες) ιη Ϛ
λ σελ(ὶς)	(ταλάντων) (μυριάδες) λδ Ηφ
λα σελ(ὶς)	(ταλάντων) (μυριάδες) ις Γϡ
λβ σελ(ὶς)	(ταλάντων) (μυριάδες) ια Εσ
λγ σελ(ὶς)	(ταλάντων) (μυριάδες) δ Ηχ

Folio 23 recto

Column i

† Page-by-page account of the merismos of the tenth indiction.

Page 1	397,200 tal.
Page 2	179,900 tal.
Page 3	85,200 tal.
Page 4	136,200 tal.
Page 5	354,900 tal.
Page 6	62,800 tal.
Page 7	216,500 tal.
Page 8	131,000 tal.
Page 9	80,900 tal.
Page 10	161,200 tal.
Page 11	329,400 tal.
Page 12	158,700 tal.
Page 13	192,000 tal.
Page 14	252,600 tal.
Page 15	123,400 tal.
Page 16	275,100 tal.
Page 17	115,600 tal.
Page 18	129,200 tal.
Page 19	289,100 tal.
Page 20	103,200 tal.
Page 21	77,400 tal.
Page 22	273,600 tal.
Page 23	140,300 tal.
Page 24	196,400 tal.
Page 25	80,800 tal.
Page 26	219,400 tal.
Page 27	82,[700] tal.
Page 28	91,300 tal.
Page 29	186,000 tal.
Page 30	348,500 tal.
Page 31	163,900 tal.
Page 32	115,200 tal.
Page 33	48,600 tal.

Folio 23 recto

Column ii

λδ σελ(ὶς) (ταλάντων) (μυριάδες) ζ Δυ
λε σελ(ὶς) (ταλάντων) (μυριάδες) ιγ Αϡ
λς σελ(ὶς) (ταλάντων) (μυριάδες) ιε// υ
λζ σελ(ὶς) (ταλάντων) (μυριάδες) λε Δσ
λη σελ(ὶς) (ταλάντων) (μυριάδες) κς Αυ
λθ σελ(ὶς) (ταλάντων) (μυριάδες) κα Γϡ
μ σελ(ὶς) (ταλάντων) (μυριάδες) λς Ασ
δ(ιὰ) εἰσπράξ(εως) τῆς
κώμ(ης) (ταλάντων) (μυριάδες) ψλδ Ετ
καὶ (ὑπὲρ) τόπ(ου) Δημέου
(ταλάντων) (μυριάδες) να Ϛϡ
ὁ(μοῦ) (μυριάδες) ψπς Βσ

(At lower right, rubbed out traces of writing apparently from another document)

ϡγ
ἀφ᾽ (ὧν) ωδ δκ( ) . .
λο( ) (ταλάντων) (μυριάδες) ϡξη
].[
νο(μισμάτια) μ κ(εράτια) αL
νο(μισμάτια) πη κ(εράτια) θL

3 ϡ corrected (to υ?)? Cf. note to 1r.30. 10 ω crossed out; ϡ very faint 12 Θϋ pap. 13 ψ ex χ? 16 Γϋ pap.; υ ex φ? see 7v.32n. 21 (μυρ.) ϊ pap. 25 Ϛϋ pap. 27 Θϋ pap. 33 Εσ, σ ex τ, overwritten 35 Δϋ pap. 36 ϊγ pap. 37 ϊε pap. 39 Αϋ pap.

[Folio 23 verso is blank]

Folio 23 recto

Column ii

Page 34	74,400 tal.
Page 35	131,900 tal.
Page 36	150,400 tal.
Page 37	354,200 tal.
Page 38	261,400 tal.
Page 39	213,900 tal.
Page 40	361,200 tal.

Through collection of the
village, 7,345,300 tal.
And for Topos Demeou
516,900 tal.
Altogether, 7,862,200 tal.

(At lower right, rubbed out traces of writing apparently from another document)

903
From which 804, . . .
(Account?) . . . 9,680,000 tal.
traces
40 sol., 1 ½ car.
88 sol., 9 ½ car.

[Folio 23 verso is blank]

Folio 24 recto (Folio 24 verso blank)

† λόγ(ος) μικρ(οῦ) λόγ(ου) κώμ(ης) Τεμσευ Σκόρ(δων) δεκάτης [ἰνδ(ικτίωνος)]

μερ(ισμοῦ) Μεχεὶρ κβ
Κουι Σνοβ ὑ(πὲρ) τιμ(ῆς) οἴν(ου) κ(εράτια) β (τάλαντα) Αϡ
Ἐνῶχ γναφεὺς δ(ιὰ) Κύρα `Ἰωσηφ(ίου)´ κ(εράτια) γ (τάλαντα) Βω
Σαραπίον Ἰακυβίου κ(εράτια) δ (τάλαντα) Γψ
Ἰωσῆφ(ις) Ὥρου δ(ιὰ) Τατιαν(οῦ) κ(εράτια) β (τάλαντα) Αω
ΠανηϪνου κ(εράτιον) α (τάλαντα) ϡ
Γεώρ(γιος) Ταυ(ρίνου) κ(εράτια) γ (τάλαντα) Βω
Ἰωάννης Παργατης κ(εράτιον) α (τάλαντα) ϡ
Ψᾶτος Κόμες κ(εράτια) β (τάλαντα) Αω
Ἰσάκ(ις) Ἡλίας νο(μισμάτιον) α π(αρὰ) L (ταλάντων) (μυριὰς) α ϛφ
[[Ἰωσῆφ(ις) Ὥρ̣[ο]υ̣ ὁμοί(ως) κ(εράτιον) α (τάλαντα) *vac*]]
Μ̣ονίου Ἑρμ̣α̣πόλ(λωνος) κ(εράτια) γ (τάλαντα) Βω
Ἀντωνίου Ὠ̣φελ(ίου) κ(εράτιον) α (τάλαντα) ϡ δ(ιὰ) Ἐνῶχ οἰκ(ονόμου)
Μηνᾶ μάγυ(ρος) κ(εράτια) η (τάλαντα) Ζσ
τῶν σκυτ(έων) δ(ιὰ) Παπνουθ(ίου) κ(εράτια) βL (τάλαντα) Βτ
Ἰερημίας Ἡλίας νο(μισμάτιον) α (ταλάντων) (μυριὰς) α Ζ
ΤϪεερ κ(εράτιον) α (τάλαντα) ϡ
Σαραπίον Ἰακ(υβίου) κ(εράτια) αL (τάλαντα) Αυ
`Φαμ(ενὼθ) ιζ´
Μηνᾶ μάγυρ(ος) κ(εράτιον) α (τάλαντα) ϡ
Μονίου Ἑρμαπ(όλλωνος) κ(εράτια) β (τάλαντα) Αϡ
Μονίου Κόμες κ(εράτιον) α (τάλαντα) ϡ
Γεώρ(γιος) μάγυρ(ος) κ(εράτια) γ (τάλαντα) Βω
Τατιαν(ὸς) Παρβας δ(ιὰ) Πα̣ύ̣λ(ου) καθ(αρουργοῦ) κ(εράτια) β (τάλαντα) Αϡ
Ἐνῶχ οἰκον(όμος) κ(εράτια) ϛ (τάλαντα) Εχ
Ἀνοῦφ(ις) ἀπὸ Τβακη (ὑπὲρ) Ἰωάν(νου) κ(ερατίου) <L> (τάλαντα) υ
Ἰσακίου Ἡλίας νο(μισμάτιον) α (ταλάντων) (μυριὰς) α Δ
Σολομ(ῶν) Φιβίου δ(ιὰ) Μονίου πρ(ωτοκωμήτου) κ(ερατίου) L (τάλαντα) υ
Τατιαν(ὸς) Παρβας δ(ιὰ) Παύλου καθαρ(ουργοῦ) κ(εράτιον) α (τάλαντα) ϡ
Ἀπολ(λῶς) ϭες κ(εράτια) γd (τάλαντα) Γ
Μονίου Κόμες κ(εράτιον) α (τάλαντα) ϡ ἀγρ( )
Γεώρ(γιος) Φιβίου (ὑπὲρ) τιμ(ῆς) τυρ̣(οῦ) κ(εράτια) βL (τάλαντα) Βτ
τῶν σκυτ(έων) κ(εράτια) ϛL (τάλαντα) ϛ
<(ταλάντων) (μυριάδες)> ι/ Ζφ

2 κουϊ pap. 4, 18 Σαραπίων 5 ϊωσηφ/ pap., κ(ερ.) β, β ex γ? 8 ϊωαννης pap. 10 ϊσακ/ pap. 11 ϊωσηφ/ pap. 14, 19, 22 μάγει(ρος) 16 ϊερημιας pap.; (μυρ.) ex α 18 Αϋ pap. 27 ϋ pap. 33 ϊ pap.

Folio 24 recto (Folio 24 verso blank)

† Account of the Small Account of the village of Temseu Skordon for the tenth indiction.

Merismos of Mecheir 22.

Koui Snob for price of wine 2 car. 1,900 tal.
Enoch, fuller, through Kyra daughter of Iosephis 3 car. 2,800 tal.
4 Sarapion son of Iakybis 4 car. 3,700 tal.
Iosephis son of Horos, through Tatianos 2 car. 1,800 tal.
Panejnou 1 car. 900 tal.
Georgios son of Taurinos 3 car. 2,800 tal.
8 Ioannes son of Pargates 1 car. 900 tal.
Psas son of Komes 2 car. 1,800 tal.
Isakis son of Elias 1 sol. minus ½ 16,500 tal.
[[Iosephis son of Horos, likewise 1 car. *vac* tal.]]
12 Monis son of Hermapollon 3 car. 2,800 tal.
Antonios son of Ophelios 1 car. 900 tal. through Enoch, oikonomos
Menas, meat-cook 8 car. 7,200 tal.
The cobblers through Papnouthis 2 ½ car. 2,300 tal.
16 Ieremias son of Elias 1 sol. 17,000 tal.
Tjeer 1 car. 900 tal.
Sarapion son of Iakybis 1 ½ car. 1,400 tal.
Phamenoth 17 (inserted)
Menas, meat-cook 1 car. 900 tal.
20 Monis son of Hermapollon 2 car. 1,900 tal.
Monis son of Komes 1 car. 900 tal.
Georgios, meat-cook 3 car. 2,800 tal.
Tatianos son of Parbas, through Paulos, baker 2 car. 1,900 tal.
24 Enoch, oikonomos 6 car. 5,600 tal.
Anouphis from Tbake for Ioannes <½> car. 400 tal.
Isakis son of Elias 1 sol. 14,000 tal.
Solomon son of Phibis, through Monis protokometes ½ car. 400 tal.
28 Tatianos son of Parbas, through Paulos, baker 1 car. 900 tal.
Apollos qes 3 ¼ car. 3,000 tal.
Monis son of Komes 1 car. 900 tal. unr.
Georgios son of Phibis, for price of cheese 2 ½ car. 2,300 tal.
32 The cobblers 6 ½ car. 6,000 tal.

107,500 <tal.>

Folio 25 recto

† Φαρμ(οῦθι) κδ ϛ σελ(ίς)

Περουϣ	κ(εράτια) ηL	(τάλαντα) Η
Ἐνῶχ Πετηνηου	κ(εράτια) ϛ	(τάλαντα) Εχ
Ἠλίας Πεϣοι Ἰων(ίου)	κ(εράτια) γ	(τάλαντα) Βω
Καβίου	κ(εράτια) ηL	(τάλαντα) Η
Κουι Σον	κ(εράτια) β	(τάλαντα) Αϡ
Φοι(βάμμων) Πιον	κ(ερατίου) Ld	(τάλαντα) ψ
Ἰερημίας Ἰερ(ημίου)	κ(εράτια) γ	(τάλαντα) Βω
κοιν(ὸν) ἐποικ(ίου)	κ(εράτια) θd	(τάλαντα) Ηψ

(ταλάντων) (μυριάδες) γ Ηφ

4 πεϣοϊ, ϊων (without abbreviation mark) pap. 6 κουϊ pap. 8 ϊερημιας ϊερ/ pap.
9 Numerals in Cols. 2 and 3 written over washed-out text

Folio 25 recto

	† Pharmouthi 24.	Page 6.	
	Peroush	8 ½ car.	8,000 tal.
	Enoch son of Peteneou	6 car.	5,600 tal.
4	Elias son of Peshoi, grandson of Ionios	3 car.	2,800 tal.
	Kabios	8 ½ car.	8,000 tal.
	Koui Son	2 car.	1,900 tal.
	Phoibammon son of Pion	¾ car.	700 tal.
8	Ieremias son of Ieremias	3 car.	2,800 tal.
	Corporation of the epoikion	9 ¼ car.	8,700 tal.
		38,500 tal.	

Folio 25 verso

† Μεχεὶρ κβ νο(μισμάτια) β τόπ(ου) Δημέου

κλ(ηρονόμοι) Παμίδου	κ(εράτια) ιβ	(ταλάντων) (μυριὰς) α Ασ
Ἡλίας Πισοι	κ(εράτια) ϛ	(τάλαντα) Εχ
Ἀνοῦφ(ις) Παμίδ(ου)	κ(εράτια) ϛ	(τάλαντα) Εχ
Ἡλίας Ἰωνίου	κ(εράτια) ϛ	(τάλαντα) Εχ
Ἐνῶχ Ὥρου	κ(εράτια) ϛ	(τάλαντα) Εχ
ὁμοί(ως) νο(μισμάτιον) α Φαμεν(ὼθ) ιβ		
Παῦλ(ος) Πέτρ(ου)	κ(εράτια) δ	(τάλαντα) Γψ
Μίνου Ἡλίας	κ(εράτια) δ	(τάλαντα) Γψ
Κυριακ(ὸς) Ϣνητ	κ(εράτια) β	(τάλαντα) Αϡ
Μηνᾶ Ἰωάννου	κ(εράτιον) α	(τάλαντα) ϡ
Ζαχαρίας	κ(εράτιον) α	(τάλαντα) ϡ
Πκῦλ(ις) Βίκτωρ	κ(εράτιον) α	(τάλαντα) ϡ
[[Σαρ]] Ἀπίων Πέτρ(ου)	κ(εράτιον) α	(τάλαντα) ϡ
Μίνου Κύρα	κ(εράτιον) α	(τάλαντα) ϡ
Γεώρ(γιος) Πέτρ(ου)	κ(εράτιον) α	(τάλαντα) ϡ
Εὖς Ὥρου	κ(εράτιον) α	(τάλαντα) ϡ
Πέτρ(ος) Φιβίου	κ(εράτιον) α	(τάλαντα) ϡ
Φαρμ(οῦθι) κδ		
Ἐνῶχ Ὥρου	κ(εράτια) βLd	(τάλαντα) Βφ
Φοι(βάμμων) Πιον	κ(εράτια) εd	(τάλαντα) Δϡ
Εὖς Ὥρου	κ(εράτια) βL	(τάλαντα) Βτ
γυν(ὴ) ΠερϪουϢ	κ(εράτια) βd	(τάλαντα) Βρ
Παχαον	κ(εράτια) βd	(τάλαντα) Βρ
Ἀπίον Πέτρ(ου)	κ(εράτια) δL	(τάλαντα) Δσ
Παῦλ(ος) Πέτρ(ου)	κ(εράτια) ιd	(τάλαντα) Θχ
Πκῦλ(ις) Βίκτωρ	κ(εράτια) β	(τάλαντα) Αϡ
Γεώρ(γιος) Πέτρ(ου)	κ(εράτια) β	(τάλαντα) Αϡ
Ἰωάνν(ης) ΠαϪεερ	κ(εράτια) αd	(τάλαντα) Ασ
Ἀνοῦφ(ις) Παμίτου	κ(εράτια) γ	(τάλαντα) Βω
Ζαχαρ(ίας)	κ(εράτια) ϛ	(τάλαντα) Εχ
(ταλάντων) (μυριάδες) θ Ασ		

2 ϊβ pap. 3 πισοϊ pap. 5 ϊωνιου pap. 7 φαμεν̄ pap. 11 ϊωαννο$^{\upsilon}$ pap. 13 Βίκτορος 17, 22 Εὖς ex corr. (υ ex τ in 17?) 25 Ἀπίων 29 ϊωαννS pap.

Folio 25 verso

† Mecheir 22, 2 sol. for Topos Demeou.

Heirs of Pamides	12 car.	11,200 tal.
Elias son of Pisoi	6 car.	5,600 tal.
Anouphis son of Pamides	6 car.	5,600 tal.
Elias son of Ionios	6 car.	5,600 tal.
Enoch son of Horos	6 car.	5,600 tal.
Likewise, 1 sol., Phamenoth 12		
Paulos son of Petros	4 car.	3,700 tal.
Minos son of Elias	4 car.	3,700 tal.
Kyriakos son of Shnet	2 car.	1,900 tal.
Menas son of Ioannes	1 car.	900 tal.
Zacharias	1 car.	900 tal.
Pkylis son of Victor	1 car.	900 tal.
Apion son of Petros	1 car.	900 tal.
Minos son of Kyra	1 car.	900 tal.
Georgios son of Petros	1 car.	900 tal.
Eus daughter of Horos	1 car.	900 tal.
Petros son of Phibis	1 car.	900 tal.
Pharmouthi 24		
Enoch son of Horos	2 ¾ car.	2,500 tal.
Phoibammon son of Pion	5 ¼ car.	4,900 tal.
Eus daughter of Horos	2 ½ car.	2,300 tal.
Wife of Perjoush	2 ¼ car.	2,100 tal.
Pachaon	2 ¼ car.	2,100 tal.
Apion son of Petros	4 ½ car.	4,200 tal.
Paulos son of Petros	10 ¼ car.	9,600 tal.
Pkylis son of Victor	2 car.	1,900 tal.
Georgios son of Petros	2 car.	1,900 tal.
Ioannes son of Pajeer	1 ¼ car.	1,200 tal.
Anouphis son of Pamides	3 car.	2,800 tal.
Zacharias	6 car.	5,600 tal.
91,200 tal.		

Folio 26 recto

† Τῦβ̣(ι) ιε	δ̣ σ̣ε̣λ̣(ίς)	
Κυριακὸς Ϣνητ	κ̣(εράτια) β	(τάλαντα) Αω
Πουρουϣ	[κ(εράτιον) α]	(τάλαντα) ϡ
Κωντα	[κ(εράτιον) α]	(τάλαντα) ϡ
Πετηνηου	κ̣(εράτιον) α	(τάλαντα) ϡ
Γεώρ(γιος) Πέτρ(ου)	κ̣(εράτιον) α	(τάλαντα) ϡ
Πκῦλ(ις) ἀρτοκ(όπος)	κ̣(εράτιον) α̣	(τάλαντα) ϡ
Μίνος Κύρα	κ̣(εράτιον) α̣	(τάλαντα) ϡ
	Μεχεὶρ δ νο(μισμάτια) γ	
	ἀφ' (ὧν) ο(ὕτως)	
Ἀτρῆτος Παματη	κ(εράτια) β	(τάλαντα) Αϡ
Ἀτρῆτος κεφαλα(ιωτοῦ)	κ(εράτια) γ	(τάλαντα) Βω
Μηνᾶς Πεσχαλ	κ(εράτια) αL	(τάλαντα) Αυ
Ἐνῶχ Πετινίου	κ(εράτιον) α	(τάλαντα) ϡ
Κυριακ(ὸς) Ϣινητου	κ(εράτια) β	(τάλαντα) Αϡ
Περουϣ	κ(εράτια) αL	(τάλαντα) Αυ
γυν(ὴ) Περϭουϣ	κ(εράτιον) α	(τάλαντα) ϡ
Ταυρίνου Παμίτου	κ(εράτια) ιε	(ταλάντων) (μυριὰς) α Δ
Ἀνοῦφ(ις) Παμίτου	κ(εράτια) ζL	(τάλαντα) Ζ
Μίνος Κύρα	κ(εράτια) αL	(τάλαντα) Αυ
Ἠλίας Ἰωνίου	κ(εράτια) δL	(τάλαντα) Δσ
Πεϣοει Ἰωνίου	κ(εράτια) βL	(τάλαντα) Βτ
Ἀπίωνος Πέτρου	κ(εράτιον) α	(τάλαντα) ϡ
Γεώργιος Πέτρου	κ(εράτιον) α	(τάλαντα) ϡ
Πκῦλις Βίκτορος	κ(εράτια) αL	(τάλαντα) Αυ
Μίνος Καβίου	κ(εράτια) γ	(τάλαντα) Βω
Ἐνῶχ Ὥρου	κ(εράτια) δL	(τάλαντα) Δσ
	(ταλάντων) (μυριάδες) ε Ζφ	

13, 16, 20, 25 Αϋ pap. 22 ϊωνιου\ pap. 27 Δσ, σ ex ρ

Folio 26 recto

† Tybi 15. Page 4.

Kyriakos son of Shnet	2 car.	1,800 tal.
Pouroush	[1 car.]	900 tal.
Konta	[1 car.]	900 tal.
Peteneou	1 car.	900 tal.
Georgios son of Petros	1 car.	900 tal.
Pkylis, baker	1 car.	900 tal.
Minos son of Kyra	1 car.	900 tal.

Mecheir 4, 3 sol.
From which, as follows:

Hatres son of Pamates	2 car.	1,900 tal.
Hatres, kephalaiotes	3 car.	2,800 tal.
Menas son of Peschal	1 ½ car.	1,400 tal.
Enoch son of Petinios	1 car.	900 tal.
Kyriakos son of Shinetos	2 car.	1,900 tal.
Peroush	1 ½ car.	1,400 tal.
Wife of Perqoush	1 car.	900 tal.
Taurinos son of Pamites	15 car.	14,000 tal.
Anouphis son of Pamites	7 ½ car.	7,000 tal.
Minos son of Kyra	1 ½ car.	1,400 tal.
Elias son of Ionios	4 ½ car.	4,200 tal.
Peshoei son of Ionios	2 ½ car.	2,300 tal.
Apion son of Petros	1 car.	900 tal.
Georgios son of Petros	1 car.	900 tal.
Pkylis son of Victor	1 ½ car.	1,400 tal.
Minos son of Kabios	3 car.	2,800 tal.
Enoch son of Horos	4 ½ car.	4,200 tal.

57,500 tal.

Folio 26 verso

Μίνος Ἐνῶχ	κ(εράτιον) α	(τάλαντα) ϡ
Π̣[ο]υ̣ρουϣ̣	κ(εράτια) αL	(τάλαντα) Αυ
Ἀπίων	κ(εράτιον) α	(τάλαντα) ϡ
γυν(ὴ) Περσουϣ	κ(ερατίου) L	(τάλαντα) υ
Μηνᾶ Πεσϫαλ	κ(εράτιον) α	(τάλαντα) ϡ
Κουντα Ἀπίων(ος)	κ(εράτιον) α	(τάλαντα) ϡ
Ἐνῶχ Πετηνηου	κ(εράτιον) α	(τάλαντα) ϡ
Γεώρ(γιος) Πέτρ(ου)	κ(εράτιον) α	(τάλαντα) ϡ
[Σ]α̣ρ̣α̣π̣ίων traces	κ(εράτιον) α	(τάλαντα) ϡ
________________		
________________Τῦβι ε		
. . . . .του	κ(εράτια) ιε	(ταλάντων) (μυριὰς) α Δ
Ἀ̣ν̣οῦ̣φ(ις) Παμίδου	κ(εράτια) ζL	(τάλαντα) Ζ
Ἠλ̣ίας Ἰωνίου	κ(εράτια) ϛ	(τάλαντα) Εχ
Γ̣εώ̣ρ(γιος) Μ̣αθ̣ί̣ας	κ(εράτια) ε	(τάλαντα) Δψ
. . . ος	κ(εράτια) γ	(τάλαντα) Βω
Φ̣ῖβ̣(ις) δ(ιὰ) Πέτρ(ου)	κ(εράτια) γ	(τάλαντα) Βω
Κ̣ά̣β̣ι̣ος	κ(εράτια) γ	(τάλαντα) Βω
Μ̣ί̣ν̣(ος) Τ̣[ι]μοτη	κ(εράτια) αL	(τάλαντα) Αυ
Π̣ο̣υ̣ρο̣υ̣ϣ	κ(εράτια) αL	(τάλαντα) Αυ
Μ̣η̣ν̣ᾶ̣ Πεσϫαλ	κ(εράτια) αL	(τάλαντα) Αυ
Ἐνῶχ Κυρίας (sic)	κ(εράτιον) α	(τάλαντα) ϡ
Μ̣ίνος̣ Κύρα	κ(εράτιον) α	(τάλαντα) ϡ
. . . ς Π. . . ου	κ(εράτιον) α	(τάλαντα) ϡ
[Π]κ̣ῦ̣λι̣ς ἀρτοκ(όπος)	κ(εράτια) αδη´	(τάλαντα) Ατ
Κ[υ]ρ̣ιακ̣(ὸς) Ϣνητ	κ(εράτια) β	(τάλαντα) Αω
Γεώρ(γιος) Πέτρ(ου)	κ(ερατίου) L	(τάλαντα) υ
[Π]κ̣ῦ̣λ̣(ις) Παμίδ(ου)	κ(εράτια) ιβ	(ταλάντων) (μυριὰς) α Ασ
[Ἀνοῦ]φ(ις) Παμίδ(ου)	κ(εράτια) ϛ	(τάλαντα) Εχ
. . . . .	κ(εράτια) β	(τάλαντα) Αω
[Ἱερ]ημίας Ἠλίας	κ(εράτια) δ	(τάλαντα) Γψ
. . . . .	κ(εράτια) β	(τάλαντα) Αω
Ἰ̣ερ̣η[μ]ί̣[ας]	κ(εράτια) δ	(τάλαντα) Γψ
Π	κ(εράτιον) α	(τάλαντα) ϡ
Ζαχαρίας	κ(εράτιον) α	(τάλαντα) ϡ
(in margin by line 24)	(ταλάντων) (μυριάδες) η Ζυ̣	

2 Αϋ pap. 4 ϋ pap. 11 ϊε pap.

Folio 26 verso

	Minos son of Enoch	1 car.	900 tal.
	Pouroush	1 ½ car.	1,400 tal.
	Apion	1 car.	900 tal.
4	Wife of Perqoush	½ car.	400 tal.
	Menas son of Pesjal	1 car.	900 tal.
	Kounta son of Apion	1 car.	900 tal.
	Enoch son of Peteneou	1 car.	900 tal.
8	Georgios son of Petros	1 car.	900 tal.
	Sarapion . . .	1 car.	900 tal.
		Tybi 5	
	. . . . .tou	15 car.	14,000 tal.
12	Anouphis son of Pamides	7 ½ car.	7,000 tal.
	Elias son of Ionios	6 car.	5,600 tal.
	Georgios son of Mathias	5 car.	4,700 tal.
	. . . . . os	3 car.	2,800 tal.
16	Phibis through Petros	3 car.	2,800 tal.
	Kabios	3 car.	2,800 tal.
	Minos son of Timote	1 ½ car.	1,400 tal.
	Pouroush	1 ½ car.	1,400 tal.
20	Menas son of Pesjal	1 ½ car.	1,400 tal.
	Enoch son of Kyra	1 car.	900 tal.
	Minos son of Kyra	1 car.	900 tal.
	. . .s P. .ou	1 car.	900 tal.
24	Pkylis, baker	1 3/8 car.	1,300 tal.
	Kyriakos son of Shnet	2 car.	1,800 tal.
	Georgios son of Petros	½ car.	400 tal.
	Pkylis son of Pamides	12 car.	11,200 tal.
28	Anouphis son of Pamides	6 car.	5,600 tal.
	. . . . .	2 car.	1,800 tal.
	Ieremias son of Elias	4 car.	3,700 tal.
	. . . . .	2 car.	1,800 tal.
32	Ieremias [ ]	4 car.	3,700 tal.
	P	1 car.	900 tal.
	Zacharias	1 car.	900 tal.
	(in margin by line 24)	87,400 tal.	

Folio 27 recto

† τόπ(ος) Δημέου Φαῶ[φι . .	β σελ(ίς)]	
Πεεῦτος	κ(εράτια) ι[.]	[(ταλάντων) (μυριὰς) α . .]
Μονίου	κ(εράτια) ιβ̣	[(ταλάντων) (μυριὰς) α Ασ]
Ἀνοῦφ(ις) Παμίτου	κ(εράτια) ιβ	[(ταλάντων) (μυριὰς) α Ασ]
Ἀτρῆτος κεφαλ(αιωτοῦ)	κ(εράτια) δ	[(τάλαντα) Γψ]
Μηνᾶς Πεσϫαλ	κ(εράτια) β	[(τάλαντα) Α⸓]
Ζαχαρίας	κ(εράτιον) α .	(τάλαντα) .
Ἐνῶχ Πετηνηου	κ(ερατίου) L	(τάλαντα) υ
Ἐνῶχ Ὥρου	κ(εράτια) εLd	(τάλαντα) Ευ̣
Εὖς Ὥρου	κ(εράτια) β	(τάλαντα) Α⸓
Ἠλίας Ἰωνίου	κ(εράτια) θ	(τάλαντα) Ηφ̣
Κυριακ(ὸς) Ϣενητ	κ(εράτια) βLd	(τάλαντα) Β[χ]
Καβίου	κ(εράτια) δL	(τάλαντα) Δ[σ]
Πουρουϣ	κ(εράτιον) α	(τάλαντα) ⸓
Πκῦλις Βίκ(τορος)	κ(εράτια) αL	(τάλαντα) Α[υ]
Ἀπίων Πέτρ(ου)	κ(εράτια) αd	(τάλαντα) Α[σ]
Γεώρ(γιος) Πέτρ(ου)	κ(ερατίου) Ld	(τάλαντα) ψ
Κο[υ]ι Σον	κ(εράτια) αL	(τάλαντα) Αυ
γυν(ὴ) Περόουϣ	κ(ερατίου) Ld	(τάλαντα) ψ
Πεϣοι Ἰωνίου	κ(εράτια) δLd	(τάλαντα) Δτ
Πιλᾶτος	κ(ερατίου) Ld	(τάλαντα) ψ
Πεεῦτος	κ(εράτια) ϛ	(τάλαντα) Εχ
Μονίου	κ(εράτια) ϛ	(τάλαντα) Εχ
Ἀνοῦφ(ις) Παμίτ(ου)	κ(εράτια) ϛ	(τάλαντα) Εχ
Ἠλίας Ἰωνίου	κ(εράτια) δL	(τάλαντα) Δ[σ]
Π̣εϣ̣ο̣ι Ἰων(ίου)	κ(εράτια) βL	(τάλαντα) Βτ
Κα̣[βί]ου	κ(εράτια) βL	(τάλαντα) [Βτ]
Ἀτρῆτος κεφαλ(αιωτοῦ)	κ(εράτια) β̣	(τάλαντα) [Α]⸓
Ἐνῶχ Ὥρου	κ(εράτια) δ	(τάλαντα) Γψ
Πκῦλ(ις) ἀρτοκ(όπος)	κ(εράτιον) α	(τάλαντα) ⸓
Πιλᾶτος	κ(ερατίου) L	(τάλαντα) υ
Εὖ̣ς Ὥρ̣ου	κ(εράτιον) α	(τάλαντα) ⸓
[Μ]ί[νος] Κύρα	κ(εράτιον) α	(τάλαντα) ⸓

(in margin of line 31) (ταλάντων) (μυριάδες) ι// Θχ

1 Φαῶ[φι, Φ ex corr. (θ?) 2 ϊ[pap. 4 ϊβ pap. 11 ϊωνιο\ pap. 13 L ex d 18 κουϊ pap. 19 γυν(ή), υ ex corr. 20 πεϣοϊ pap. 25 ϊωνιō pap. 26 πεϣοϊ ϊων pap. 31 ϋ pap.

Folio 27 recto

† Topos Demeou, Phao[phi . .Page 2.]

Peeus	1[.] car.	[tal.]
Monis	12 car.	[11,200 tal.]
Anouphis son of Pamites	12 car.	[11,200 tal.]
Hatres, kephalaiotes	4 car.	[3,700 tal.]
Menas son of Pesjal	2 car.	[1,900 tal.]
Zacharias	1 [+?} car.	[ ] tal.
Enoch son of Peteneou	½ car.	400 tal.
Enoch son of Horos	5 ¾ car.	5,400 tal.
Eus daughter of Horos	2 car.	1,900 tal.
Elias son of Ionios	9 car.	8,500 tal.
Kyriakos son of Shenet	2 ¾ car.	2,[600] tal.
Kabios	4 ½ car.	4,[200] tal.
Pouroush	1 car.	900 tal.
Pkylis son of Victor	1 ½ car.	1,[400] tal.
Apion son of Petros	1 ¼ car.	1,[200] tal.
Georgios son of Petros	¾ car.	700 tal.
Koui Son	1 ½ car.	1,400 tal.
Wife of Perqoush	¾ car.	700 tal.
Peshoi son of Ionios	4 ¾ car.	4,300 tal.
Pilatos	¾ car.	700 tal.

Peeus	6 car.	5,600 tal.
Monis	6 car.	5,600 tal.
Anouphis son of Pamites	6 car.	5,600 tal.
Elias son of Ionios	4 ½ car.	4,[200] tal.
Peshoi son of Ionios	2 ½ car.	2,300 tal.
Kabios	2 ½ car.	[2,300] tal.
Hatres, kephalaiotes	2 car.	[1,]900 tal.
Enoch son of Horos	4 car.	3,700 tal.
Pkylis, baker	1 car.	900 tal.
Pilatos	½ car.	400 tal.
Eus daughter of Horos	1 car.	900 tal.
[Minos] son of Kyra	1 car.	900 tal.

109,600 tal.

Folio 27 verso

[†] λόγ(ος) τόπ(ου) Δημέου
Μεσ(ορὴ) ιε ἀφ᾿ (ὧν) δ(ιὰ) τῶν κτητ(όρων)

After these lines, on the left-hand side of the leaf was a normal three-column account. In these lines, only a few remains of the first column can be seen. Down to line 21, everything has been crossed out with Xs.

	]	(ταλ.) [
	]	(ταλ.) [
	κ(εράτια) ιδ	(ταλάντςν) (μυριὰς) α Γρ
	κ(εράτια) .]	(τάλαντα) ..
	κ(εράτια) ς.	(τάλαντα) Ϛ.
].υρ( )	κ(εράτια) [ς .]	(τάλαντα) Ϛ.
]ιας	κ(εράτια) ι	(τάλαντα) Θτ
].	κ(εράτια) ι	(τάλαντα) Θτ
	κ(εράτια) βL]	(τάλαντα) Βτ
	κ(εράτια) β	(τάλαντα) Αω
	κ(εράτια) γ	(τάλαντα) Βω
	κ(εράτια) δ	(τάλαντα) Γψ
	κ(εράτια) β	[(τάλαντα Αω]
	κ(εράτια) β	[(τάλαντα) Αω]
	κ(εράτιον) α	[(τάλαντα) ϡ]
	κ(εράτια) γ	(τάλαντα) Βω
	κ(εράτια) β	(τάλαντα) Αω
	κ(εράτιον) α	(τάλαντα) ϡ
	κ(εράτια) αL	(τάλαντα) Αυ

] ῥωκάτωρ δ(ιὰ) Ἀπολ(λῶτος) ἐλαιουρ(γοῦ) [
] ψωμί(ου) ζεύγ(η) μ
ψω]μί(ου) ζεύγ(η) λ
(traces of 5 lines)
δ(ιὰ) τῆς] ἁγίας ἐκλ(ησίας)

Μη]νᾶ μάγυρ(ος)	(τάλαντα) Ερ
Γε]ώρ(γιος) μάγυρ(ος)	(τάλαντα) Ερ

22 ῥωγάτωρ 30 ἐκκλησίας 31, 32 μάγειρος

Folio 27 verso

[†] Account of Topos Demeou,
Mesore 15, from which, through the landowners:

After these lines, the left-hand side of the leaf was a normal three-column account. In these lines, only a few remains of the first column can be seen. Down to line 21, all is crossed out with Xs.

			] tal. [
4			] tal. [
		14 car.	13,100 tal.
		. car.	. . tal.
		6 car.	6,000 tal.
8	]ur( )	[6 car.]	6,000 tal.
		] 10 car.	9,300 tal.
		] 10 car.	9,300 tal.
		2.5 car.]	2,300 tal.
12		2 car.	1,800 tal.
		3 car.	2,800 tal.
		4 car.	3,700 tal.
		2 car.	[1,800 tal.]
16		2 car.	[1,800 tal.]
		1 car.	[900 tal.]
		3 car.	2,800 tal.
		2 car.	1,800 tal.
20		1 car.	900 tal.
		1 ½ car.	1,400 tal.

	] rogator, through Apollos, oil-worker [	
	] 40 pairs of loaves of bread	
24	] 30 pairs of loaves of bread	
	(traces of 5 lines)	
	through the] Holy Church	
	Me]nas, meat-cook	5,100 tal.
32	Ge]orgios, meat-cook	5,100 tal.

Unplaced fragment

β εἴσπραξ(ις) ὁμοί(ως) Παχ(ὼν) ι [

Κύρα Ἰωσηφ(ίου) (ὑπὲρ) τιμ(ῆς) ψωμ(ίων) κ(εράτια) .[
Ἀπολ(λῶς) Ἰωάνν(ου) (κεράτια) [
Τατι<α>ν(ὸς) ϭες (κεράτια) [
ἀπόδοσ(ις) λόγ(ου) traces
δ(ιὰ) κοιν(οῦ) τῆς κώμ(ης) Θὼθ ι κερ(ατισμοῦ) νο(μισμάτια) ϛς [
Φῖβις Τοοσε νο(μισμάτια) γ [
Μηνᾶ μάγυρ(ος) νο(μισμάτιον) α [
remainder blank and verso blank

2 ϊωσηφ/ pap. 3 ϊωαννS pap. 6 κώμ(ης), ω ex corr. (ex α?) 8 Μηνᾶ, η ex corr.; μάγειρος

Unplaced fragment

2nd collection, likewise, Pachon 10

Kyra daughter of Iosephis, for price of loaves car. [
Apollos son of Ioannes [.] car. [
Tatianos qes [.] car. [
Payment on the acount of . . .
through the corporation of the village, Thoth 10, for keratismos, 96 sol. [
Phibis son of Toose 3 sol. [
Menas, meat-cook 1 sol. [
remainder blank and verso blank.

Notes to the Text

Folio 1
Width is 13.3 cm.

Folio 1 Recto
Chipped, rectangular fragments broken off at the upper right cause no loss of text. At the lower left side, a thin, tall strip of papyrus (2.5 x 15 cm) has been lost. This results in slight damage to the beginning of line 17 and losses at the beginnings of lines 18–29. The entries from lines 2 to 16 show in their margins oblique checking strokes, each such stroke surmounted by a small x except at lines 5 and 8; the x is heavily overwritten in line 7. These presumably ran through the rest of the entries as well; the stroke is partly visible in line 17 but lost after that owing to the physical damage to the papyrus at lower left. In line 16, the x/ is seemingly followed by a thin chrism. The alignment of the second column (carats and solidi) is erratic. Column 3 (the talents column) is more regular, but demonstrates for the first time a tendency to shift gradually leftward (in accordance with Maas's law) as the scribe proceeds with his writing from top to bottom. The lower margin is at least 4 cm, reduced to 3 cm after entry of the page total (line 30).

1 There was originally at least one additional folio, since page 1, with 397,200 tal. in payments (23r.2), is missing. That it was also dated Thoth 29 is indicated by the ὁμοίως on page 2.

10 We have here the first instance of a scribal behavior found also in 6r.8 and 6v.23, in which the second of two consecutive entries for 1 solidus has what appears to be a pi with following diagonal stroke beginning at the foot after the alpha for 1. We do not know what it means. It does not affect the number of talents given in any of the three cases, so it is not a fraction of a solidus or a number of carats. The simplest explanation (adopted in translation) is that the scribe prepared to indicate a discount or deduction from the solidus, thus π(αρά), as, e.g., in 19r.15–16, but then did not write a number of carats after it; but we do not see why he would have done this three times.

18 There is room for only 4 letters at the start, so the scribe did not write Ἀτρῆτος as elsewhere (1r.7, for example). The only other payer in the codex with a father named Georgios was Choor. It is uneconomical to suppose that this entry represents some other, unknown taxpayer. The name Γεώργιος is fairly common, including in first position, in this register. There is no clear case of the occupational term γεωργός, nor any reason to expect it, since this is evidently a list of owners, not lessees. In Column 2, the scribe first wrote κ(εράτια) ε in its normal place, then rewrote it farther to the left and added after it the d for ¼, followed by two oblique strokes, over what he had originally written. These both mark the fraction and cover up the rest of the original epsilon.

22 Only the end of a diagonal stroke (upper left to lower right, as alpha, lambda, or mu), followed by a short diagonal mark of abbreviation, survives. Of the six known carpenters, only Abraamis seems a possible restoration. But that name is usually abbreviated with a sinusoidal curve after rho, so it is less than certain here.

29 Part of the nu of νο(μισμάτιον) is visible descending from the epsilon of Τοοσε, which projects into what would normally be the space for the second column. The placement of the third column is maintained, so there is barely room for the solidus entry to be crowded in before the third column.

30 The summary (23r.3) gives a total of 179,900, which agrees with the page total. The sampi here appears to have a short diagonal stroke before it, giving the impression of upsilon. This might suggest that there was correction. If so, that could have resulted from changes either in the last digit in line 7 (originally omega, corrected to sampi) or in line 18 (where the carats amount was corrected). But it could just be slight carelessness in writing the sampi.

Folio 1 Verso

As in 1r, the oblique strokes in the left margin are regularly topped by X's, clearly visible in lines 2–7 and again at line 11 through line 27, except perhaps for the canceled entry at line 21. There is a slight loss of papyrus at the line beginnings of the upper left, removing the oblique marginal strokes before lines 9 etc. In addition to the oblique strokes that are virtually universal in codex entries, numerous entries in this line are followed by dots, mostly at mid-line level. They are evident at lines 8–20 (faint if present in 19), 22–26. These are presumably to be taken as stemming from a second round of double-checking. The alignment of the carats column (Col. 2) is far more regular than in 1r, but note the leftward drift of Col. 3 from top to bottom of the text. The bottom margin is 2.5–3 cm before the entry of the total (line 28); 1.5 cm after.

5 For Tbake, a Hermopolite village, see Drew-Bear 1979: 270.

8 There is a stroke by the edge at the start of line 8 that does not look like an x. If it did not precede the diagonal stroke, one might think of δ(ιά). There may have been something similar in line 21, but less is preserved.

11 This is the first instance of the scribes' difficulties with the name Τατιανός, which is deformed in a number of ways through the codex. The alpha is likewise missing at 9v.28, but see the scribal insertion of the missing alpha at 9v.2. See further p. 19 for the scribe's other difficulties with this name.

12 The overlining on this Coptic name is unusual.

22 There may be a dot below [[ἀγρ( )]] (on which see introduction, p. 22) at the end of this line. Between Cols. 2 and 3 there is ink, perhaps 2–3 letters, resembling alpha and nu. We do not know what its significance could be.

28 The total agrees with that reported on 23r.4. The sum of the payments, however, is 84,900 tal.

Folio 2
Width is 13 cm.

Folio 2 Recto
This folio is cut very close to the left edge, with the loss of the left margin but not the beginnings of names. The papyrus surface is abraded. For this reason, oblique strokes are not consistently visible. There are faint remains in lines 2–4, and perhaps in 28–29; elsewhere they are either faint because of abrasion to the papyrus or lost because of missing papyrus. Tremas are sometimes hard or impossible to identify; even names are difficult to recover. The right margin is clean except for the insertion between lines 13 and 14. The bottom margin was at least 1.5 cm. Once the total was entered (line 30), the margin was eliminated (and is now blocked by the lower frame).

1 The scribe's abbreviation of Φαῶφ(ι) with double obliques through the lower hasta and his use of trema over iota in the following number both serve to eliminate any possible confusion between Phaoph(i) 15 and Phaophi 5 as the intended date. Unusually, there is no long horizontal line below this line as there is on other pages, only a faint, short stroke.

4 The short form of abbreviation κλ/ is squeezed in in this line, but it is also used below, line 20, where there was plenty of space.

10–12 Note the presence of three persons with same description as ϭεc in succession. Cf. the introduction, pp. 18 and 64, for this word.

13–14 The payments down to line 13 bring to an end the payments connected with an initial apodosis on Thoth 29 and completed on Phaophi 15; we do not have the number of solidi included in this payment, which would have been mentioned on page 1. Here starts a payment of 23 ½ solidi by Antinoite standard. This includes lines 14–29 of 2r, all of 2v, and all of 3r. These payments total 486,700 tal. That would give a value for the Antinoite solidus of 20,710.6. This disagrees with 3v.2.

25 We do not have another instance of 9,600 tal. to compare, but since 10 car. equates to 9,300 tal., the additional 300 tal. seems more likely to represent a quarter-carat than a half-carat.

30 The total of 136,200 agrees with the summary listing (23r.5). The total of the payments listed on this page is, however, 130,100.

Folio 2 Verso
The writing is very clear except for the last few lines, and of a pretty consistent thickness. Note the leftward drift of Col. 2 and, by attraction, Col. 3. Oblique strokes against the taxpayers' names in the left margin are universal and clear. The right margin is clear. The bottom margin was 1 cm. The total was entered in line 30, leaving no margin (it is now in any case blocked by the frame).

4 The number of carats has been written over an erased numeral (probably plus fraction), as has the number of talents in Column 3. We cannot recover the original number in either case.

7 An ink smudge between the start of lines 6 and 7 obscures the trema expected over the iota of Ἰσακίου.

12 Phi in Φῖβις is blotted.

18 The initial alpha is blotted.

21 The scribe seems to have written 2 ½ ¼, then blotted it out and written a gamma above the beta. The figure in column 3 agrees with the gamma.

30 The amounts add up to 355,200 talents, against the scribe's 354,900 given here, and tallied at 23r.6. The scribal correction in line 21 would have increased the total by 300 or 400 talents, depending on whether 2 ¾ was thought of as 2,400 or 2,500 tal. (both occur in this account). If the total written depended on the original amount, 300 talents would cover the difference. No sign of correction is visible in the final column, however.

Folio 3

A very regular sheet; width (at widest) 13 cm. Right side (viewed from recto) very evenly cut.

Folio 3 Recto

The page has only 18 entries, presumably because it finishes off entries for Phaophi 15 from the two preceding pages. The bottom margin is at least 9 cm, 7 cm after the entry of the page total at line 20. There are oblique strokes in the left margin against all preserved entries, although sometimes faint to the point of near-invisibility or even lost with the papyrus edge. Column 2 maintains its alignment, but Column 3 drifts leftwards, the right margin increasing from 3 cm at line 2 to 4 cm at line 19. The right margin is clean apart from line 8.

14–15 Two sons of Kollouthos in a row make their payments.

20 The total of 62,800, also found in 23r.7, agrees with the total of the payments listed.

Folio 3 Verso

The writing is very clear. Cols. 2 and 3 have the characteristic leftward drift. There are oblique strokes in the left margin, occasionally hard to see (8, 11, 16) but apparently universally in the original state of the papyrus. The 1.5 cm bottom margin is reduced to 0.5 cm after entry of the page total at line 27.

1 This line was squeezed in as an afterthought in the top margin of the page. The writing is minuscule.

2 The payment of 18 solidi by the Antinoite standard seems to cover the 216,500 tal. on this page and the entries in lines 1–19 of the next page, totalling 312,200 tal. The Antinoite solidus would by this reckoning be worth 17,344.4 tal.

4 There is a dot in the right margin after phi, perhaps to draw attention to the correction.

10 Below the end of this line, between the talents symbol and the numeral, there is some canceled writing of unknown nature; which line it concerns is unclear.

24 This place name appears four times in the register, as follows:

3v.24	αρμοτ/
4v.27	αρμοθ/
14r.8	αρμοτν/
16r.19	αρμS

Drew-Bear 1979: 73–74 includes the first three references (in alphabetical order) as instances of an Hermopolite village named Ἁρμῶτνις, attested in other Greek documents of the third to sixth century. F. Morelli, in *CPR* XXX, pp. 107–110, has now discussed the village further, based on an attestation in 643/4. It was part of the 11th pagus.

28 The amount of 216,500 tal., also listed on 23r.8, agrees with the total of the payments.

Folio 4

The width is 13.2 cm.

Folio 4 Recto

Lines 2–19 record 18 payments for Phaophi 24. A heading for an "old account" is found at line 20, set off by horizontal strokes above and below. The lines that follow record ten entries for Hathyr 9. At the upper left a strip of the top layer of papyrus is lost; the result is that the usual oblique strokes are not consistently apparent; they (or traces) can be seen in 2, 4–5, 6–19, and 21–30. Cols. 2 and 3 more successfully retain their alignments than on other pages, except for a repositioning of Column 2 rightward at line 7. There is no bottom margin.

8 We have no idea why the scribe spells φομντ here in such a divergent fashion.

20 Ἁθὺρ θ has been squeezed in above line 20. A total of 33,700 tal. of the payments on this page are to be credited to the delivery of 7 solidi by village standard, which begins here and continues on the next page.

32 The total is to be found in the right-hand margin at a level with lines 24 and 25. The payments add up to 129,400 talents, rather than the scribe's 131,000 (repeated on 23r.9). Of these, 95,700 tal. are in the first section (to line 19), the balance of 33,700 tal. in the second section. It appears (cf. 4v.32–33n.) that we should suppose that 114,700 or 114,600 tal. were delivered for these 7 solidi by village standard, so 16,385.7 tal. per solidus.

Folio 4 Verso

The writing is fainter than on other verso pages. The page is fully packed top to bottom. There are oblique strokes against all entries except at line 10 (unless it was off to the left) and 12 (no papyrus remains to the left of hori); those in 19–20 are faint. Lines 8 and 16 are interlinear insertions. The writing, especially in the lower third or so of the page, is vertically very compressed. The total (line 33) is entered in the righthand margin at line 27. The figures entered on the papyrus at line 32 are blocked by the mounting frame. See note on 32–33 below.

27 See note above on 3v.24.

32–33 23r.10 gives the talents total for this page as 80,900, as does line 33 here. Everything before line 32 adds up to 72,400 (or 72,100, if one omits the entry in line 8). That means we are looking in line 32 (on the assumption the scribe is correct in his addition on this page) for a figure of 8,500 talents representing 9 carats. Because of the binding, we cannot make out any number with confidence, but MacCoull originally thought to see the top of epsilon, which may suggest that theta is correct. At the end of the line, the top of a vertical stroke, perhaps the top of phi, is visible. Since 9 car. is typically 8,500 tal. in the register, we have restored this figure.

Folio 5

Width 13 cm.

Folio 5 Recto

This side is quite dark at the left, but lighter at column 3. The papyrus surface is seriously abraded. Presumably there were more tremas than can now be discerned. There are oblique strokes in the left margin throughout, but they are sometimes very faint. The total is entered in the right margin opposite line 24. The bottom margin is 1 cm. There is a generous right margin, 3 cm toward the top of the page, 4 cm below.

2 The initial phi of Φοιβάμ(μων) is crossed by the rising stroke of schima in the next line, making it at first look as if there is an abbreviation there. The next two letters are somewhat obscured.

13 Ματρώv(ας), cf. 6r.16 for the same resolution. "Matrona" never appears in the first slot, always in second. The name is spelled out as Matrona in 3v.12, 4v.32, 7v.22, 8v.6, 11r.5, 13r.30, 14v.12; abbreviated at nu in 5r.13, 6r.16, 16v.18, 18r.31. There are no examples of a fully-written spelling of a genitive Ματρώνας.

33 The payments (including the crossed-out figure in line 2) total 170,100 against the scribe's 161,200 (also 23r.11), a difference of 8,900. It happens that the last three entries (lines 30–32) total exactly 8,900. It is possible that these were late entries, written after the total was calculated. They do look somewhat compressed. A less exact reconciliation, however, can be produced by supposing that the entry in line 2, for 8,500 tal., was crossed out before the total was calculated.

Folio 5 Verso

The papyrus is lighter than on the recto, the writing correspondingly clearer (though lines 20, 24–29 are faint). Oblique strokes stand against all 25 entries. The page is therefore a short one with a bottom margin of 6.5 cm. Columns 2 and 3 have the characteristic leftward drift: a margin of 1.7 cm against line 2 increases to 3.3 cm against line 28. A probable second hand in lines 26–27 (see introduction, p. 13) enters two payments for Choiak 10, compared to the date at the top of the page, Hathyr 27. Because there is plenty of space, the line with totals comfortably fits at the bottom.

26 This line indicates a payment of 41 car., which is then given further definition in line 27 as belonging to the heirs of Konstantinos. The sum is there equated to 38,700 tal., which indicates an equation of 1 car. = 943.9 tal., consistently with the rest of the account. We do not understand the function of ἀποδομ( ) here before the sum of 41 car. is repeated. If a single word, it must be an aorist participle of ἀποδίδωμι, presumably ἀποδόμ(ενα), but its purpose here is unclear to us. Taking it as two words—there is a slight space after omicron, probably however the result of a descending stroke from the line above—yields no useful explanation. The use of an amount of carats as high as 41 is also not in keeping with usual practice in this register.

28 The total of 329,400 matches the entry on 23r.12. It agrees with the total of the payments in lines 2–25, excluding the Choiak 10 payments in lines 26–27.

Folio 6

Width is 12.8 cm.

Folio 6 Recto

There are 31 entries, one of which (line 31) is deleted. Oblique strokes seem to be universal, although not visible at line 16 because of loss of papyrus and often hard to see elsewhere. The total (line 33) is in the right margin between lines 29 and 30. The leftward drift of Columns 2 and 3 leaves a right margin of 1.5 cm against line 2, increasing to 4.5 cm in the last few lines of text. The right margin is clear except for the insertion of the page total.

8 For the pi after the numeral for the solidus here, see 1r.10n.

27 We have restored the number of talents (3,300) so that the actual total of the payments is 158,700, in accordance with the scribe's 158,700 in the margin (line 33; as also in 23r.13). We cannot be absolutely certain, however, whether the amount was written and then erased, or even never written at all as a result of the scribe's uncertainty. The correct number of carats to match 3,300 tal. would be 3 ½. The symbol for ½ in the statement of carats is faint, giving the impression of having been washed out, whereas the symbol for ¼ is clear. It is impossible for us to be sure just what the writer's final intention was and if he executed it consistently and fully.

31 The surface is blank after the talents sign here, suggesting that the amount of carats was crossed out before any amount in talents was written.

Folio 6 Verso

A very full page, with 31 entries. There are oblique strokes against all entries, mostly clear and doubled at lines 11 and 15. A change of papyrus color, clearly defined, runs vertically at the right edge of the writing of column 3, signalling a kollesis.

23 For the pi after the numeral for the solidus here, see 1r.10n. The αΖ are almost invisible.

26 It is not obvious what the purpose of the horizontal stroke beneath the line is.

32 The scribe gives a total in the margin opposite line 31 of 192,000 tal. This total is carried forward to 23r.14. The surviving amounts equal 180,800 tal. The difference is 11,200 tal., or exactly 12 car. The entry for 12 car. is clear, but there is no sign that the scribe ever wrote the 11,200 tal. in the proper place, even though he included them in his total.

Folio 7

Width is 12.8 cm. At the bottom are unusual, triangular losses of papyrus, a smaller inside and a larger outside loss, attended respectively by shorter and longer diagonal cracks, fortunately without loss of text on either side. Halfway preserved, at the top, is a stub to facilitate the codex's binding. Better, in fact fully preserved, are those stubs still attached to Folios 12 and 13 (below). See also Folio 8.

Folio 7 Recto

There are oblique strokes against all entries, although hard to see in line 17. The bottom margin is 3.5 cm. The total inserted in line 30 leaves a remaining margin of 2.0 cm. The papyrus is relatively light but turns darker and more difficult to read at about line 19.

11 It looks as if the scribe made some kind of error or changed his mind about abbreviating Λουλοῦτος; perhaps he wrote a third lambda, then corrected to tau.

19–27 To the right of these lines, but not quite aligned with them, we find Τατιαν(ὸς) Ἑρμ(), written ΤατιανS ΕρμS, eight times. We see no sign of numbers after the name. The writing is rather faint, and we are not certain if the writing was intended to be washed out or not.

23 The sense of ὁμοίως here escapes us, as neither payer nor amount corresponds to anything preceding on this page.

30 The scribe's total of 252,600 is repeated on 23r.15. It agrees with the total of the payments recorded.

Folio 7 Verso

This is a darkish and therefore difficult page, especially in its lower half. The left edge is a bit ragged. The usual oblique marginal strokes can nevertheless usually be seen, down to line 16, after which abrasion or loss makes them difficult to follow. Longer, desperately compressed entries in

Col. 1, lines 8–10, push Col. 2 farther to the right. It is repositioned at line 11 but then proceeds to drift leftward as the text proceeds. Column 3 tends to retain its initial alignment better, but it too shares a leftward drift. A right margin of 1.8 cm at line 2 increases to 3 cm by the end of the page.

1–1a The reading of Choiak 6 is secure, but the preceding page (7r) is dated Choiak 10 and the next (8r) appears to be Choiak 20, although this is not completely certain. For this reason we print here <ι>ς. The line below is a case in which an interpretation as ο(ὕτως) is attractive, cf. above, p. 21.

30 We have been unable to read the name of the payer here, partly because a glob of adhesive obscures part of it. We certainly do not see any of the known payers with the patronymic Apollos (Anouphis, Victor, Piter).

32 The scribe's total is 123,500. On 23r.16 we find 123,400, but a faint phi can be seen washed out to the right of upsilon. This figure (123,400) agrees with the total of the payments recorded.

Folio 8

The folio proper is 12.5 cm. wide, but here as for Folio 7 a binding stub has been preserved (in better condition than in 7) for the top half of the sheet: 3 x 14.5 cm.

Folio 8 Recto

This page records 8 payments made for Choiak 20 (?), 24 for Tybi 5. There are strokes above and below to set off the new date, Tybi 5, at line 10. Oblique strokes are visible before all individual entries, especially thickly written or overwritten at line 29. They are hard to see at lines 33–34 because they are obscured by a roughly oval-shaped discoloration, which looks like glue, at the lower left corner of the papyrus. There is a rightward shift in the alignment of Cols. 2 and 3 especially, caused by the lengthy and much compressed entry at Col. 1 line 12. An analogous but less dramatic rightward shift is caused by Col. 2 entries at lines 23–26. Both shifts fight against the scribe's natural tendency to move his second and third columns gradually leftwards. The total for this page is recorded in 23r.17 (275,100), but is not to be found either in the bottom of the text (as far as visible) or in the right margin. In neither location was there available space. It agrees with the total of the entries, including the restored amount in line 34.

10 The double slash after Tybi assures there will be no confusion between Tybi 15 and Tybi 5.

11 The scribe wrote nominative Ἀπολλῶς, then "corrected" to genitive Ἀπολλῶτος.

13–14 Lakon pays for himself in 13, then stands as agent for Kor Jij in 14.

23 "Son of Iosephis" here would seem to be an error for "son of Ioannes," as Apollos son of Ioannes is well-attested and Apollos son of Iosephis otherwise unknown.

34 The lower right corner of the papyrus is abraded, and the end of the line is also obscured by a large circular blob of discoloration (probably glue).

Folio 8 Verso

The left margin is almost entirely lost. Oblique strokes are visible at lines 2–11, but then are either lost or (partly) blocked by the frame of the glass sandwich in which the papyrus is mounted; they are partly visible at lines 20–23. The writing on this page is thick and clear—except for the very faint record of the page total at line 33. Cols. 2 and 3 drift steadily leftward, until reoriented rightward by the extra-wide entries beginning in Col. 1 at line 19. Columns 2 and 3 then resume their inexorable leftward drift, especially noticeable from line 24 to the end. The right margin is 2.5–3 cm not counting the extra flap.

There are curious assorted horizontal streaky smudges over lines 19 and 25; a smudge of ciphers in line 5.

19–25 One individual (Pessoous, line 18) serves as agent for no fewer than seven individuals. Cf. below, 13v.18–20.

33 The scribe's total is 115,600 tal. This is reported on 23r.18. This agrees with the total of the recorded payments.

Folio 9

The folio measures 13.5 in width. A thin vertical strip has been lost at the lower left (see below on 9r).

Folio 9 Recto

There is a clearly defined kollesis at the edge of the writing of column 1. There is a more than usually radical leftward drift of Cols. 2 and 3. At the top (though gradually diminishing) there is a distinct space between Cols. 1 and 2; by the bottom they nearly touch. Oblique strokes are visible till line 22; the rest are lost because of the loss of a tall (10 cm), thin (0.8 cm) strip of papyrus at the lower left. The right margin is 1.5 cm at top, 4 cm below.

15, 17 In both lines stigma was, atypically, written before the carats symbol. In 15 it was canceled and rewritten after the carats symbol; in 17 it was not.

26 In erasure after the name, perhaps [[σιδ(ηρουργός)]], but the reading is very unsure.

35 The very top of this line is all that is visible, with the rest blocked by the frame of the mounting. The scribe's figure of 129,200 tal. is read on the model of 23r.19. This agrees with the total of the entries on the page.

Folio 9 Verso

On this page, there *seem* to be numerous changes of hand, including and in addition to the hand of the principal scribe, especially between lines 5 and 11. See introduction, pp. 13–14, for the problems of identifying different hands here. There are oblique strokes in the left margin against all entries except the canceled entry in line 9. They are clear until line 16, when the left edge darkens considerably. From line 25 to line 36 they are again clear. There is a dark vertical swath running from line 3 to the bottom of the page. It obscures readings in the talents column, especially from line 18 on.

14 The notation of "through" whom the payment was made seems to have been squeezed in between Cols. 1 and 2 as an afterthought.

28 This line appears to correspond to earlier headings giving figures for an *apodosis* in solidi and is not included in our count of payments on p. 23. The difficulty with line 36, however, makes it hard to be certain if the payments in lines 29–36 correspond accurately to this amount. If our restoration of line 36) is correct, we would have 1 solidus (counted as 17 carats) plus 16 ¼ car., for a total of 33 ¼ car., leaving us 1 ½ car. short of the amount specified in line 28.

36 The total (in the margin by line 33) of 289,100 agrees with 23r.20. The total of the entries other than that in line 36 is 268,900. The amounts in line 36 are almost entirely obscured by the binding strip. An amount of 1 sol., 3 ½ car., equating to 20,200 tal., would be necessary to make the amounts agree. The tops of the symbols for talents and myriads are visible, followed by a hole where a beta would have stood. The scanty traces of the tops of letters where the amount in gold should stand support the restoration better on the original than on the photograph.

Folio 10

A narrow sheet, 11.5 cm. wide.

Folio 10 Recto

There are oblique strokes throughout except for losses caused by a lost strip of papyrus at the lower left, which affects only lines 22–25. The writing in the upper part of the page, lines 1–12, is thick—apart from a very thinly written entry at line 10; the writing becomes progressively thinner in the lower parts of the page.

There is no visible total on the page; it may be hidden by the binding of the pane. In 23r.21 we find a total of 103,200 tal. That agrees with the total of the payments on the page.

11–12 The payments relevant to the account of the gnoster Victor continue on page 21. Those in lines 13–31 of the present page total 42,500 talents.

13 The reference to the intermediary Panejnou is squeezed in, in very tiny writing—an afterthought, it seems.

Folio 10 Verso

There are oblique strokes for every entry. The ink is thicker and clearer in the top half (lines 1–15), thinner below. Lines 1–2 and 12–13 provide two-line headings, one for Tybi 9, the other for Mecheir 4. The first of these is a continuation of the payments on the previous page. A finer pen starts with the stroke under line 15.

Again, no page total is preserved on this page, or else it is hidden. In 23r.22 we get a total of 77,400 tal. But the payments listed total 77,800 tal. even without figures for the last two payments, where the numbers are missing. There is no sign of cancellation of any entry.

1 The payments in lines 3–15 total 26,400 tal. Added to the figures for the same payment in the previous page (10r.11–12n.), we get 68,900 tal. That was 4 solidi, 5 ¾ carats. We would expect 4 solidi to be 68,000 tal., and 5 ¾ solidi to be 5,300 tal. (as in 10r.13). The overall total thus seems short of the mark by 4,400 tal. The presence of a payment of precisely 5 ¾ car. in 10r.13 is striking; we should therefore find exactly 4 solidi made up in the rest of the payments, but we do not.

16 For the treatment of this line, see 9v.28n.

30–31 In principle, the amounts here could be in solidi; but the considerations above suggest that these amounts were in fact small.

Folio 11

12.5 cm at widest. There is a very ragged right edge (viewed from the recto side). It is darker on the left than on the right half (vertically). Seemingly there is a kollesis running midway from top to bottom of the folio.

Folio 11 Recto

The darkness of the left side of the papyrus (see above) covers most of Col. 1 and makes it hard to verify tremas in the expected places. There are oblique strokes against all entries, abraded at lines 21–23 and doubly thick at line 27. The usual extended horizontal stroke under line 1 is not apparent. Cols. 2 and 3, written close together (more so than usual), tend to retain their initial alignments, though thrown rightwards by the long, albeit compressed, Col. 1 entry at line 18. Between lines 22 and 29 the figures in Column 3 are faint, the papyrus is dark and sometimes damaged, and readings are difficult.

Palaeographically unusual on this page are several genitives in omicron-upsilon (14, 15, 22, 25) where omicron appears as a large dot, upsilon as a short horizontal superstroke.

12 The iota in the carats numeral has been written thickly and probably more than once; it intrudes on the lower leg of kappa and the abbreviation stroke, so it was probably omitted on first writing, then inserted with force.

33 The scribe's total, which agrees with that at 23r.23, is 273,600 tal. The total of the payments recorded, however, is 189,000 tal., a discrepancy of 84,600 tal., unparalleled in the account. As only two amounts in talents are restored, and in both cases the number of carats is preserved, there is no significant uncertainty about the readings. As we saw in 6v.32, where an unwritten figure figures in the total, the scribe was not actually dependent on adding the figures in the right-hand column to reach his total figure for talents. It may have been derived from the total number of solidi and carats reckoned. One could hypothesize a writing of carats for solidi by mistake in one entry, but there is no entry that would yield the difference on such a supposition. It seems more likely that an entry, or more than one entry, has been omitted from the page but included in the total. The number is large enough to represent an entire page, but we can see no process by which an unnumbered and inserted page would have been included in this page's total.

Folio 11 Verso

The left edge is very ragged; the oblique marginal strokes are nonetheless preserved although faint at lines 22–23 and 25. It has not been possible to locate tremas on this page. That might suggest a different hand, but this does not appear to be the case. The right margin at top is 1.5–2.5 cm. The pen, especially at the top, is very thin.

7 We are not sure if the number of talents here (which is the correct figure for 3 carats) has been remade or corrected; there is a thick stroke overwriting the fairly faint omega, but also a thicker vertical to the left of the first stroke of beta. It is generally striking that Bω is written three different ways in lines 6–8, open-topped beta in 6 and thick strokes; standard beta and thick strokes in 7; and the thinly drawn line 8, with beta overwritten and a thick vertical stroke through the center of omega.

32 The line with the page total is lost except for the talents sign. The figure in 23r.24 is 140,300, which is indeed the total of the entries on this page, including the incorrect 2,800 in line 7.

Folio 12

This folio preserves the binding stub from top to bottom. Widths: folio 12.5 cm, stub 3.3 cm.

Folio 12 Recto

Oblique strokes are universal and well preserved. The spacing of the writing is more generous at the top; at the bottom it is more compressed, especially from line 28 on, in an effort to get everything in. Cols. 2 and 3 are close together and well aligned, though hard pressed by (e.g.) the long Col. 1 entry at line 15. The numbers in column 3 are often very faint, especially after line 15. The total (line 37) is in fact entered in the right margin opposite line 28. There is an extra-wide margin at left, 1.5–2 cm (3 cm before the oblique strokes), plus the extra vertical strip of 2–3 cm (3 at top, 2 below). This is a very full page, top to bottom.

36 The name is blocked by the mounting frame.

37 The last digit is not visible on this page and has been restored from 23r.25. The figure given there is 196,400; as the last entry is entirely invisible thanks to the binding strip, it is impossible to verify this. We have restored that entry as being another 6-carat payment, like the one preceding it, which would bring us to 196,400. But the uncertainty of this restoration should not be disguised.

Folio 12 Verso

The oblique strokes in the left margin are not entirely preserved. The left side of the papyrus is dark and abraded, like the right side of the recto. Strokes are very clear in lines 2 and 4–9. Partial traces are visible after that, but either loss of papyrus or the mounting frame interferes with visibility, the latter from line 21. There is only one entry for Mecheir 4 (a carryover from the preceding page); then come 28 entries for Mecheir 22. Cols. 2 and 3 get realigned rightward for the Mecheir 22 entries, then show the characteristic leftward drift, if only slightly. The right margin without the flap is ca 2.5 cm. The flap is 3.3 cm at the top, 2.5 cm below.

26 The line is written smaller than the rest. It is not completely clear whether it is to be connected with line 25 or line 27, but the first of these seems more likely.

33 The total of 80,800 tal. agrees with the summary on 23r.26. The entries on the page also add up to this sum.

Folio 13

This folio also preserves its binding stub. The sheet width is 12.8 cm, stub width ca 4.2 cm. Total width: 17 cm. Kollesis toward right?

Folio 13 Recto

There are oblique strokes throughout. The stroke at line 20 is triply thick and runs through initial sigma. At line 22, the left part of the stroke is a thick, filled-in triangle. A slight leftward drift of Cols. 2 and 3 is observable, with a displacement rightward at line 18 owing to inclusion of an agent in Col. 1. This is a very full page, with 32 individual entries and (page fullness notwithstanding) the total at the bottom in line 34. Except for line 5, the right margin is 2 cm toward the top, 3 cm toward the bottom. Oblique strokes fill the left margin, which would otherwise have been 1 to 1.5 cm top to bottom.

6 ἐργάτης: γατης is written in tiny strokes.

34 The text gives 219,400 tal. as a total, confirmed in the summary at 23r.27, but the figures actually add up to 219,500.

Folio 13 Verso

The oblique strokes are preserved in the left margin but abraded at lines 13–18. Cols. 2 and 3 tend to drift leftward. The wide Col. 1 entries at lines 18–20 force Col. 2 back to the right for a short distance. There is a wide right margin, 3.5 cm.

7 2,800 talents is the correct conversion for 3, not 3¼, keratia (Col. 2). The writing of beta and omega is faint. It is displaced to the right to avoid the descender from sampi (900) in line 6. We have looked for traces to suggest that it was erased in favor of the expected gamma (3,000), but we see none in an inspection of the original.

18–20 For Pessoous as intermediary cf. 8v.19–25.

33 The scribe's 82,700 is repeated on 23r.28 except that the hundreds character is lost. The actual sum of the payments recorded is 82,500. The scribe's total may have assumed the correct 3,000 tal. in line 7 (see note ad loc.) rather than the 2,800 tal. he apparently wrote.

Folio 14

This folio is narrower than other folios, measuring 12 cm wide at the top, 10 cm below. There is an unusually ragged left edge (as viewed from the recto side).

Folio 14 Recto

There is a possible kollesis at left. The left edge itself is ragged and torn. Even so, oblique strokes are visible, if abraded, in lines 2–9; but after this, the left edge preserves no strokes except in lines 20–21. A dark vertical stripe runs down near the left edge of the papyrus for 18 cm until it ends where the ragged left edge gives out. The stripe obscures the initial letters of the names in Column 1, especially in the upper half of the sheet. Tremas are hard to locate on this page. The right margin is 2.5 cm at top, 3.7 cm below. Line 10 juts into the right margin. The bottom margin is 1 cm. No total is given as far as the visible text goes; one could be hidden by the binding strip.

The scribe's total as reported on 23r.29 is 91,300 tal. This agrees with the total of the reported payments on the page.

19 It is hard to say if the absence of sigma at the end of γναφεύϛ indicates abbreviation or is to be construed as omission. We have printed it as if the first is correct, but there is no sign of abbreviation.

30 The same man appears in 18r.28, but with a hellenized form, Πασῶθιϛ, in place of Παϣοτη.

Folio 14 Verso

The bottom margin is 1.5 cm; into this space the total (line 33) has been inserted. There is a small left margin filled with oblique strokes, which are present throughout, although at times abraded or truncated by loss of papyrus, especially at lines 16–20. The right edge is ragged and torn; the preserved right margin is 3 cm toward the top, 2 cm toward the bottom. A dark vertical stripe runs between and through Cols. 2 and 3. This is not a bleeding through of the recto's dark stripe.

33 The scribe's total is 186,000 tal., reported on 23r.30. This agrees with the total of the listed entries.

Folio 15

The folio is 12.2 cm wide near the top, but only 10 cm toward the bottom.

Folio 15 Recto

There are oblique strokes against all entries; the one in line 4 starts with a small triangle. The alignment of Cols. 2 and 3 is fairly regular, although they press closer together toward the bottom. The left margin is 1–1.5 cm and is occupied by the oblique strokes. The right margin, as preserved, is 2.5 cm at top, 1.5 cm at bottom. There is a bottom margin of 2 cm, into which the page total (line 31) has been entered.

31 The scribe's total is 348,500 tal., as also on 23r.31. This agrees with the total of the listed entries.

Folio 15 Verso

The right margin is 3 cm at top. The usual oblique strokes in the left margin are visible at lines 2–7. The loss of papyrus at the left causes the loss of the rest of these strokes. In addition, there are X-marks at the end of lines 19–29, apparently an indication of a second cross-checking for some entries. As the readings of the lower right corner are difficult, the X-marks may have continued in lines 30–33. There is a slight leftward drift of Cols. 2 and 3, written very close on Col. 1. The right margin at top is ca 4 cm. Lines 17–18 force a wider realignment at line 19, and a much reduced margin, but the leftward drift (albeit very slight) resumes.

30 No known payer fits the traces here, which after a fragmentary letter seem to be omega, mu, and a sinusoidal abbreviation stroke.

34 The total is—uniquely—recorded between Cols. 1 and 2 in line 27. The figure of 163,900 tal. (so also 23r.32) cannot readily be reconciled with the reported entries. A particular puzzle is line 16, where a payment of 17 car. is not represented by an amount in talents, although the talents sign is present. A payment of the same amount for the same person occurs in 17v.12 but is there crossed out. Leaving out of consideration the canceled payment in line 8, the 17 car. in line 16, and the payment in line 33, where the amount is lost, we obtain a total of 163,400, just 500 tal. less than the scribe's total. But no amount of 500 tal. ever occurs by itself in the register, as it would have represented something between half and three-quarters carat. It therefore seems best to leave the restoration of line 33 open.

Folio 16

The folio is well preserved though only 12.5 cm in width. A worm track is visible in the lower left quadrant. There may be a kollesis toward the right (as viewed from the recto side).

Folio 16 Recto

Oblique strokes occur throughout except the canceled entry in line 6. Those at lines 3–4 start with little blobs. There are X-marks after every line (see 15v), fainter at lines 9, 10, and 20, more elaborate at 16, farther to the right in 21. Cols. 2 and 3 are reasonably well aligned. The left margin is 1–1.5 cm before the oblique strokes.

9 It is hard to say if the scribe has simply omitted sigma at the end of Κωμήτα or there is haplography with the sigma beginning the patronymic. Our text reflects a preference for the first explanation. There is an interesting family cluster at lines 9–11, two grandsons (Kometas and Ioannes) and a son (Sarapion) of Theonilla.

21 The second and third columns were forced below the proper line level by the previous line. The numerals in both the second and third columns appear to have been erased and corrected, but they are in their final form too ghostly for us to read with confidence.

30 The traces visible in this line could belong to a total. Folio 23r.33 gives a total of 115,200 tal. The actual entries yield a total of 112,300, however, excluding the canceled line 6 and line 21. It therefore seems more likely that the traces in line 30 belong to one additional entry, perhaps of 2,000 tal. (2 ¼ car.).

Folio 16 Verso

There are X-marks at line ends except for in lines 6, 12, 14, 24, and 27. There are oblique strokes throughout except at the canceled entry in line 27. The writing gets smaller toward the bottom of the page (to fit more entries in). Cols. 2 and 3 have the characteristic leftward drift. The right margin of 2.5 cm at line 2 (not counting X) increases to 4.5 cm at line 28 (again not counting X). The oblique strokes leave very little left margin.

31 The scribe gives the total as 48,600, reported on 23r.34. The entries actually add up, excluding the canceled 2,800 of line 27, to 48,700.

Folio 17

The width of this well-preserved folio is 12.8 cm.

Folio 17 Recto

Left marginal oblique strokes are found throughout the small left margin; they are doubly thick at lines 5–6. There are X-marks at the ends of all entries, written up against the figures in the talents column, except perhaps for line 4. Some of them are very faint. The right margin measures 3 cm at the top, as much as 4.5 cm below, at lines 23–24.

27 The mu of Κλεμ( ) is flush against the kappa for κ(εράτια). There was not enough space to include the usual indication of abbreviation (S) after mu. This omission must indicate the scribe's consciousness of column alignments and his attempt to keep to them.

30 The scribe's total, partly obscured by the binding strip, is 74,400 tal., as in 23r.35. The figures, none of which is uncertain, really add up to 70,400, a shortfall of exactly 4,000 tal.

Folio 17 Verso

The left margin is filled with oblique strokes, sometimes abraded, except before the canceled entry at line 12. The stroke at line 17 is written twice. There is an ample right margin, at places 4 cm, filled with X-marks (but not at lines 9, 12, 16, 24–25; very faded at lines 20–21). The bottom margin is 3 cm at left, 2 cm at right (the frame intrudes) into which the page total (line 29) has been centered and entered.

14 This line is an insert, in tiny writing. The date is hard to read, but 8 gives us a known collection day rather than, with 20, one otherwise unattested. What stands at the start, we cannot say; it is very faint.

29 The scribe's total of 131,900 tal. appears also in 23r.36. This agrees with the listed payments, omitting the entry in line 12, which has been crossed out.

Folio 18

This folio is in near perfect condition in terms of size, except for a short vertical worm track at its lower left. 12.5 cm wide.

Folio 18 Recto

There are oblique strokes in the left margin throughout, but they are abraded at lines 26–30 and missing at 31 with the papyrus. There are X-marks at most line ends, but not lines 3, 9, 19, 21, 24 (both of these perhaps just faded), and 28.

20 Παύλ(ου) is squeezed in with tiny writing and no formal indication (a stroke through right leg of lambda is the scribe's usual method) of abbreviation.

28 See 14r.30 for this person.

32 The scribe's total of 150,400 tal., also in 23r.37, is correct.

Folio 18 Verso

There are oblique strokes in the left margin throughout, smudged at lines 11 and 17. X-marks are present at most line ends, but missing at lines 3, 8, 14, 21–22, and 25–26. The right margin is ca. 3 cm (it varies). A dark streak runs vertically through the talents column (Col. 3). There is a bottom margin of ca. 1.2 cm, into which the page total (line 33) has been inserted.

4, 15 In the patronymics (Ἰακυβίου and Παχυμίου), the strokes indicating genitive case upsilons are written over the iotas, not over the omicrons.

33 The scribe's total (also in 23r.38) is 354,200 tal. This agrees with the sum of the entries on the page.

Folio 19

12.8 cm. at its widest.

Folio 19 Recto

The page is discolored and abraded at the left side, especially in the lower two-thirds. The entry in line 13 forces a format shift on the page and realignments of Cols. 2–3. There are payments for Pharmouthi 8 in lines 1–18. Then come two payments on Pharmouthi 11—Apa Ionios and the Holy Martyrion, in lines 19–20; this is then followed by payments for Pharmouthi 24 (lines 21–33). The small left margin is filled with oblique strokes against the entries, an X-mark at line 13. At 18 there is a very faint oblique, and all of the obliques in 27–33 are faint and abraded. The right margin increases to 3.5 cm at line 11; it is eliminated at lines 13–20 and resumes though more modestly at line 22 (averaging 2.5 cm though varying line by line). There are X-marks written at right in lines 2–10, 14, 27, and 29. The bottom margin is a bit above 1 cm, into which the page total (line 34) has been entered.

1 It is hard to be certain whether the stroke after the theta of Pharmouthi is iota or an abbreviation stroke. The purpose of the abbreviation stroke would be to avoid confusion between "18" and "8" following the month name. Such diagonal strokes occur after month-names ending in iota on occasion. We therefore think this is the more likely reading.

16–17 At proof stage we observed that the letters ϊα stand between these lines, with the iota under the mu of Ἰερημίας. This is likely to refer to the date, Pharmouthi 11, which stands already in line 19. We do not know whether it is intended to indicate that the payment in line 17 was made on that date, that the payments in both lines 17 and 18 were made on that date, or something else. We have not relocated either payment to the 11th in the table on p. 24, given this uncertainty.

17 In the second column, the characters after beta are a clear gamma under the horizontal stroke of which is written a lunate or circular character, represented here by a degree sign. We have not seen a parallel in the text and do not know what its significance is. As indicated above, pp. 30–31, 2 1/3 works well in the framework of the equations of solidi and talents in the accounting, but that would normally require only a gamma with a short number-stroke.

26 We do not know what the marginal writing at the right is intended to indicate. The first two letters could indicate the 26th of the month, but the next two would seem most likely to be the numerals 800 and 400, and we do not know why they would stand together in this way.

34 The total is to a large degree obscured by the binding strip. We are not confident that we see any trace of the stigma, but the alpha is compatible with the remains and upsilon is certain. The number is given much more clearly in 23r.39. The total of the entries is actually 261,100. The difference is only 300 tal. On the reckoning of the solidi in lines 15–17, see the introduction, pp. 30–31.

Folio 19 Verso

There are oblique strokes in the modest left margin more or less throughout: written double at lines 3 and 8, omitted before the canceled entry at line 4, missing at lines 7 and 13 (?), thick at 14–15, repeatedly overwritten at 25–26, abraded or missing at 32. The alignment of Cols. 2–3 holds up pretty well. The right margin is 2 cm at the top, 3 cm at the bottom. There is an X-mark after line 2 (only). It is unclear why these marks cease after this point.

9 The use of ὁμοί(ως) here with no further information is remarkable. It may indicate simply a second payment by Victor.

33 The scribe's total is 213,900 (duly reported to 23r.40). The entries really add up to 218,500 or 4,600 more than the scribe allows. That would indicate an entry of 5 carats, but there is no such entry on this page.

Folio 20

The folio is 12.3 cm wide at its narrowest point, 13.0 cm at bottom. There may be a kollesis dividing the folio roughly in the middle.

Folio 20 Recto

This is a short page, with only 24 entries; the bottom margin is thus at least 7.2 cm, or 6.0 cm after insertion of the page total (line 26). Cols. 2–3 are well aligned until they squeeze together in the last two entries (lines 24–25). There are oblique strokes in the slender left margin throughout, although very faint at lines 3–4, 14, and 25; thick and short at 6, doubled at 18–20. The right margin averages 2.5 cm.

15 This is the only such entry for an unnamed daughter of a taxpayer in the register, in contrast to the several for sons (8r.12, 9v.28, 12v.5, etc.; see Index IIA s.v. υἱός).

18–19 There seem to be traces of writing in the left margin between these lines: a short vertical stroke followed by a c-shaped character.

22 There appear to be traces of writing squeezed in between lines 21 and 22, running from above the omicron of Φοι(βάμμων) to above the omicron of Πινουτίων, but not extending into the columns of figures. The background is extremely dark here, and we have not succeeded in deciphering any of the traces.

26 The scribe's total survives in full in 23r.41 and the somewhat doubtful reading here is verified from that information as 361,200 tal. This agrees with the total from the payments enumerated here.

Folio 20 Verso

This side is very abraded. The small left margin is occupied throughout with oblique strokes, but they are extraordinarily faint and abraded beginning at line 11 (where there is also loss of papyrus), then clearer in 21–27 before becoming faint again in 28–31. This is the beginning of the second collection for the tenth indiction, and a number of new names occur. The entries in the lower right part of the page are very difficult to see.

1a We did not identify this line as an instance of ο(ὕτως) until lines were already numbered.

2 The letter (or letters; it could be two letters) between the epsilons of the name have evaded interpretation. As there are no other ἀρτοκόποι in the text, we cannot find help in a parallel.

9 Or the name Χῶλος; the nominative case would support the descriptive adjective, but in this text such an argument has little force.

28 The reading of the zeta is extremely uncertain.

32 The summary on 23r does not include this page. The total is partly obscured by the binding, leaving a kappa as the only visible numeral, and that only partly. It is, however, necessitated by the addition. If all of the uncertain readings in the column are correct, the total would be 269,100 tal., which is restored here.

Folio 21

This folio is an intrusive insert, measuring 8.1 cm. x 22.2 cm. It is thus much smaller in both dimensions than the standard folios.

Folio 21 Recto

In a large, unfamiliar hand, the text is short, with plenty of room left. It is important for preserving the indiction number (10) and the village name. There is a bottom margin of 11.7 cm, or roughly half the height of the papyrus. The lower half of the papyrus, in a sharp line, is a different shade from the top (it is a darker tan with a flatter finish, in place of tan with yellowish highlights). This seems to have been caused by an erasure that has not entirely eliminated the beginnings of lines. The left margin is ca 1.5 cm. Lines 1, 6, and 9 run to the right edge of the papyrus—as do some end-of-line strokes that obviously serve as fillers stretching toward the papyrus' right edge: the abbreviation stroke of ἰνδ(ικτίωνος) in line 2, a short extension to the bar of E, end of line 5, and the horizontal stroke of sigma, end of line 10.

1 There is a short diagonal stroke above and right of the chrism. Omicron of λόγος is a circular ink blot; so also the second omicron of ὁμοί(ως) in line 6.

10 See 23r.46. The remainder (not given by the scribe) is 1,167,800.

Folio 21 Verso

There are only six lines of text, leaving a big (16.5 cm) lower margin. The writing is crammed to the top as if to allow for further entries never written. The hand is again the main hand.

1 There seems to be enough space for a single-digit day-date after Θώθ if the scribe had wished to write one. It may have been intended to be filled in later.

4–5 For παραλ(ληλισμοῦ), as a charge for a calculation of amounts necessary to align weight standards, see Banaji 1998: 192–93; Maresch 1994: 38 ff. We do not regard παραλλαγή, attested in eighth-century documents, as a plausible alternative. It is not evident if these payments refer to line 3, or to some other base. The Oxyrhynchite rate of 1 sol. per 144 sol. (= 2 pounds of gold) would, applied to the total of 4 sol. here, give a base of 576 sol. or 8 lbs. of gold, considerably in excess of the total amount for the *pakton* mentioned in 21r.5.

Folio 22

The width returns to a more normal 13.3 cm (and 29 cm high) after the smaller format of the intrusive Folio 21.

Folio 22 Recto

Blank

Folio 22 Verso

Lines 2–7 record the page-by-page tally for Topos Demeou, which the heading in line 1 shows is also for indiction 10; line 8 gives the total. The canceled section below (lines 16–23) is pertinent to the Temseu Skordon pages of the codex.

The hand of lines 1–8 is surely not the codex's main hand. Murch apparently thought the present hand was the same as that for the page-by-page summary for Temseu Skordon on 23r, and we have followed him in that judgment in Section 2 of our introduction. But, on closer look, the writing of 22v.1–8 seems less skilled even than that for the crudely drawn 23r and the work of someone really struggling with his assignment. The hands are, nevertheless, likely to be the same.

2 Probably the 132,700 tal. was the total from the now badly preserved 27v, dated Mesore 15, which was Topos Demeou, page 1.

3 The sum is that from 27r.34, cf. 27r.1: Phao[phi x; Page 2]. Since Topos Demeou and Temseu Skordon collection dates significantly coincide (see Introduction, Section 4), and collections were made at Temseu Skordon on Phaophi 15 and 24, the date for Topos Demeou was probably also either 15 or 24.

4 The sum is that for 26v, before and on Tybi 5 (line 10) [Page 3], 87,400 tal.

5 The sum is that for 26r, Tybi 15, Mecheir 4, Page 4, 57,500 tal.

6 The sum is that for 25v, Mecheir 22, Phamenoth 12, and Pharmouthi 24 [Page 5], 91,200 tal.

7 The sum is that for 25r, Pharmouthi 24, Page 6, 38,500 tal.

8 The total for the six pages as given, 516,900 tal., is correct.

16–23 These lines have been canceled by the scribe. It is important to note that the names recovered in the transcript (Isakios heir of Elias, Enoch oikonomos, and Tatianos son of Elias) all frequently figure in the Temseu Skordon pages of the codex even though the tallies at the page's top are for Topos Demeou. On keratismos, see the note to Frag. 6–8.

Folio 23
The width is 13.5 cm.

Folio 23 Recto
This page is written in a different, cruder hand than the main hand. Nonetheless, it is very regular in its formations. The left-hand column tends to drift ever so slightly rightwards (in opposition to the main scribe's tendency). Tremas seem not to be consistent. Line 45 of Col. 2 is positioned between lines 11–12 of Col. 1. The line 46 total in Col. 2 is opposite Col. 1 line 15.

The two-column format is matched by the *kataselis* of *P.Lond.Copt.* 1076 (= MS.Or. 6047), Fol. 10, but there the list accounts for 55 pages and both columns are packed: 25 entries in Col. 1 (which also has the heading), 30 entries in Col. 2 (where the writing gets smaller, apparently so as to get all 55 entries in on a single page).

22 There is a blot of ink between the two zetas.

39 It appears that this line has been corrected; as it stands, it agrees with the figures partly visible in 19r.34 (see note ad loc.) and differs only slightly from the actual total of the payments on 19r.

Folio 23 Verso
Blank.

Folio 24
The width is 13.5 cm.

Folio 24 Recto
The sheet has been mounted upside down. The right margin is 3 cm (toward the top), 4 cm (below). The small left margin is filled with oblique strokes against almost all entries; these are missing before the canceled entry at line 11 and also at lines 29–32. The stroke at line 26 is written double.

This page concerns the account of a "small account" for Temseu Skordon for the tenth indiction, dated Mecheir 22. Just what the "small account" represents is unknown. Φαμ(ενὼθ) ιζ has been squeezed in between lines 18 and 19. Like Mecheir 22, it is one of the busier dates for tax payments represented in the codex. See Introduction, Section 4. It is not completely clear if it refers only to the following entry or to more. We have assumed in the table (p. 24) that it concerns the remainder of the page.

5 The beta for the number of carats has an overwritten left vertical and a mark above it, the meaning of which we do not know.

14 The eta in the carats column looks more like an open-topped beta, but it is possible that some sort of correction has been at work.

24 There seems to be a short horizontal stroke through the chi of Ἐνῶχ, perhaps without significance. The iota of the following οἰκ is oddly written, with a pronounced curvature.

25 The scribe seems to have omitted the sign for a half carat; there is no space between the carats sign and the talents sign for anything to have been written. There is, however, the characteristic dot that usually follows the half sign.

33 The scribe's total is 107,500 tal. The sum of the preserved entries (excluding the canceled entry in line 11) is 107,100. We may then restore the one missing entry, in line 25, as ½ carat = 400 tal.

Folio 24 Verso
Blank

Folio 25
The width is 13.5 cm.

Folio 25 Recto
The sheet is mounted upside down. This page seems to be work of the main scribe, but the writing is larger than normal because there was plenty of room on this page. There was a bottom margin of 19.5 cm into which the total has been inserted (line 10), leaving a bottom margin of 18 cm below the tail of phi (the number 500). The right margin is at least 3 cm through all ten lines. Oblique strokes fill the small left margin (1 cm at line 2); those in lines 8–9 run through the initial letters.

1, 10 The figure is reported on 22v.7.

Folio 25 Verso
The right margin is 2.5 cm at lines 8–10; 4 cm at line 18; 3.3 on average. Oblique strokes against all individual entries (but not the indented line 7) fill the left margin of 1.5–2 cm. Some of these are topped with or include what seem to be secondary dots, most noticeable at lines 11–12 and 15. The strokes are doubled or thicker between lines 20 and 31, except for 27 and 30; that at line 28 has a thick circular bulge at its lower left. There is a bottom margin of 1 cm into which the total has been entered (line 32). This is evidently by the main hand.

There are five payments for Mecheir 22, eleven (of which one is canceled) for Phamenoth 12, and twelve for Pharmouthi 24. In the first set of entries (Mecheir 22), Cols. 2 and 3 are written close to Column 1. In the subsequent two sets, Col. 2 is distanced a bit from Col. 1, but Cols. 2 and 3 are themselves close together (closer in the Phamenoth 12 entries than in the Pharmouthi 24 entries). Each new date therefore has introduced its own alignment.

1 This is not stated, but it is Page 5 for Topos Demeou.

14 As indicated, Σαρ has been canceled, in fact erased. The oblique stroke against the remaining name ("Apion") stands in the erasure and not in the left margin.

18 The sampi has an extraneous oblique stroke bisecting its left rising stroke.

21 There is an extraneous oblique stroke between the talents symbol and delta, as if perhaps the writer had begun to write a differently-shaped delta but reverted to his standard form.

32 The scribe's total is 91,200 tal., which is reported on 22v.6. This agrees with the total for the actual entries in Col. 3, which break down as follows: (a) Line 1 gives 2 solidi for the entries that follow. Lines 2–6 actually add up to 33,600, even though the conversion rate for 2 solidi elsewhere is 34,000 talents. (b) Line 7 enters 1 solidus (normally 17,000 talents), but the entries in lines 8–18 yield a total of only 16,500 talents. (c) Line 19 gives no solidus figure, but the entries in lines 20–31 add up to 41,100 talents.

Folio 26

The folio is 13.5 cm. wide. There is a significant vertical split at 7.5 cm from the left edge (on the recto side). In Section 1 of the introduction we have explained why what is labeled in the British Library as recto and verso of this folio have been reversed here.

Folio 26 Recto

This sheet is mounted upside down with label also upside down. There is a lower margin of 5.5 cm into which the total has been entered (line 28), leaving a margin of 4 cm (from the tail of the phi = 500). The right margin is 3.3–4 cm. Line 10 is perhaps a late insertion.

Written in the main hand, but larger than usual and perhaps more carefully, this page is as clear as 26v is faint. There are oblique strokes against all entries, except perhaps for line 25, where there is loss of ink at the start. The strokes are cleanly drawn even where thinly doubled. A vertical split runs between Cols. 1 and 2 from line 8 to 24. Additional vertical damage occurs slightly right of this split from the top of the papyrus to line 10. This removes or damages some of the carat entries in Col. 2, but these readings are guaranteed by the 900-talent entries in Col. 3, lines 3–8. There are some minor losses of papyrus at the right edge, especially in the upper right corner, but these are without effect on the text.

The page contains seven payments for Tybi 15 and seventeen payments for Mecheir 4. The scribe's resistance to abbreviation is notable and unusual, but the Col. 1 entries are after all very simple, mostly name plus patronymic without further complication.

1 Page 4: see 22v.5. The top of line 1 is hidden beneath the mounting, making it difficult to be certain of the text.

28 The scribe's total given here, 57,500 tal., corresponds to 22v.5. It agrees with the total of the entries.

Folio 26 Verso

The sheet is mounted upside down and not on the label side of the glass frame (another indication that this is actually the verso rather than recto). There are oblique strokes against all entries, although much abraded. The right margin is 3–4 cm at top; it becomes much smaller after the Tybi 5 date in line 10. This page is very abraded and hard to read. This is Page 3 of the Topos Demeou section of the codex, but there is no visible indication of this fact.

10 The heading in this line has been written over a three-column entry, in the remains of which we can see an amount of 6 car. and the talents sign to the right of the date. It is not clear if this was erased or not.

35 The total of 87,400 tal. corresponds with the figure at 22v.4. Addition of the entries, however, yields a total of 90,500 tal. Unless an entry is obscured along with the header at the top, we do not see a means of reconciling these figures.

Folio 27

This is much more damaged than other folios and measures 10.5 cm at its greatest width.

Folio 27 Recto

Mounted upside down. Width (at greatest) is 11.2 cm. Right margin is lost. Lower margin 1.2 cm. Loss of papyrus at right is substantial until the last six lines. Lost readings are restorable from the conversion table (p. 30). There are oblique strokes as usual against all entries, but these strokes are also surmounted by an X. At lines 26–27, they are difficult to see because of abrasion, and they are missing from line 28 onward, where a strip of papyrus at the lower left has been lost. The entries in lines 8–15 are, perhaps accidentally, alphabetical. Analysis of the order of entries on this page might repay close attention. Cf. introduction, pp. 26–27.

1 For the restoration of the page number, see 22v.3 and note.

7 The partially-preserved fraction is probably a half; in that case the number of talents should be 1,400, and the surviving trace of the numeral is part of an alpha. But the remains are not sufficient to guarantee that reading.

21 The strokes below this line seem to indicate a new set of entries for an unspecified date, later than that for 27r.1–21 but before Tybi 5 (26v.10). Most of the people mentioned in the earlier section are entered again with additional payments. See Introduction, Section 4.

34 The total (= Page 2) of 109,600 tal. is found also in 22v.3. If our suggestion for restoring line 7 is correct, the gap between this and the 107,000 that the payments total (as we have reconstructed and restored them) is 2,600 tal., or 2.75 car. This could be restored in line 2, with the carats as 12.75 and the talents as 12,600; no traces survive to control this conjecture.

Folio 27 Verso

The two lines of writing at the top, in a tiny hand, are surely not in the hand of our main scribe. This is presumably the first page concerning Topos Demeou.

22–32 These lines mention Apollos the oil-worker (22), the meat-cooks Menas and Georgios (31–32, restored), all frequently met with at Temseu Skordon (Index II.A). We suppose therefore that they concern that village rather than Topos Demeou, despite the mention of the epoikion at the top of the page. It is impossible to say confidently which place is involved in the fragmentary intervening lines. Lines 22–24 certainly concern military rations. On the rogator, a military requisitioner, see *P.Horak* 31–59.

Unplaced Fragment

9.7 x 12 cm. Verso is blank.

Recto

The papyrus seems to have been cleanly sliced at top. There is a free space of 5.7 cm under line 8. There are oblique strokes in the left margin. This could be our principal scribe again—though the writing is larger than usual. That fact and the names present suggest that this fragment concerns Temseu Skordon rather than Topos Demeou, and we have indexed it on that basis.

5 This line seems very much an interlinear insert.

6, 7, 8 As in lines 2–4, we are missing a third column with the relevant conversions to talents. With the solidus normally reckoned at 17,000 tal., the amounts were presumably 102,000, 51,000, and 17,000 tal. What the basis for the calculation of keratismos (the term appears also in the deleted 22v.17, again abbreviated as here) is, we do not know. The term is rare, found hitherto only at Aphrodito. P. Maraval, *P.Stras.* VII 699.18n., calls it "la perte qui se produit lors du change des *solidi* en *kératia*," without citing any references or evidence for the statement, but perhaps relying on John Lydus 3.70; cf. J. Schamp's remarks, pp. CCXXI–CCXXII in his Budé edition (2006) of *De magistratibus* 2–3. *P.Cair.Masp.* I 67058 ii.11 is the only other instance found in a search of the DDbDP. The Strasbourg fragment is re-edited in Zuckerman 2004, column X; lines 378–381 record the keratismos of the guild of the carpenters, totalling probably 3 5/6 car. There is no translation or note for this passage. The term appears again in line 630 of Zuckerman's edition, heading a recapitulation of amounts in carats on the 6 pages with payments stated in carats (Cols. XI–XVI), to which the koinon's amount is added. The total of the deductions in carats from payments listed in solidi is then subtracted to get a net amount of carats. Zuckerman's calculation (p. 271, note to line 637) should apparently read "1829 2/3 car. + 3 5/6 car. = 1833 ¼ car. – 1807 ¼ car. = 26 car.") From all of this it is clear that in this account the term *keratismos* refers to payments denominated in copper, not to a charge or subtraction. But it remains unclear to us how to interpret it in the present context.

References

Bagnall, R. S. 1985. *Currency and Inflation in Fourth Century Egypt*. Atlanta.

Bagnall, R. S. 2005. "Village and city: geographies of power in Byzantine Egypt," in J. Lefort, C. Morrisson, and J.-P. Sodini, eds., *Les villages dans l'Empire byzantin (IVe–XVe siècle)*: 553–65. Paris. (Réalités byzantines, 11.)

Bagnall, R. S. 2008. "Village Landholding at Aphrodito in Comparative Perspective," in J.-L. Fournet (ed.), *Les archives de Dioscore d'Aphrodité cent ans après leur découverte*: 181–90. Paris.

Banaji, J. 1998. "Discounts, Weight Standards, and the Exchange-Rate between Gold and Copper: Insights into the Monetary Process of the Sixth Century," in G. Crifò and S. Giglio (eds.), *Atti dell'Accademia romanistica costantiniana: 12 convegno internazionale in onore di Manlio Sargenti*: 183–202. Naples.

Banaji, J. 2001, 2007². *Agrarian Change in Late Antiquity*. Oxford.

Brunsch, W. 1984. "Index zu Heusers 'Personennamen der Kopten'," *Enchoria* 12: 119–53.

Brunsch, W. 1985. "Index der koptischen und griechischen Personennamen in W. E. Crums Coptic Dictionary," *Enchoria* 13: 133–54.

Carrié, J.-M. 1980. "Monnaie d'or et monnaie de bronze dans l'Egypte protobyzantine," in *Les dévaluations à Rome* 2: 253–69. Rome.

Crum, W. E. 1905. *Catalogue of the Coptic Manuscripts in the British Museum.* London.

Crum, W. E. 1939. *Coptic Dictionary*. Oxford.

Derda, T. and E. Wipszycka. 1994. "L'emploi des titres Abba, Apa et Papas dans l'Egypte byzantine," *JJP* 24: 23–56.

Drew-Bear, M. 1979. *Le nome hermopolite. Toponymes et sites*. Missoula, Mont.

Fikhman, I. F. 2006. "Sur quelques aspects socio-économiques de l'activité des corporations professionelles de l'Égypte byzantine," in A. Jördens (ed.), *Wirtschaft und Gesellschaft im spätantiken Ägypten. Kleine Schriften Itzhak F. Fikhman*: 302–23. Stuttgart. (Reprinted from *ZPE* 103 [1994] 19–40).

Gascou, J. 1989/2008. "Les codices documentaires égyptiens," in A. Blanchard (ed.), *Les débuts du codex* (*Bibliologia* 9, 1989) 71–101 = Gascou, *Fiscalité et société en Égypte byzantine* (Paris 2008) 351–74.

Hasitzka, M. 2004. *Namen in koptischen dokumentarischen Texten* (http://www.onb.ac.at /files/ kopt_namen.pdf).

Heuser, G. 1929. *Die Personennamen der Kopten.* Leipzig.

Hickey, T. M. and K. A. Worp. 1997. "The Dossier of Patermouthis sidêrourgos: New Texts from Chicago," *BASP* 34: 79–109.

MacCoull, L. S. B. 1987. "Money and People in the Late Antique Hermopolite: BM 1075 and Related Texts," *Tyche* 2: 99–105.

MacCoull, L. S. B. 1994. "Accounting in BM 1075," in A. Bülow-Jacobsen and H. Cuvigny (eds.), *Proceedings of the 20th International Congress of Papyrology, Copenhagen, 23–29 August 1992*: 484–87. Copenhagen.

Maresch, K. 1994. *Nomisma und Nomismation: Beiträge zur Geldgeschichte Ägyptens im 6. Jahrhundert n.Chr.* Opladen.

Papaconstantinou, A. 2001. *Le culte des saints en Égypte des Byzantins aux Abbassides. L'apport des inscriptions et des papyrus grecs et coptes*. Paris.

Rémondon, R. 1965. "P. Hamb. 56 et P. Lond. 1419 (notes sur les finances d'Aphrodito du VIe siècle au VIIIe)," *Cd'E* 40: 401–30.

Vycichl, W. 1983. *Dictionnaire étymologique de la langue copte*. Leuven.

Worp, K. A. 2004. "Notes on Coptic Containers of Liquids in Greek Papyri," in M. Immerzeel and J. van der Vliet (eds.), *Coptic Studies on the Threshold of a New Millennium* I: 553–72. Leuven.

Zuckerman, C. 2004. *Du village à l'Empire*. Paris.

Indexes

I. Chronological

A. Indictions

B. Months and days

II. Names of persons

(d. = daughter; f. = father; gf. = grandfather; gs. = grandson; m. = mother; s. = son)

A. Temseu Skordon

B. Topos Demeou

III. Geographical

IV. Religious offices, institutions, and titles

V. Offices and occupations

VI. Weights, measures, and coinage

VII. Greek and Coptic words

PLATES

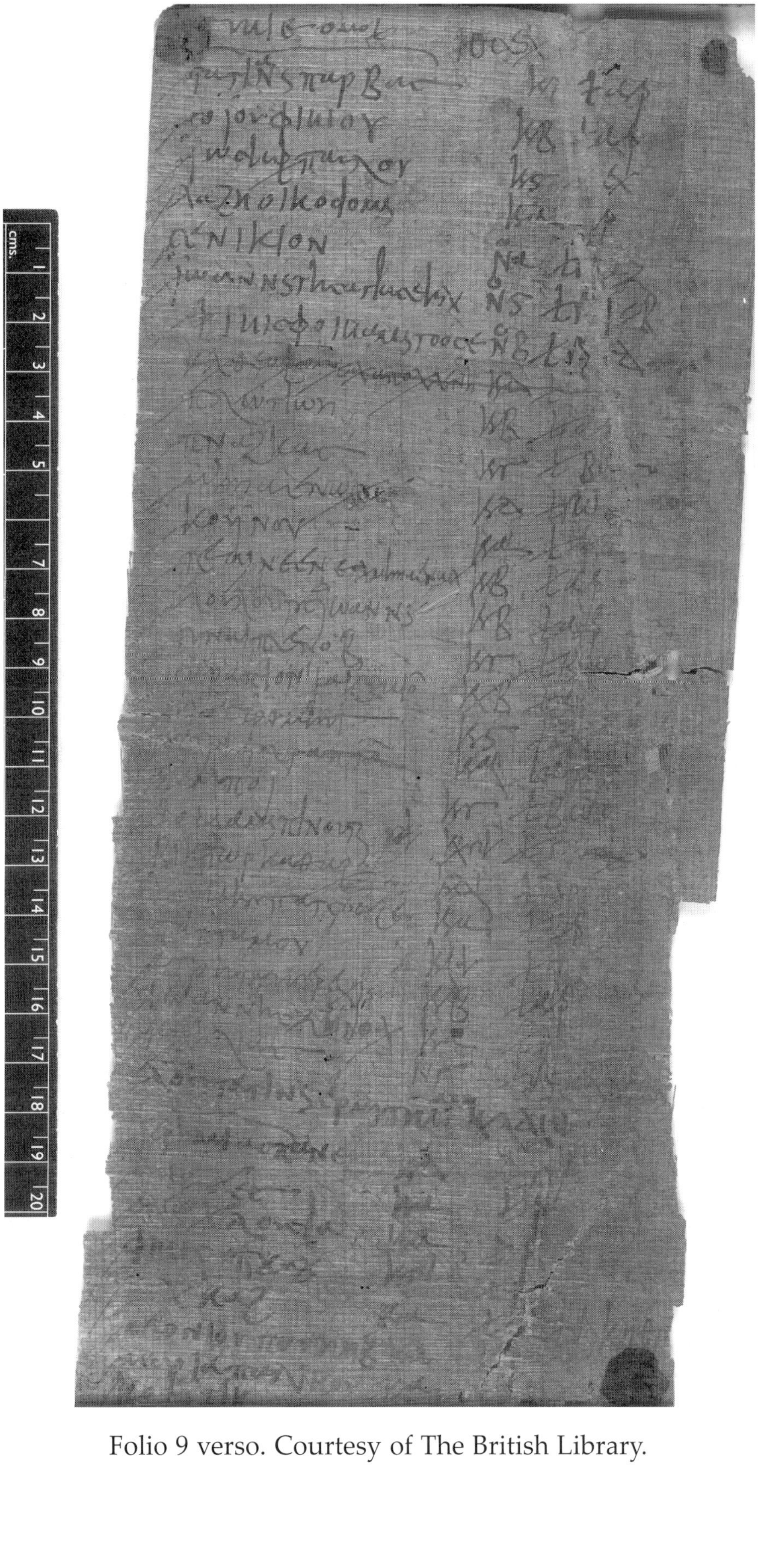

Folio 9 verso. Courtesy of The British Library.

PLATE 2

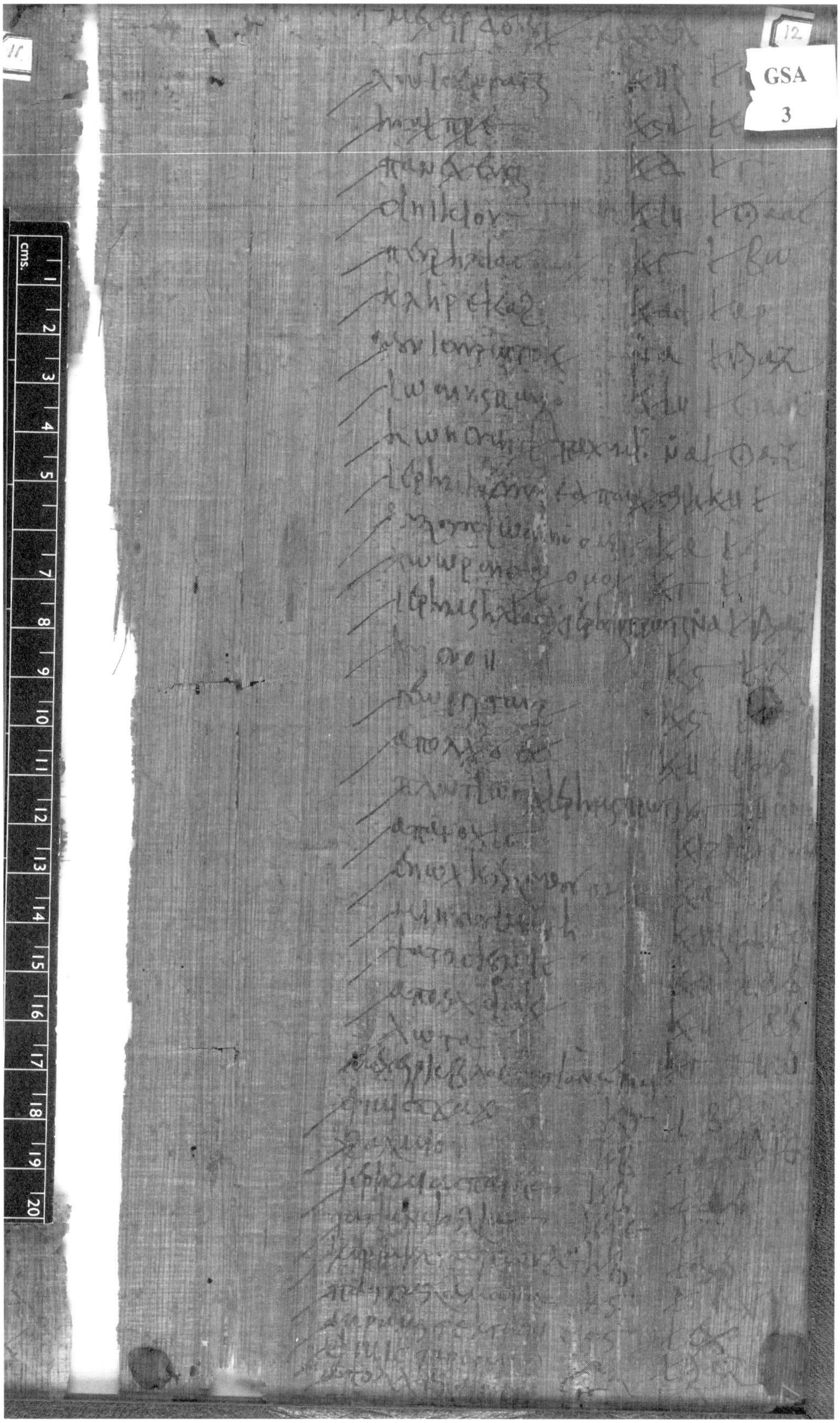

Folio 12 recto. Courtesy of The British Library.

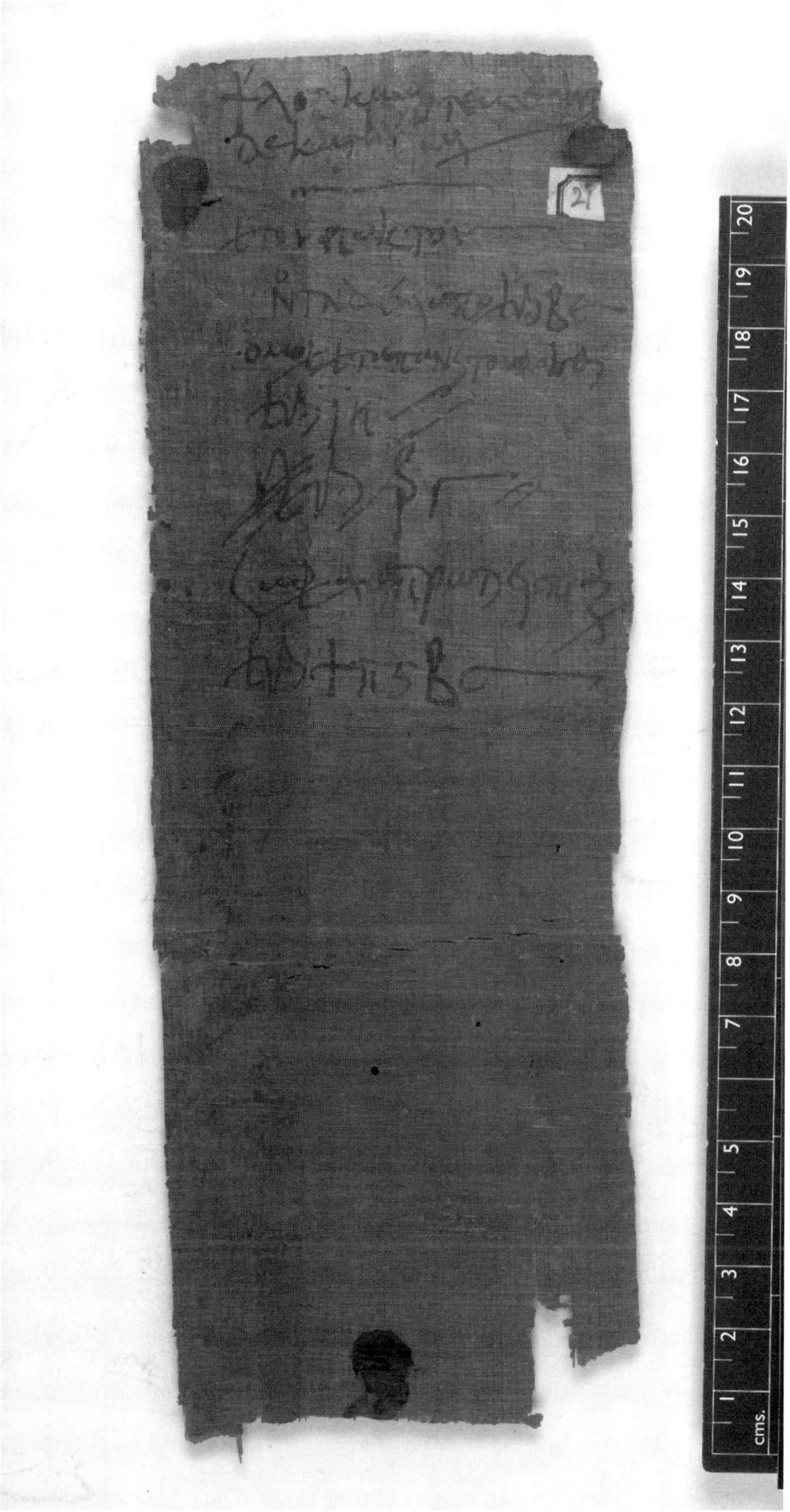

Folio 21 recto. Courtesy of The British Library.

PLATE 4

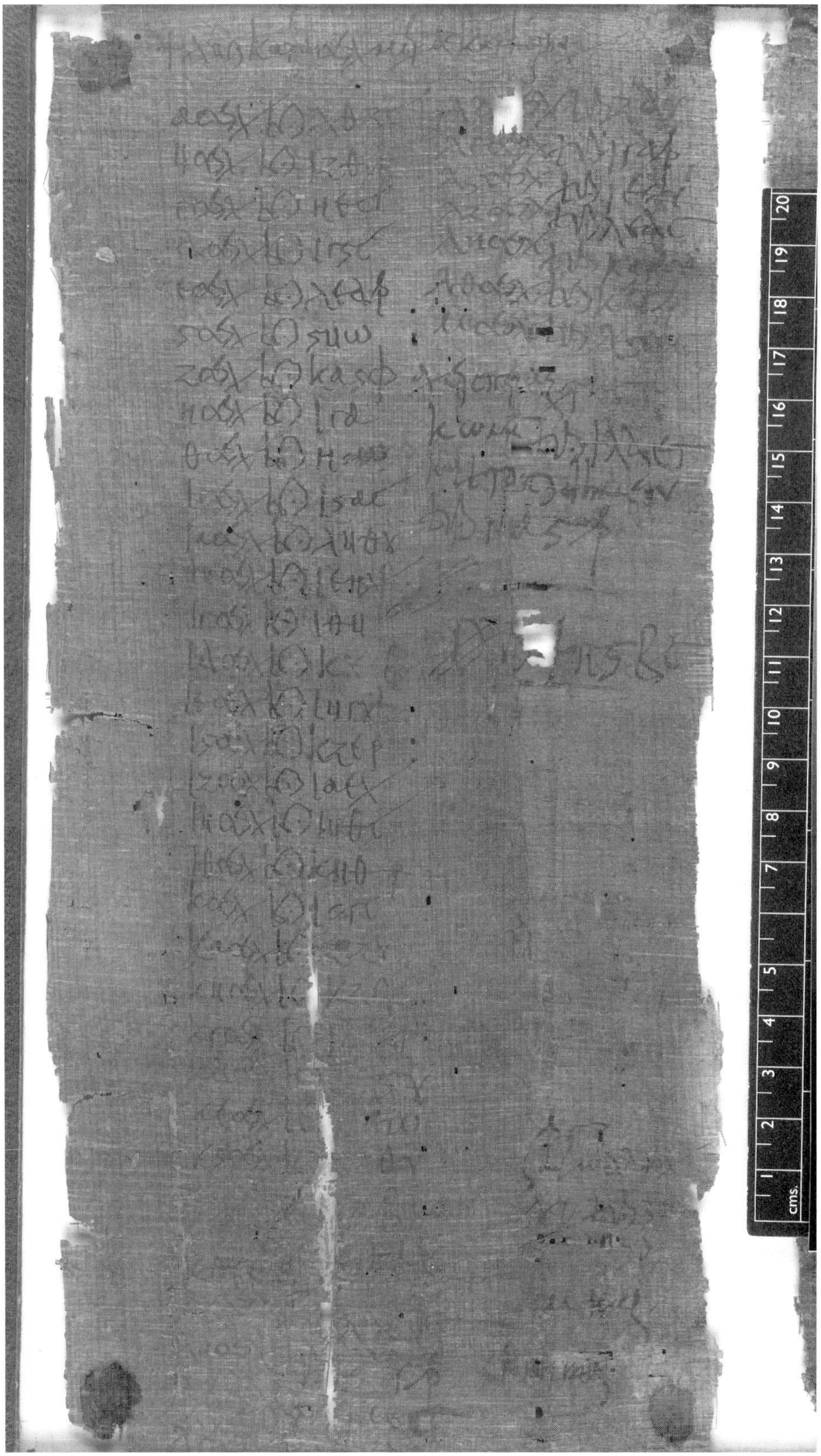

Folio 23 recto. Courtesy of The British Library.